ISBN 978-1-331-16682-5
PIBN 10153059

1 MONTH OF
FREE
READING

at

www.ForgottenBooks.com

By purchasing this book you are eligible for one month membership to ForgottenBooks.com, giving you unlimited access to our entire collection of over 700,000 titles via our web site and mobile apps.

To claim your free month visit:

www.forgottenbooks.com/free153059

* Offer is valid for 45 days from date of purchase. Terms and conditions apply.

Library of New-England History

No. II

CHURCH'S PHILIP'S WAR

PART I

The History

OF

KING PHILIP'S WAR

By BENJAMIN CHURCH

WITH AN INTRODUCTION AND NOTES

By HENRY MARTYN DEXTER

Boston

JOHN KIMBALL WIGGIN

MDCCCLXV

No.

Entered according to Act of Congress in the year 1865, by

JOHN K. WIGGIN

In the Clerk's Office of the District Court of the District of Massachusetts

EDITION

Two Hundred and Fifty Copies, Small Quarto
Thirty-five, Royal Quarto

Press of John Wilson and Son

TO

JOHN GORHAM PALFREY, D.D., LL.D.,

WHO ADDS THE MINUTE AND PATIENT ACCURACY OF THE ANTIQUARY TO THE
BROAD AND PHILOSOPHICAL INSIGHT OF THE HISTORIAN;

AND WHO HAS, MORE FAITHFULLY THAN ANY OTHER WRITER, CONCEIVED
AND DEFINED THE REAL POSITION OCCUPIED BY THE
ABORIGINES OF NEW ENGLAND IN THE
CIVIL AND SOCIAL SCALE:

This Edition of a homely but invaluable Tract,

HAVING LARGE REFERENCE TO THEM,

Is by Permission, most respectfully Inscribed.

PREFATORY NOTE.

HE need of the literal reprint of so valuable a contribution to the history of New England as Church's "ENTERTAINING PASSAGES RELATING TO PHILIP'S WAR," has been widely felt; and the more, because the re-issue of 1772, from which all later editions have been copied, was defective in some important particulars affecting the use of the work as an historical authority. Two instances of this may be here particularized; viz., where (page 18) the words occurring on page 10, "and of the black Rocks to the Southward of them," offering an important hint of the exact locality of the "pease-field fight," were dropped out altogether; and where (page 30) the words occurring on page 17, "in about *a* Months time," were reprinted "in about *three* months' time," thus seeming to hint an expedition into the *Nipmuk* country in March, 1676, referred to by no other writer. The endeavor has accordingly been made to put the purchaser of this edition in possession of as exact a reproduction of the original of 1716, as it has been possible for modern antique types and skill to do · the minuteness of the imitation having been designed to be extended to every misprint, mispunctuation, and even inverted comma, — of which the word "discocovered" (page 31, line 11 from the top), the word *Pl mouth* (page 140, line 8 from the bottom), and very many other seeming blunders of the printers of this edition, will be found to be only faithful illustrations.

In the Notes, the endeavor has been made to straighten the involved and crooked chronology from other sources; to identify the exact localities made for ever classic by their association with this rude warfare; to give some account, from contemporary records, of the various actors; and, generally, to shed all possible light upon the narrative.

Familiar with most of the country traversed over by the story, from a childhood that was fascinated by the graphic simplicity of Church's description of his campaigns, the Editor indulges the hope that he may have done something to aid future readers of these " Entertaining Passages " to comprehend them in their exactness of time and place and circumstance.

The original, from which this reprint is made, — now a very rare volume, — was printed in small quarto, pp. 120, in Boston, in 1716, by B. GREEN. A second edition, itself now becoming rare, was published fifty-six years after at Newport, R.I., in 1772, by SOLOMON SOUTHWICK, in small 8vo, pp. 199. It is made clear from the Diary* of Rev. EZRA STILES, D.D., (then Pastor of the Second Congregational Church in Newport), that he aided SOUTHWICK, and really edited the volume.

The following extracts bear upon the subject; viz, —

"1771. Dec. 18. . . . . . Correcting the press for Col. Church's Hist. of K. Philip's War in 1675.

"1771. Dec. 19. . . . . . Reviewing Col. Benj. Church's History of K. Philip's War, 1676, at the request of the printer ; — adding English or present Names of places written in Indian names in the Original. Mr. Southwick is printing a Second Edition ; first Edit. 1718 [*Sic*].

"1772. Apr. 9. . . . . . Finished writing the Life of Col. Benjamin Church, to be affixed to the new Edition of his History of the Indian war, called K. Philip's War, now printing. He was born 1639, and died at Little Compton, Janry. 171⅞, *Æt.* 78.

"1772. Apr. 10. . . . . . Inspecting the Press."

Dr. STILES appended to the volume, also, an "Ode Heroica," which [*N. E. Hist. and Gen. Reg.*, xi. 155] was composed by BENJAMIN CHURCH of Boston, "Venduemaster," son of the old Colonel's son Edward, who was also a "Vendue-master," — as that age styled the useful person whom we call an Auctioneer, — and was father of Dr. BENJAMIN, of sad Tory memory. He not only glori-

---

* This Diary is now in the Library of Yale College, of which Rev. Dr. STILES was President at the time of his death.

fied his grandfather in a tongue unknown to the brave old warrior (although, as he wrote Dr. STILES, "almost too old for such juvenile attempts; being upwards of 67"), but furnished the Doctor with the materials for the biography of the Colonel.

The glorification was as follows: —

"ODE HEROICA,

" [a Nepote Heroïs composita]

" BIOGRAPHIAE PRAECEDENTI AFFIGENDA SIT.

" NUNC permitte Nepos Lector, magnalia Avi ejus,
    Et vitam ut brevitér caneret, quoq; pauca loquendo,
Traduce de veteri, celebrata et, versibus, ex quo
Magnanimusq; Heros frondebat: deinde locoque:
Quo fuit intrepidus Phoenix, memorandus et ortus!
Agricola ecce Pater manuum gaudebat in omni
Tumve labore suo, nutritus frugibus Arvi!
Mater pauperibus curas, casusq; relaxans,
Omnibus afflictis passim mater fuit alma!
Numinis arbitrioq; bono, sine murmure mentis,
Acquievêre, suis contenti sortibus ambo —
Cordibus elatis, gratiq; fuêre Parentes,
Filius ut talis mortalibus hisce daretur!
Qui patriaeq; suae perluxit gloria longè,
Donec erat victus truculentae mortis ab ictu!
Duxburiae dictum est, Genioq; fuisse beatum
Oppidum, et exultans, tanto quòd munere Martis
Distinctum fuerat! Vicinis majus ab illo!
Historicus suprà probitér canit arma virumq;
Quiq; erat in pugnâ multis, magnisq; periclis

Expositus !   Natos nemoris fuscosve secutus
Armipotens ; sylvas, Dumosq ; arbustaq ; densa
Pervolitans, nigros scloppo ejus perdidit Angues
Monstraq ; quos natura parens crudelia dixit !
Victoriisq ; suis pacem stabilivit in Orbis
Terrarum occasû — jam, jam sub vitibus omnis
Hic sedeat salvus — terrore absente Mavortis !
Mortuus est Heros !   Nomen sed vivet in aevum —
Spiritus ascendit Coelos, Jesûq ; triumphans ;
Dum latet in tumulo corpus cum pulvere mixtum !

Sic cecinit Nepos BENJ. CHURCH, *Sen.*"

This edition was also adorned with what purported to be portraits, on copper, of Colonel CHURCH, and of King PHILIP, both from the graver of PAUL REVERE; of which more will be said in another place.

The third edition of this winsome narrative was edited, fifty-three years later, by Mr. SAMUEL GARDNER DRAKE, and was the first contribution of that since accomplished archæologist to this department of Aboriginal research; in which, without injustice to others, it may safely be said that he has no superior. Travelling through the Old Colony in the summer of 1824, he, for the first time, saw [*N.E. Hist. and Gen. Reg.*, xvii. 202], and became possessor of, a copy of SOUTHWICK'S reprint; and, circulating proposals, he obtained nearly a thousand subscribers for a new issue. He published in 12mo (Boston: Howe and Norton, 14, State Street, 1825), pp. 304; prefixing eight pages of Index, and two pages of Introduction, and adding an Appendix of forty pages, comprising a brief sketch of the settlement of this country, of the Indian wars, &c., &c. It was mainly a reprint of Southwick's edition,—the editor having then never seen the original, — with the omission of the "Ode Heroica," and the addition of a few foot-notes. It was embellished with a fancy portrait of King PHILIP, decidedly more prepossessing in appearance, and quite as authentic in character, as that of PAUL REVERE of a half-century before.

The success of this effort was so marked as to induce Mr. DRAKE to prepare and issue a second edition (the fourth of the work), which he did, early in 1827, from stereotype plates; being among the first fruits of the stereotype press in Boston. This, also, was in 12mo, pp. 360. He added many more notes, and gave an Introduction of five pages, an Index of six pages, and an Appendix of sixty-eight pages, of the same general character as that of the previous edition, but rewritten and enlarged. The old head, purporting to be a likeness of CHURCH, was re-engraved for this issue, and other plates were added.

All the (nominally new) editions of this work, from that time to the present, have been re-issues of this last; the plates having long since passed out of Mr. DRAKE'S hands, and having been used by various publishers.

The present is, therefore, the fourth reprint (fifth edition) of these "Entertaining Passages," and the first from the original, — as well as the first which has not avowedly sought to amend the text.

The map has been adapted from the State map, by the Editor, with great care, from his own personal knowledge of the ground; and he believes it to be a thoroughly accurate guide to all those localities which it purports to point out

The dates have been suffered to stand in Old Style, as written.

The Publisher has sought to produce this copy, so far as possible, in *fac-simile* of the original, as well as in literal exactness; and the headings, initial letters, &c., &c , have been accordingly engraved for that purpose.

It only remains, here, that just thanks be given to all who have aided the Editor in his labor: among whom he would gratefully mention the Hon. JOHN RUSSELL BARTLETT, Secretary of State of Rhode Island; his Honor, Judge WILLIAM R. STAPLES, of Providence; General G. M. FESSENDEN, of Warren, R. I.; RICHARD SHERMAN, Esq., of Portsmouth, R. I. ; Mr. HENRY M. TOMPKINS, the Town Clerk of Little Compton, R. I.; Hon. WILLIAMS LATHAM, of Bridgewater, Mass.; SAMUEL F. HAVEN, Esq., Librarian of the American Antiquarian Society in Worcester, Mass.; Rev. JOHN LANGDON SIBLEY, Librarian of Harvard College; and Mr. GEORGE H. TABER, of Fairhaven, Mass. Two gentlemen deserve more special mention for the unwearied pains they have taken to aid the Editor in some portions of the work; viz., his friend and kinsman, Mr. FRANKLIN B. DEXTER, now Tutor in Yale College, to whom he owes the extracts from the Diary of Dr. STILES, the identification of the site of JOHN COOK's house in Cushnet, and other kindred helps; and the Hon. J. HAMMOND TRUMBULL, Secretary of State of Connecticut, to whose disinterested and indefatigable aid much of what may be thought to be of special value in the work will be largely due. The Editor knows nothing about the Indian tongue; and the reader is desired to take notice here, once for all, that for all the interesting and valuable suggestions having reference to that, which are scattered through the book, his thanks will be wholly due to the learning and gen erosity of that eminent *savan*.

It has not been found possible — without too great enlargement of the volume — to insert herein the Second Part of the original work, giving "a further account of the Actions in the more later Wars against the Common Enemy and *Indian* Rebels in the Eastern Parts, under the Command of the aforesaid Capt. *Benj. Church*;" which makes sixty-six of the solidest quarto pages. That is in preparation, and will follow as a separate issue.

H. M. D.

HILLSIDE, ROXBURY,
   15th July, 1865.

INTRODUCTORY MEMOIR.

N his preface to thefe "Entertaining Paffages," Colonel Church makes the apologetic remark, that "every particle of hiftorical truth is precious." That remark has been conftantly in mind in the preparation of what follows, having reference to events in the hiftory of this fimple-hearted, yet noble-hearted man. It would be more exact to ftyle what is here offered "Materials toward a Memoir," than fuch a Memoir itfelf. Moft of the official records in which various actions of his bufy life would naturally leave their footmarks, have been fearched, and their various references to his career have been gathered together and arranged chronologically here; fo as to put the reader in poffeffion of thefe fragmentary, yet faithful, evidences of what he was. The man himfelf has exhaled; but fome rude impreffion of him remains in them, which may ferve as a matrix in which imagination may fhape fome image;

which, if far from being a reproduction of the perfon whom his cotemporaries knew, muſt yet have some fac-fimile lineaments. The humble office of the editor is to furniſh the mould; leaving to the reader the re-creative work.

BENJAMIN CHURCH was a fon of Richard. Richard came to Maſſachuſetts probably in the fleet with Gov. Winthrop;* was a carpenter by trade; 19 Oct. 1630, was propounded to be a freeman in the Maſſachuſetts Colony; in 1630, was at Weſſaguſſet and Plymouth; 2 Jan. 163⅔ was freeman of Plymouth; 16 Feb. 163⅔ hired William Baker to faw timber into boards for him; was "rated for public uſe" £1 16s. in March following, and £1 7s. the next year; married Elizabeth, daughter of Richard Warren, in 1636; was often a member of the "Grand Enqueſt," and was occaſionally made referee; ferved as fergeant in the Pequot war; with John Tompſon helped build the firſt meeting-houſe (as ſuch) in Plymouth about 1637; lived at Eel-river; 9 April, 1649, fold his eſtate there to Robert Bartlet for £25; was in Charleſ-town in 1653, but finally fettled down in Hingham, where he made his will 25 Dec. 1668, and died two days after, at Dedham, leaving at leaſt nine children.†

---

* Savage's *Gen. Dict.* i: 386; Win-for's *Duxbury*, 245; Deane's *Scitu-ate*, 234; Mitchell's *Bridgewater*, 363; *N. E. Hiſt. & Gen. Reg.* xi: 154; *Plym. Col. Rec.* i: 6, 8, 11, xii: 165, &c. &c.

† Church ſpeaks [*B. C. D.* i: 91] of

BENJAMIN was born at Plymouth in 1639, and was bred to his father's trade. No other circumftance of his early life has found record. 26 Dec. 1667, — when at the age of twenty feven or eight — he married Alice, fecond daughter of Conftant and Elizabeth (Collier) Southworth, of Duxbury; who was then not far from twenty-one, having been born in 1646. It is prefumed that their early married life was paffed in Duxbury, though it is probable that he was temporarily refident in various portions of the Colony, in the purfuit of his vocation. His firft appearance upon the Plymouth Colony Records is 25 Oct. 1668, when [*P C. R.* vii: 150] he is named as on a trial jury in the cafe of Jofias Winflow *vs.* Kenelm, and in that of John Doged.

1 *June,* 1669, lefs than fix months after his father's death, the Court granted him " land att Taunton River " which William Pabodie had taken up and then furrendered, [*P. C. R.* v: 20] "for full fatisfaction for all the right his father, Richard Church, deceafed, hath to land in this Collonie."

7 *March* 1670 [*P. C. R.* vii: 163], he was one of a petit jury at Plymouth for the trial of feveral actions. 29 *May,* 1670, [*P. C. R.* v: 275], his name appears upon the lift of

Sarah, wife of James Burroughs, of Briftol, tailor, as his fifter, though no fuch name appears upon the fulleft publifhed lift of Richard's children which I have feen. [*N. E. Hift. and Gen. Reg.* xi: 154.]

freemen of "Duxburrow," then tranfcribed by Secretary Morton.

5 *June*, 1671 [*P. C. R.* v: 54], he was Conftable of "Duxburro."

30 *October*, 1672 [*P. C. R.* vii: 174], he was one of a trial jury at Plymouth, for the fecuring of juftice in feveral criminal cafes.

4 *July*, 1673 [*P. C. R.* vii: 181], he was one of a trial jury at Plymouth for eight civil and criminal cafes. He alfo made return [*P. C. R.* v: 126], with John Rogers, Daniell Wilcockes, Conftant Southworth, William Pabodie and Edward Gray, that, purfuant to the order of the Court, they had bounded out "the fouthfyde of thofe lands formerly graunted vnto the inhabitants of Plymouth at *Punckateefett*," &c. At the fame time [*P. C. R.* v: 126], liberty was granted him with John Tompfon, by the Court to purchafe land of " Tufpaquine, the blacke fachem, and William his Son, for the inhabitants and propriators of the towne of Middleberry," &c. The proprietors were to have until the laft of the November following, to repay Church and Tompfon, and take the land; but it appears [*Ibid*, 146], that they failed to do fo, and that the Court, 3 June, 1674, granted Church and Tompfon "one third p^t_e of the faid land, for theire cecuritie and evidence." 23 July, 1673 [*Proprietor's Records Saconet*], he met with the newly organized Company to purchafe and fettle the *Saconet*

lands; appearing in the right of Richard Bifhop and Richard Beare. Sometime in this year his oldeft fon Thomas was born.

10 *April,* 1674 [*P. R. S.*], the Saconet company met at Duxbury, and Church drew the lots numbered 19 and 29. He proceeded during the fummer following to clear and erect buildings upon lot No. 19 (fee note 21 *poft*).

2 *March,* 167⅘ [*P. C. R.* vii: 195], he was on a trial jury at Plymouth, fhowing that his removal to the very outfkirts of the Colony was not defigned, by him or by the Colonifts, to diffociate him from their conftant fervice. Church's own account of himfelf in connection with the outbreak of the war which now began to defolate the land feems to begin about 15 June, 1675 [note 14, *poft*]; but the "Brieff Narrative of the beginning and progreffe of the p'fent trouble between vs and the Indians," fubmitted to the Commiffioners of the United Colonies, by the Plymouth Commiffioners, in the November following, and which bears the marks of having been carefully drawn, fays [*P. C. R.* x: 363], " on the 7ᵗʰ June, Mr. Benjamine Church being on Rhod Ifland; *Weetamoe* and fome of her Cheiffe men told him that Phillip Intended a warr fpeedily with the Englifh," &c. It would feem to have been about 15 June that he had an interview with *Awafhonks* and *Weetamoe,* as narrated in his own account, and went to Plymouth to fee the Governor. The Punkatees fight was

9 July; 19 July the Pocaffet Expedition began: in the laft of that month, Philip got acrofs *Titicut* river in the night, and fled for the *Nipmuk* country. 27 October [*P. C. R.* vii: 196], thefe warlike proceedings were interfperfed with a civil fuit againft Church, of Richard French of Marfh-field, Executor of the eftate of Richard Beare, claiming damages of 40*s*, in an action of debt, concerning which the record is, "the jury find for the plaintiffe the coft of the fuite." The fecond week in December, Church ftarts for the war again as "a Reformado" with Gen. Winflow, and on the 19th of that month was wounded in the famous Narraganfett fwamp fight, and carried over to Rhode-Ifland to be cured.

27 *January*, 1676 (note 140, *poft*), he ftarted with the army for the *Nipmuk* country; 29 Feb. (note 152, *poft*), he feems to have met with the Plymouth Council of War, at Marfhfield; 11–13 March (note 159, *poft*), arrived at Capt. Almy's, on Rhode-Ifland, with his wife and fon Thomas; 12 May, his fon Conftant was born; 6 June, he arrived at Plymouth by way of Wood's Hole; foon went back the fame way, faw the *Saconet* Indians on the rocks, and procured a formal meeting with *Awafhonks*, refulting in a treaty, and, 25 June, difpatched *Peter* to Plymouth with the "Articles"; met Maj. Bradford and his army, re-turned to Plymouth, and went to meet *Awafhonks* at *Mat-tapoifett*, 8 July; was commiffioned, and went out to

capture the *Monponfets*, 10 July; 24 July, had his commiffion enlarged, and ftarted to guard the carts to Taun
ton, whence he went to *Acufhnet*, and captured many
prifoners, and returned to Plymouth by way of *Sippican;*
30 July, ftarted for Bridgewater, chafed Philip over into
the fwamps in Norton and Rehoboth, and took many prifoners, with whom he got fafe back to Plymouth, 4 Auguft; 7 Auguft, he "rallied" for Dartmouth, and by 10
Auguft ftarted for *Pocaffet* woods, went over to the ifland,
and down to Maj. Sanford's to fee his wife, and next
morning killed Philip in the fwamp fouth of Mount-Hope,
and got back to Plymouth on the 17th; early in September, he fet his fuccefsful trap for *Tifpaquin*, and foon
ftarted out once more after *Annawon*, whom he took on
the night of 11 September.   17 October, the Maffachufetts
General Court wrote to Plymouth [*Mafs. Col. Rec.* v: 126]
afking to be affifted againft the Eaftern Indians " with fome
Englifh, & alfo fome of your Indians, and *Capt. Church*,
whom we have fpoken with here & finde him ready to
ferve God and the country, &c."; 1 November, he was
appointed [*P. C. R.* v: 215] by Plymouth Court, with
William Pabodie and Nathaniel Thomas, to lay out lands
granted to David and Thomas Lake near *Saconet* and *Punkateaft*; alfo, with the fame, to lay out fome lands in aid of
a ferry at *Pocaffet;* while he and John Simmons are granted
[*Ibid.* 216] a leafe for pafturage at *Pocaffet.*   4 November

[*P. C. R.* xi: 242], the Court ordered as follows: "Captaine Beniamen Church haueing; for and in the behalfe of the Collonie, engaged to feuerall Indians; about fiue or six; That incase they did carry well they fhould abide in this Jurifdiction; and not fold to any fforraigne p^rtes; accordingly this Court doth confeirme the faid engagement and doth hereby tollarate theire ftay as aforfaid; notwithftanding any law of this Collonie to the contrary; excepting; if any of them fhould appeer to haue had a hand in any horred murder of any of the Englifh p^rticularly excepting one Croffman; whoe is accufed to haue had a fpeciall hand in the crewell murder of Mr Hezekiah Willett."

15 *January*, 167⅚, Capt. Church was commiffioned again by the Plymouth government, and went out again and [p. 181, *poft*] took "divers parties of Indians." 6 March [*P. C. R.* v: 225], the Plymouth Court granted leave to eight of Church's Indian foldiers to fettle at *Saconet*, he fupplying them with land, on condition that they hold themfelves ready for military fervice under him, "hee, fatisfying the Indians, to haue the whole prophett of fuch an adventure." 7 June [*P. C. R.* v: 234], he is authorized to act as a magiftrate to iffue warrants, &c., at *Saconet* and *Pocaffet*; 13 July [*Ibid.* 242], he is recognized by the Court as agent of the widow of Daniel Haward, for the management of the lands of her late hufband; 30

October [*Ibid.* 246; vii: 208], he was on a trial jury at Plymouth.

5 *March*, 167⅞, he was appointed by the Court [*P. C. R.* v: 252], with John Richmond of Taunton to divide fome land at *Saconet* belonging to children of the late John Irifh; 5 July [*Ibid.* 265], he was empowered, by fpecial order, to adminifter to John Irifh the oath to ferve as conftable at *Saconet.*

8 *March*, 167⅘ [*P. C. R.* vi: 7] he was re-appointed to be a magiftrate for *Saconet* and *Pocaffet.*

4 *March*, 1679 [*Briftol County (Mafs.) Deeds*, ii: 144], he buys of Arthur Hathaway of Dartmouth, for £16, one fhare in *Punkateaft* neck, with one fhare of the Court grant of which faid neck was a part; fame date [*Ibid.* ii: 146], he buys a fimilar fhare of Edward Gray of Plymouth, for £12.

1 *January*, 16⁷⁹⁄₈₀ [*Ibid.* ii: 143], he bought a fimilar fhare of Richard Wright, tailor, of New Plymouth, for 40s. Sometime before March of this year, with feven others [*Proceedings of Mafs. Hift. Soc.*, Sept. 1857, 238], he became a purchafer of *Pocaffet* lands, and agreed to endeavor the well fettling of a plantation there, and to "joine with Succonnitt Proprietors in the calling of a Gospell Mineter & for his incouragement as to his outward fubfiftence &c."; 7 July [*P. C. R.* vi: 43], he was appointed, with Nathaniel Thomas and William Pabodie, "to bound out *Tatamanucke's* thoufand acres of land att or about Saco-

nett"; 14 Sept. [*Briftol, R.-I., Town Records*, i: 26], he figned and fealed the "Grand Articles" for the fettlement of Briftol, R.-I.

1 *March*, 168$\frac{0}{1}$ [*P. C. R.* vi: 58], with Nathaniel Thomas and Edward Gray, he petitioned to have the lines run between their *Pocaffet* purchafe and the "freemen's land" at Fall River, and the Court ordered William Pabodie to do it; 7 July, 1681 [*P. C. R.* vi: 69], he was authorized by the Court "to cutt and cleare" a more direct way from Mount-Hope to Bofton, there being "great need" of one; at the fame Court [*P. C. R.* vii: 241], he, with others, by N. Thomas, their attorney, fued David Lake for £500, for interrupting them from quiet and peaceable poffeffion of their *Pocaffet* lands; 1 Sept. [*B. T. R.* i: 46], the firft proprietors of the Mount-Hope purchafe met (76 in number, "Capt. Benjamin Church" heading the lift), and agreed that the name of the town fhould be Briftol; 10 Nov. [*B. T. R.* i: 49], with N. Byfield and Sergeant John Cary, he was appointed to make a rate upon the new town.

7 *March*, 168$\frac{1}{2}$ [*P. C. R.* vii: 247], he, with others, by N. Thomas, attorney, fued William Earle of Dartmouth for forcibly hindering the running of the boundary line of the *Pocaffet* purchafe; 22 May, 1682 [*B. T. R.* i: 49], he was chofen Deputy to reprefent Briftol in the Colony Court, and firft Selectman for the year enfuing; 7 July [*P. C. R.* vi: 93], he was commiffioned as a magiftrate,

and authorized to folemnize marriages; 27 Oct. [*P. C. R.* vii: 257], he made an official return to the Court covering the teftimony of *Wayewett* (*Awafhonks's* hufband) and three other *Saconet* Indians, that to their knowledge the little ifland of *Cheffawanucke* (Hog Ifland) belonged to *Maffafoit* and his fon *Wamfutta.*

28 *May*, 1683 [*B. T. R.* i: 51], he was re-elected Deputy; 5 July [*B. C. D.* ii: 146] with Wm. Pabodie of Little Compton, he agrees that the 23d lot at *Saconet* fhould be his; 7 July [*P. C. R.* vii: 263], John Saffin, merchant, · fues him for £100, for " daming a certain watercourfe into a coue on *Poppafquafh* necke "; 24 Oct. [*B. T. R.* i: 54], he agrees with the voters of Briftol to make three wolf-pits in a month's time, and, with others, was clothed " with full power in the towne's behalf in reference to rates now due from Mr. J. Saffin "; 31 Oct. [*P. C. R.* vii: 269], Saffin complained to the Court of him and his affociate raters of damage of £24 for unjuft affeffment, but the Court found for defendants, and affeffed Saffin £4 5*s.* cofts of Court; fame date, fame Saffin fued Church for £80, for the old caufe of " daming " his creek, and the jury found for Saffin £3 and cofts.

3 *March*, 168¾ [*B. T. R.* i: 43], he agrees with Nathaniel Byfield to maintain a fence of 393 rods in length, between their farms, each to build and keep in repair 196½ rods; 9 Feb. 1684 [*B. C. D.* i: 311], he buys of John Walley

D

and others, for £10, certain houfe-lots, &c., &c., in Briftol; 20 Feb. [*Ibid.* 309], he buys of the fame parties, for £87 feveral houfe-lots and other lands, with $\frac{1}{16}$ of a mill, and $\frac{1}{16}$ of the "ferry farm," in Briftol; 26 March [*Briftol Births*, i: 56], his then only daughter, Elizabeth, was born; 21 May [*B. T. R.* i: 55], he was re-chofen Deputy, and elected third Selectman; 16 Sept. [*Ibid.* 57], with Capt. Walley, he was chofen "for the ufing endeavors to bring £5, from next October Court of the Cape money for the Incouragement of a School-mafter"; 13 November [*B. C. D.* i: 50], he effected the divifion of the Haward land in *Saconet*, to which he had been appointed by the Court; 28 Novem ber [*B. C. D.* i: 181], he fells, for £45, to Rowland Rob infon of Newport the 24th lot at Saconet, and 40 acres at *Tyonfunbe.*

23 *June*, 1685 [*B. T. R.* i: 62], he "difburfed" 10s. to help make up £5, to pay for the freight of the goods of "Mr. Cobbit, the fchoolmafter"; 22 September [*Ibid.* 63], he was chofen one of three "raters," and one of a Town Council of five, "to join with the Commiffion officers ot this town by way of ordering concerns in any exegences relating to meletia affairs."

17 *May*, 1686 [*Ibid.* 68], he was chofen firft Selectman; 1 July [*Briftol Births, &c.* i: 18], his third fon, Nathaniel, was born (who died 29 Feb. following); 9 November [*B. T. R.* i: 70], he engaged "to deliver in four cords of fire-

wood for the Rev. Mr. Lee," to help make 42 cords; 18 November [*B. C. D.* ii: 271], he fells 20 acres of land at *Saconet*, for £11, to William Pabodie.

11 *February*, 168⁶⁄₇ [*B. C. D.* iii: 290], he buys of W. Pa bodie and W. Southworth of *Saconet* an 18-acre lot, for £13; 4 May [*B. T. R.* i: 72], he was chofen the firft of four Selectmen at Briftol; 8 May [*Rev. Dr. Shepard's Two Difcourfes*, 10], he became one of the original eight members of the Firft Congregational Church in Briftol.

23 *January*, 168⁷⁄₈ [*B. C. D.* iii: 370], he buys of Seth Arnold of Duxbury, one-half of the 33ᵈ lot in *Punkateaft* neck ; 19 February [*Ibid.* ii: 145], he exchanged with John Roufe of Marfhfield the 29ᵗʰ lot (which was the fecond he originally drew) at *Saconet* for the 18ᵗʰ (which adjoined the 19ᵗʰ, the firft which he originally drew, and on which he had built his houfe there) ; 21 May 1688 [*B. T. R.* i: 73], he was chofen again the firft of four Selectmen at Briftol; 16 July [*B. C. D.* i: 91], he buys for £100, a whole fhare of land in Little Compton, of Jofiah Cook and Jofeph Harding of Eaftham; 29 September [*Ibid.* 97], " for the love, goodwill and affection which I have and beare toward my loving friend and Brother-in-law James Bur- roughs of Briftol, Tailor, and Sarah, his now wife (being my fifter) " he gave his " home-lot " on the corner of Hope

and Queen Sts. in Briftol,* being 131 ft. by 59 ft., with other lands enumerated; 17 October [*Ibid.* vii: 572], for £33, he fold to James Peckham, of Little Compton, lands in that town, and fame date [*Ibid.* iii: 326], bought of faid Peckham for £13, two lots in faid town; 21 November [*Ibid.* i: 338], he bought for £6, of Samuel Sanford of Portfmouth, land at Little Compton; 28 November [*Ibid.* 1: 75], he exchanged certain lots in Little Compton for certain other lots there owned by John Cufhen of Scituate; 6 December [*Ibid.* i: 75], he fold for £90, lands in Little Compton to Peter Tailer of Newport; 26 December, [*Ibid.* 82], for £24, he fold land at Little Compton to Mathew Howard of that town.

24 *January*, 168⅞ [*Ibid.* 81], for £16, he fold to James Cafe and Anna his wife, of Little Compton, 40 acres of land in that town; 6 February [*Ibid.* ix: 173], he fells, for 42*s.* a ferry lot at *Pocaffet* to William Wodel; 6 September [*Entertaining Paffages, &c.* 56], he was commiffioned Major, and Commander-in-Chief, of Plymouth forces for the firft Eaftern Expedition; 7 September, 1689 [*B. C. D.* iii: 368], he buys of William Fobes, for £10, a lot in Little Compton; 18 September [*E. P.* 59], received his inftructions from the Commiffioners of the United Colonies, and

---

* Rev. Dr. Shepard fays, in a note to his *Two Difcourfes*, (p. 51) "tradition fays that the old Talbee houfe, in this town, [Briftol] ftanding near to the corner of Thames and Conftitution ftreets, the ftone chimney of which only remains (1857), was built by Col. Church."

started for Casco; 21 September [*Original letter of Church, in Mass. State Paper Office*], had an engagement with the enemy, in which eleven of his soldiers were killed and ten wounded; 13 November [*Willis's Hist. Portland* 280], he had a Council of war at Falmouth, soon after which he returned home; 25 December [*P. C. R.* vi: 228], a committee was appointed by the Colony to settle with him and others "the charges of the warr, &c." and the Court ordered him 40s. a week and £10, over, besides what he might receive "from the Bay."

6 *February*, 16$\frac{89}{90}$ [*E. P.* 65], he wrote to the Governor and Council of Massachusetts appealing on behalf of the poor inhabitants of Maine; 10 May, 1690 [*B. C. D.* ii: 66], for £7, he sells to Edward Gray of Little Compton land in *Sapowit* neck in said town; 30 May [*Ibid.* 147], he buys of Captain Christopher Almy of Rhode Island, for £11 10s. four thirtieths of lands left by the purchasers of *Pocassett*, at Fall-river, for erecting a mill or mills; 2 September [*E. P.* 69], was Commissioned for the second Eastern Expedition; 9 September [*Ibid.* 70], received his instructions, and started; was back to Bristol in three or four weeks; 4 November [*P. C. R.* vi: 255], was appointed by the Court to take charge of a contribution proposed in the County of Bristol for the relief "of ye town of Wells & parts adjacent;" 27 November [*E. P.* 77], wrote from Bristol to "the Eastern parts;" 2 December [*B. C. D.* iii: 369; v: 521], ex-

changed with W. Pabodie of Little Compton two lots in faid town.

8 *June*, 1691 [*B. C. D.* i: 199], he fells to Nathaniel Byfield, for £50, one fixteenth part of *Poppafquafh* neck being 43 acres more or lefs; 28 Auguft [*Ibid.* i: 111], he buys of his brother Caleb Church of Watertown, "mill-wright," for £100, 13½-30ᵗʰˢ of *Pocaffett* purchafe, being 30 rods in breadth, "and containes yᵉ river commonly called yᵉ Fall-river & yᵉ benefit of yᵉ ftream, and yᵉ ftrip of land defigned for yᵉ ufe of a mill, or mills, with yᵉ ½ part of yᵉ fawmill, &c. &c."; 23 September [*Ibid.* ii: 257], he buys for £70, of N. Thomas, of Marfhfield, lands at *Saconet.*

25 *July*, 1692 [*E. P.* 82], he was commiffioned for the third Eaftern Expedition; 11 Auguft, had his inftruétions, and ftarted for Penobfcot, — did what fervice he could and returned.

6 *March*, 1693 [*B. C. D.* vii: 154], he fells, for £21, to Samuel Crandall land at Little Compton; 23 May [*Ibid.* v: 11], he buys of W. Wodel, of Portfmouth, for £3, lands in Fall-river; 1 Auguft [*Ibid.* ii: 149], he buys of Thomas Burge of Little Compton, for £7 10*s.*, a meadow lot of 3 acres in that town; fame date [*Ibid.* ii: 142], he fells to faid Burge for £15, 40 rods fquare of land in the fame town.

in that town; 16 February [*Ibid*. iii: 397], he buys of Benjamin Woodworth of Little Compton, for £10, meadow lots in that town; 20 April, 1694 [*Ibid*. vi: 177], he buys of Gerſhom Wodel of *Pocaſſet*, for £3, lands at Fall-river; 23 July [*B. T. R.* i: 92], "Major Church" was choſen by the town of Briſtol the firſt of its 5 aſſeſſors; 30 July [*B. C. D.* i: 97], he bought back, for £50, his "home-lot" in Briſtol which he had ſold (29 Sept. 1688) to his brother-in-law, James Burroughs; 6 September [*Ibid*. 385], he buys of Iſrael Hubbard and Jonathan Dodſon of Scituate, for £150, one "great lot" in Freetown, "being the ſecond lot from yᵉ Fall-river."

29 *December*, 1695 [*Ibid*. ii: 21] he ſells to Joſeph Taber of Tiverton 80 acres at *Nomquid*, with a griſt mill, and alſo 39 acres in *Punkateaſt* neck, with other lots, for £360, ſaid Tabor agreeing to maintain the griſt-mill, as Church had done, with the agents of the proprietors of *Saconet*.

23 *March*, 1696 [*B. T. R.* i: 96], Major Church was choſen Moderator of Briſtol town-meeting, — the laſt time his name is mentioned on the records of that town, indicating his removal very ſoon after to Fall-river; 2 May [*B. C. D.* i: 290], he depoſed that in 1680 he ſaw Hugh Woodberry fencing "the 11th lot of yᵉ freeman's land," &c., in Freetown; 27 July [*Ibid*. ii: 217], he ſells, for £18, to John Palmer, carpenter, of Little Compton, 40 acres of land in that town; 3 Auguſt [*E. P.* 87], he was commiſſioned to

go on the fourth Expedition caſt; 12 Auguſt [*Ibid.* 88] had his inſtructions, and went out, returning in the Autumn.

18 *January*, $\frac{1699}{1700}$ [*B. C. D.* iv: 390], Major Church "late of Briſtol now of Tiverton" * — ſhowing that he had now become a reſident of Fall-river — "for natural love" gives to his ſon Thomas, of Briſtol, ſeveral parcels of land, with a houſe, &c.; 5 September, 1700 [*Ibid.* iii: 183], he buys of Joſeph Church of Little Compton for £100, ſeveral lots of land at *Saconet* Point; 20 December [*Ibid.* iii: 291], he buys of Latham Clark, of Newport, for £140, a whole half ſhare of the freeman's lot at Freetown.

7 *March*, 170$\frac{0}{1}$ [*Ibid.* iv: 29], he with others, deeds land in Little Compton to William Hiliard; 10 December, 1701 [*Ibid.* v: 161], he buys of Henry Head of Little Compton, for £10, land in that town.

27 *March*, 1702 [*Ibid.* iv: 17], "in conſideration of natural love and affection," he deeds to his ſon Edward large tracts of land in Briſtol, "his houſe on Hope St. & Queen St.," &c. &c.; 7 October [*Ibid.* iv: 37], he buys of John Bayley of Newport, for £40, certain lands in Little Comp-

---

* "His (Col. Church's) dwelling-houſe ſtood between the preſent dwelling-houſe of Col. Richard Borden, and that of his brother Jefferſon, and remained till within 40 years." Fowler's *Hiſt. Sketch of Fall River*, p. 19 [A. D. 1841]. This was on the fouth ſide of Annawon St., near Pond St., from 50 to 75 ft. from the former. The late extenſion of the Old Colony and Fall River R. R. to Newport, paſſes directly through the premiſes. [*MS.* letter from Hon. Jefferſon Borden.]

ton; 30 October [*Ibid.* 100], he buys, for £4 10*s.* of D. Wilcocks of Portſmouth, John Woodman of Little Compton, and Thomas and Roger Cory of Tiverton, lands at Fall-river.

12 *January*, 170$\frac{2}{3}$ [*Ibid.* 67], "Lieut. Col. Church of Tiverton, i.e. Fall River, for £3, buys of Conſtant Southworth $\frac{1}{30}$ part of land for a Mill at Fall-river, with $\frac{1}{30}$ of ſaid Fall-river; 16 January [*Ibid.* 99], he buys of Job Almy, of Tiverton, for £7 10*s.*, "one ſhare at Fall-river for a mill, &c."

5 *February*, 170$\frac{3}{4}$ [*E. P.*99], Col. Church wrote to Governor Dudley, offering a plan for a fifth Expedition eaſt; 18 March, he was commiſſioned; 4 May, received his inſtructions, and ſpent moſt of the ſummer on this buſineſs; 29 Nov. [1 *Maſs. Hiſt. Coll.* ix: 205], a Congregational Church was formed in Little Compton which he is believed to have aided to eſtabliſh, and of which he remained a conſiſtent member to his death.

20 *November*, 1705 [*Little Compton Town Records* i.], Col. Church firſt appears as if a reſident for the ſecond time in Little Compton, conſenting to changes in the roads for common convenience; 11 April [*B. C. D.* iv: 415], he deeds to his ſon Thomas a part of his Little Compton lands, with 10 cows, 100 ſheep, &c.; 20 July [*Ibid.* v: 100], he deeds to "my onely natural daughter Elizabeth Roſbotham, and to my ſon-in-law Capt. Joſeph Roſbotham (her now huſband) of Briſtol," lands in that town.

5 *June*, 1706 [*L. C. T. R.* 1], he was chofen Reprefentative of Little Compton for the year enfuing.

3 *February*, 170$\frac{6}{7}$ [*B. C. D.* v: 142], "for love, &c." he deeds to his fon Charles the 18th and 19th lots at Little Compton (that on which he built in 1674, with that adjoining it, which, in 1688, he had fecured by exchange with John Roufe), with the buildings, &c. &c.; 12 April, 1707 [*Ibid.* v: 214], " for love " &c. he deeds to his fon Conftant (after his own deceafe), the mill fhares and mills in Tiverton, with lands in Freetown; 26 April [*B. C. D.* v: 162], "for love " &c. he deeds to his fon Thomas of Briftol, his houfe * (after his deceafe and that of his wife), called " the little farm," containing 120 acres, with other lands; 7 Auguft [*L. C. T. R.* i.], he married at Little Compton, William Cuthbert and Mary Head; 18 September [*L . C. T. R.* i], the town voted him £18 7s. out of the town rate for his fervices as Reprefentative.

17 *March*, 1708 [*L. C. T. R.* i.], he married Edward Southworth and Mary Fobes; 24 March [*B. C. D.* v· 343], he fold for £30, to Henry Wood, of Newport, land at Little Compton; May, 1708 [*L . C. T. R.* i.], he married

---

* When he went back to Little Compton in 1705, or thereabouts, he built on the lots which he had long owned juft fouth of *Awafhonks's* ¾ mile fquare of referved territory [fee note 12 *poft*]. His houfe ftood back in the field; and the well, and traces of the cellar remain. The fpot is now owned by Mr. George H. Peckham. It is a little S. of W. from the two Windmills which ftand near together on the road from *Saconet* Point to Tiverton, and is perhaps 1¾ miles S. W. in a ftraight line, from the Common.

John Irifh and (his fifter) Prifcilla Church; 23 June [*B. C. D.* v: 471; vii: 241], he exchanged with Thomas Burge of Little Compton lands valued at £40; 22 December [*L. C. T. R.* i.], he married Amos Sheffield and Sarah ——.

29 *January*, 170⅞ [*B. C. D.* v: 463], he buys of John Irifh, for £15, meadow land in Little Compton; 4 April, 1709 [*B. C. D.* v: 488], at the inftance of the government he exchanged fome lands in Little Compton, to accommodate the Indians; 6 September [*L. C. T. R.* i.], he was chofen in Little Compton to the Grand Jury.

4 *January*, 1710 [*L. C. T. R.* i.], he married John Bailey and Lydia ——; 16 May [*Ibid.*], he was chofen Reprefentative of the town in the next General Court ; 28 September [*Ibid.*], he married William Shaw and Content Irifh.

24 *December*, 1711 [*Ibid.*], he was allowed £13 4*s*. for his fervices as Reprefentative.

25 *December*, 1712 [*B. C. D.* vii: 462], " for love," &c. he deeds land in Freetown to his daughter and her hufband, Capt. Jofeph Rofbotham; and, fame date, [*Ibid.* 463] for £100, to the fame parties more land in Freetown.

24 *January*, 171⅔ [*L. C. T. R.* i], he married Samuel Tompkins and Sarah ——; 23 February [*B. C. D.* vii: 583], for £15, he fold to his fon Thomas, of Little Compton, lands in Tiverton; 18 March, 1713 [*L. C. T. R.* i.], he was chofen moderator of the town meeting in Little

Compton; 25 September [*Ibid.*], he married William Briggs, jun., and Deborah Church; 16 November [*Ibid.*], he married Jonathan Blackman and Sarah ———

14 *January*, 171¾ [*B. C. D.* vii: 480], "for love" &c., he deeds feveral valuable tracts of land in Little Compton; 25 March, 1714 [*Ibid.* viii: 583], he buys, for £33 15*s*. lands in Tiverton of Samuel and Mary Snell; 31 March [*Ibid.* viii: 582], he fells, for £24, to William Wilbor, lands in Little Compton; 18 November [*Ibid.* 583], for £32 10*s*. he fells to Richard Ward and Lion Arnold of Newport, lands in *Pocaffet*.

14 *April*, 1715 [*Ibid.* ix: 738], with Conftant, he fells land in Freetown to Thomas Turner; 7 June [*Ibid.* 451], for £6, he fells his fon Thomas land in Little Compton; 1 November [*L. C. T. R.* i.], he married Peter Taylor and Hannah Wood. During this year alfo he doubtlefs dictated to his fon Thomas his "Entertaining Paffages."

8 *April*, 1716 [*Ibid.*], he married Samuel Coe and Mary Chadwick; 13 May [*Ibid.*], he married Jonathan Hilliard and Abigail Wilbor.

3 *March*, 171⁶⁄₇ [*B. C. D.* x: 637], he gave lands in Freetown to his fon Conftant, referving the right to improve them during his life; 20 June, 1717 [*L. C. T. R.* i.], he married William Wilbor and Efther Burges; 11 September [*Briftol Marriages*, &c. ii: 23], "Mr. John Sampfon and Mrs. Elizabeth Rofbotham of this town (Briftol) were

joined in marriage by Benjamin Church, Efq.”; 13 November [*L. C. T. R.* i.], he married (his laſt couple) Thomas Tibbets and Elizabeth Wood.

———

The account which was given by Dr. Stiles on the authority of a member of the family, of the old Colonel’s death, is as follows: — “the morning before his death, he went about two miles on horſeback to viſit his only [furviving?] ſiſter, Mrs. Iriſh, to ſympathize with her on the death of her only child. After a friendly and pious viſit, in a moving and affecting manner, he took his leave of her, and ſaid, ‘ It was a laſt farewell; Telling her, he was perfuaded he ſhould never fee her more; but hoped to meet her in heaven.’ Returning homeward, he had not rode above half a mile before his horſe ſtumbled, and threw him over his head: And the Colonel being exceeding fat and heavy, fell with ſuch force that a blood veſſel was broken, and the blood guſhed out of his mouth like a torrent. His wife was foon brought to him; he tried but was unable to ſpeak to her, and died in about twelve hours. He was carried to the grave in great funeral pomp, and was buried under arms, and with military honours.”

———

His monument — a huge flat ſtone laid horizontally over the grave, ſupported by ſtones under each ſide and end, in the graveyard adjoining the Congregational Church in Little Compton — ftill bears the following infcription: —

" Here lyeth interred the [body]
of the Honourable
Col. BENJAMIN CHURCH, Esq.
who departed this life,   January
the 17, 171⅞, in yᵉ 78 yeare of
his age."

The Probate Record of his Eftate, is as follows: —

The fifth day of March Administration Granted to Madam Allice Church on the Estate of Collᵉ Benjā Church deceased

[Bristol Co. Probate Records, iii : 363.]

A true Inventory of Estate both Reall & Personall left by the Honᵉᵃᵇˡᵉ Collᵉ Benjāⁿ Church Esqᵉ Late of Little Compton decᵈ Taken by us the subscribers the 5ᵗʰday ffebᵉʸ 1717–18

To his Sword and Belt	05	00	00
To a Cane & Gloves	00	12	00
To Wearing Apparell.	28	15	00
To 2 Gold Rings 1ˡ & 3 pair of Buttons 1ˡ 10 : 0 all .	02	10	00
To one pair of Plate Buckles	00	15	00
To one Tanker one cup one Porringer & 2 salt sellars plate and seven spoons all weighing 42 Ounces	25	00	00
To a Case of knives & forks	00	08	00
To Sundry Books	02	00	00
To land in Tiverton one Six Score acre lot & half being 18 aᵉ [acres].	180	00	00
To Two Gunns	03	00	00

To one Bed 2 Blankets one Rug curtains and Vallence & two Pillows and Bedstead &c	24	00	00
To one other Bed Bedstead and 4 Blankets or Coverlids Two Pillows and Curtains.	18	00	00
To one other Bed Bedstead Bolster & 3 Blankets .	12	00	00
To 14 pair of Sheets	21	00	00
To nine Pillow cases . . . . . . ·	01	16	00
To two Doz of napkins & Towels	03	12	00
To 4 Table Cloathes	02	00	00
To three Tables	03	10	00
To one Cubboard	03	00	00
To six Chests	02	02	00
To seven Turkey worked chairs	04	02	00
To 16 Wooden Chairs	02	08	00

Puter To 21 plates 1 17 0 To 7 platters 3ˡ all .   04 17 00

To 11 Basons 1 13 00 & 3 Chamber Potts 8ˢ   . 02 01 00

Tinn To one Collender one Cauldron & on Tea pott all . 00 03 00

Brass To one Chaffing Dish & one warmingpan   . 01 10 00

To two Kettles and one Bellmettell skillet 06 00 00

Iron To three Potts and one Kettle 01 10 00

To one spit 3 AndIrons two pair of Tongs one fire shove two Trammels one hook and one frying pan all 02 02 00

To 8 Keelers 8 pails 3 Piggins 3 Trayes & one Sugar Box all 02 15 00

To 5 Cheese fatts one churn & 3 Cedar Tubs all . 02 04 00

To one Mealtrough & Corrill & one Tray all . . . 00 06 00

To 3 Bags 12ˢ to Earthenware 6ˢ & 12 Glass Bottles 4ˢ all 01 02 00

To two Ropes 6ˢ to 5 old Sythes 5ˢ To 3 old Iron hopps & 3 Iron Boxes 8ˢ all 00 19 00

To a Bettle and wedges 6ˢ & 3 Sythe Snaths 3ˢ all . 00 09 00

To 3 hones 6ˢ one Bill hooke & 4 Axes 11ˢ all . . . 00 17 00

To Iron ffetters horse traces one Coller Harnes & old Iron 00 14 00

One Hmmer & one square 00 08 00
One old Tennant Saw 2 pair of sheers & 2 pᵣ of Stel-
   liards 00 08 00
To one girdle 3 Stirupp Irons & one Lanthorn all . 00 04 00
To three Riddle Sives 3ˢ & 14 old Cask — 1 08ˢ all . 01 11 00
To 25 bushells of salt 3ˡ 15ˢ & 2 Cheese presses 8ˢ all 04 03 00
To 2 pair of Spinning Wheels and one pair of Cards 00 10 00
To 2 Barrills of Beef one Barrill of Pork . 05 00 00
To nine Cows 54 00 00
To 4 heifers 20 00 00
To a pair of Oxen 14 00 00
To a pair of Steers 12 00 00
To one Bull 02 10 00
To Seven Two Year old Cattle. 21 00 00
To a cart and Wheels 2 Yoaks 2 Chains & Clevis &
   pin 04 10 00
Two Iron Barrs and one Sledge 01 00 00
To Yarn and flax 03 15 00
To about 25ᶜ weight of Cheese 04 00 00
To 13 Bushels of Barley 02 00 00
To 2 old Barrills and Some Beanes 00 10 00
To Twenty Bushells of Oates 02 10 00
To about 40 Bushells of Indian corn 08 00 00
To one Tubb & Pork 04 00 00
To 2 Barrills of Cider 1ᵉ & three empty Cask 6ˢ . 01 06 90
To one sorild horfs 12 00 00
To one black horfs 16 00 00
To the Collafh with the Horfs saddle & Brydle &c 12 00 00
To one Bay mare 18 00 00
To 2 old ploughs and one Brake 01 05 00
To ten yearling Cattle 15 00 00
To 5 Swine 02 10 00
To a looking Glass and hour Glass 00 08 06
To 3 Scivers one pair of tongs & pair of Bellows all . 00 05 06
To one pair of holdsters & an old Portmantle 00 12 00

To about 15 pound of Butter 00 10 00
To a Negro man Clothing and bedding &c . . 60 00 00
To a Negro woman clothing & Bedding &c . . . 40 00 00
To a Servant Boy called William Hood. 10 00 00
To John Tomlin. 03 00 00
To three rakes and Two pitch forks 00 06 00
To an Iron Bark 01 10 00
To a score of Sheep 06 16 00
To a Clasp Stale pan a pair of Specticles & Inkhorn 00 09 00
To Silver and Gold Buttons 02 02 06
To Cash 02 18 06
To his Right in a Small lott of land Tiverton . . . 05 00 00

This Inventory was taken the day and year
above written by us   JOHN WOOD   ⎫
                      THOMAS GREY   ⎬ *Prifers*
                      WILLIAM PABODIE ⎭
[Bristol Co. Probate Records, iii: 381, 382.]

To all People to whom these presents Shall come   Know Yee that we who are the Children of our Hon^ed ffather Coll^e Benjamin Church late of Little Compton in the County of Bristol in the Province of the Mafsachuset Bay in New England dec^d Who Dyed Intestate   And that the law of this Province doth Provide that all Just Debts & funerall Charges shall be payd out of the Personall Estate which will be a great Damage to our Hon^ed Mother Mrs Allice Church who is Administratrix to said Estate

These are therefore to give full power and lawfull Authority to our above named Mother as Administratrix to our above s^d Hon^ed ffathers Estate To Bargain Sell Alin & Dispose of all our Right Title Claime or Demand of one Six Score acre lot and one halfe in the Township of Tiverton in pocafet Purchafs the whole lot being the fourteen in number and the half lot being the Thirteenth lot in number which lot and half being mentioned in the Inventory of our s^d ffathers estate and is

F   xli

I append here fuch few fcattering genealogical facts in regard to the defcendants of Colonel Church as have come incidentally to my notice, — as materials for whoever may, at any future time, attempt to catalogue the complete defcent from him.

BENJAMIN CHURCH,[1] b. at Plymouth, 1639, m. 26 Dec. 1667 ALICE SOUTHWORTH (b. Duxbury 1646, d. Little Compton 5 Mar. 171$\frac{7}{8}$, æt. 73), d. 17 Jan. 171$\frac{7}{8}$, at Little Compton, R.-I. æt. 78. They had (1) Thomas,[2] b. Duxbury, 1674, d. Little Compton, 12 Mar. 1746, æt. 73; (2) Constant,[3] b. Portsmouth, R.-I. 12 May, 1676, d. 26 Mar. 1726? [*N. E. Hist. & Gen Reg.* xi: 155.] (3) Benjamin,[4] b. 1678; (4) Edward,[5] b. 1680; (5) Charles,[6] b. 1682, d. Bristol Jan. 1747; (6) Elizabeth,[7] b. 26 Mar. 1684; (7) Nathaniel,[8] b. 1 July 1686, d. 29 Feb. 1687; (8) Martha.[9]

THOMAS CHURCH,[2] m. *first*, 21 Feb. 169$\frac{8}{9}$, SARAH HAYMAN, had (1) Sarah,[10] b. 15 Jan. 1700, d. 29 Aug. 1701; (2) Elizabeth,[11] b. 9 Sept. 1702, d. 27 Sept. 1702; (3) Thomas,[12] b. 20 Aug. 1704, d. young; m. *second*, 16 April 1712 EDITH, 2d dau. and 4th child of John and Hannah [Timberlake] WOODMAN [b. 7 Sept. 1685, d. 3 June 1718], had (4) Elizabeth[13], b. 10 Jan. 1713; (5) Hannah[14] b. 23 Sept. 1714; (6) Priscilla,[15] b. 6 Jan. 1717, d. 15 Mar. 1744; (7) Thomas[16] b. May 1718, d. 21 Aug. 1718; m. 1719 *third*, SARAH ———? had (8) Thomas,[17] b. 31 May, 1720, d. 4 July, 1720; (9) Sarah,[18] b. 15 May, 1721; (10) Thomas,[19] b. 13 July, 1722, d. 5 Oct. 1722; (11) Benjamin,[20] b. 9 Sept. 1723, d. 27 Sept. 1723; (12) Mary,[21] b. 2 Jan. 1725; (13) Thomas,[22] b. 1 Sept. 1727; (14) Benjamin,[23] b. 10 Jan. 1732, d. 4 Aug. 1749; (15) Mercy,[24] b. 18 Sept. 1734.

CONSTANT CHURCH.[3] [I have seen no trace of his family, if he had any.]

BENJAMIN CHURCH.[4] [It is said died unmarried.]

EDWARD CHURCH[5] lived in Boston, where, before 1764, he had a place of business as vendue-master, on Newbury Street, "two doors south of the sign of the Lamb." He m. Elizabeth ———? who d. 18

April, 1766, æt. 27. He had an only son Benjamin,[25] who was probably also a vendue-master, and the father of two sons (one of whom was
Dr. Benjamin Church, of Tory memory in the Revolution), and a daughter who m. Mr. Fleming, a stationer.

CHARLES CHURCH[6] was High Sheriff of the County, and Rep-
resentative to the General Court; m. 20 May, 1708, Mrs. HANNAH
PAINE of Bristol, had (1) Constant,[26] b. 12 Dec. 1708; (2) Elizabeth,[27]
b. 24 Dec. 1710; (3) Hannah,[28] b. 20 Feb. 171$\frac{2}{3}$, d. Jan. 174$\frac{7}{8}$.

ELIZABETH CHURCH,[7] m. *first*, 1700? Capt. JOSEPH ROS-
BOTHAM of Bristol, had (1) Benjamin,[29] b. 21 Dec. 1701; (2) Alice,[30]
b. 26 Aug. 1704; (3) Elizabeth,[31] b. 9 Sept. 1708; (4) Hannah,[32] b. 20
June, 1711; m. *second*, 11 Sept. 1717, Mr. JOHN SAMPSON, of Bristol,
[d. 12 Jan. 173$\frac{4}{5}$]; had (5) John[33] and (6) Elizabeth,[34] (twins) b. 20
Jan. 171$\frac{8}{9}$; (7) John,[35] b. (at New Haven) 31 May, 1722; m. *third*,
18 June, 1739, Capt. SAMUEL WOODBURY.

NATHANIEL CHURCH,[8] [died an infant.]

MARTHA CHURCH[9]. [I find no trace of her except her signa-
ture to the document accompanying the settlement of her father's
estate.]

SARAH CHURCH,[18] m. 29 Apr. 1742, SAMUEL BAILEY of Little
Compton, had (1) William,[36] b. 25 Aug. 1742, m. 4 Mar. 1770, SARAH
BRIGGS, d. 17 Feb. 1825; (2) Samuel,[37] b. 3 Jan. 1744, m. ELIZABETH
CHURCH; (3) Francis,[38] b. 4 Oct. 1745; (4) Ruth,[39] b. 24 Apr. 1747, d.
6 Dec. 1771; (5) Sarah,[40] b. 23 Sept. 1749, m. 1 Mar. 1772, JOHN MAN-
CHESTER; (6) George,[41] b. 29 Apr. 1751, d. 27 Mar. 1764; (7) Hannah,[42]
b. 25 July, 1760.

MARY CHURCH,[21] m. 31 Mar. 1748, AARON WILBOR [3d son
and 6th child of John, who was 2d son and 3d child of William, an original settler], had (1) Sarah,[43] b. 25 Dec. 1748; (2) Benjamin,[44] b. 22
Oct. 1750; (3) Aaron,[45] b. June, 1753; (4) Francis,[46] b. 4 Aug. 1755, d.
15 June, 1844; (5) Thomas,[47] b. 23 Sept. 1756, d. 13 Sept. 1840; (6)
John,[48] b. 4 May, 1762.

THOMAS CHURCH,[22] m. *first*, 31 Jan. 1748, RUTH BAILEY
[youngest dau. and child of William, and so youngest sister of the husband of Sarah,[18] b. 3 Aug. 1727, d. 31 Jan. 1771], had (1) Constant,[49]

b. 9 May, 1748; (2) Sarah,[50] b. 12 Feb. 1750, d. 17 Nov. 1750; (3) Sarah,[51] b. 24 May, 1751; (4) Elizabeth,[52] b. 25 Dec. 1752; (5) Benjamin;[53] (6) Mercy,[54] b. Mar. 1756, d. 31 Mar. 1837; (7) Thomas,[55] b. 26 Nov. 1757; (8) Obadiah,[56] b. 21 Apr. 1759; (9) William,[57] b. 7 May, 1761; (10) Charles,[58] b. 10 Mar. 1763; (11) Francis,[59] b. 19 Dec. 1764; (12) Thomas,[60] b. 3 Mar. 1767; (13) Ruth,[61] b. 5 Dec. 1768; (14) Mary,[62] b. 30 Jan. 1771, d. 1 Feb. 1771; m. *second*, MARY RICHMOND, [b. 26 Dec. 1735, 2d dau. and 8th child of William, oldest son of Sylvester]; had (15) George,[63] b. 30 May, 1773; (16) Gamaliel,[64] b. 1 Mar. 1775; (17) Mary,[65] b. 12 Feb. 1777, d. 17 July, 1777.

MERCY CHURCH,[24] m. 3 Feb. 1754, PEREZ RICHMOND [4th son and 5th child of William, d. 1801], had (1) Sarah,[66] b. 24 Aug. 1756; m. 27 Apr. 1776, JOB CLAPP; (2) Ruth,[67] b. 6 Sept. 1758; (3) Elizabeth,[68] b. 9 Mar. 1760; (4) Thomas,[69] b. 5 Mar. 1764; (5) Benjamin,[70] b. 11 July, 1765; (6) Anna,[71] b. 24 Mar. 1767; (7) Mary,[72] b. 5 Apr. 1770; (8) Charles,[73] b. 9 July, 1773; (9) Hannah,[74] b. 17 Dec. 1775.

CONSTANT CHURCH,[49] m. 20 June, 1771, KEZIA BRIGGS [3d dau. and child of Jeremiah, who was 4th son and child of Job, who was 4th son and 7th child of William, b. 13 Oct. 1751, d. 17 Dec. 1818.], had (1) Ruth,[75] b. 19 Dec. 1771; (2) Sarah,[76] b. 29 May, 1774; (3) Jeremiah Briggs,[77] b. 22 Jan. 1776; (4) Benjamin,[78] b. 23 Jan. 1778, d. 20 Sept. 1778; (5) Kezia,[79] b. 14 Mar. 1780; (6) Charles,[80] b. 16 Mar. 1782, d. 14 Sept. 1805; (7) Betsey,[81] b. 17 Sept. 1784; (8) Anna,[82] b. 11 Feb. 1787; (9) Constantine,[83] b. 5 Jan. 1789, d. 1 Nov. 1826; (10) Hannah,[84] b. 9 Oct. 1781, d. 2 Sept. 1828; (11) William,[85] b. 27 Apr. 1795, d. 14 Oct. 1796.

ELIZABETH CHURCH,[52] m. 23 Oct. 1774, SAMUEL BAILEY [b. 3 Jan. 1744, was 2d son and child of Samuel, who m. SARAH[18]], had (1) Sarah,[86] b. 31 Mar. 1775; (2) Cornelius,[87] b. 8 Oct. 1776; (3) Benjamin,[88] b. 18 Aug. 1780; (4) Ruth,[89] b. 26 Feb. 1782; (5) Thomas,[90] (6) Samuel,[91] (twins), b. 6 May, 1785; (7) George,[92] b. 26 April, 1788; (8) Charles,[93] b. 5 Apr. 1790; (9) Hannah,[94] b. 1 June, 1794.

CONSTANT CHURCH,[26] of Bristol, m. 25 Jan. 173⅔, MARY REYNOLDS, of Bristol, had (1) Peter,[95] b. 1 Dec. 1737; (2) Mary,[96] b. 2 Apr. 1740; (3) Charles,[97] b. 5 Nov. 1743.

PETER CHURCH [95] [as the records seem to say] m. 22 Mar. 1764, Mrs. SARAH FALES, of Bristol, and, for second wife, HANNAH ———? had (1) George,[98] b. 1 Apr., 1771 ; (2) William,[90] b. 5 Apr. 1776 ; (3) Peter,[100] b. 26 Apr. 1791 ; (4) Hannah,[101] b. 13 Sept. 1792.

This Peter[100] I suppose to be the Col. Peter, now living in Bristol, whose son, Captain Benjamin, commanding a company in the 8th Michigan V. M., was killed by a shot through the head, 16 June, 1862, while gallantly leading a charge upon the rebels, in the battle of James Island. [*Stone's R.-I. in the Rebellion*, 298.]

xlvii

INTRODUCTORY NOTE.

I T had been intended to give, in this place, a full ftatiftical ftatement of the condition of New England in population, refources, towns, churches, minifters &c., &c., at the date of the breaking-out of thofe hoftilities which are commonly known as Philip's War; and to add a careful eftimate of the caufes of that ftrife, and the effects of it upon the Colonies. But the neceffary length of fuch a ftatement and eftimate, and the unexpected voluminoufnefs of the preceding biographical matter, compels the refervation of that hiftorical introduction until the iffue of that remaining portion of thefe "Entertaining Paffages," which has efpecial reference to the Eaftern Expeditions; when it will be given as preliminary to thofe brief ftatements which may be further needful to make clear the caufes and iffues of thofe later conflicts.

Meanwhile, the reader who defires to perufe thefe exploits and experiences of Captain Church, with the moft intelligent comprehenfion of their relation to the general matters of the war, and the condition of the country at that date, is refpectfully referred to the third volume of Dr. Palfrey's "Hiftory of New England," where [pp. 132–239], he will find the moft lucid, careful and truthful expofition of the fubject, which has yet been given to the prefs.

1

Entertaining Paſſages

Relating to

𝕻𝖍𝖎𝖑𝖎𝖕'𝖘 WAR

W H I C H

Began in the Month of June, 1 6 7 5.

AS ALSO OF

EXPEDITIONS

More lately made

Againſt the Common Enemy, and Indian Rebels, in the Eaſtern Parts of New=England·

W I T H

Some Account of the Divine Providence

T O W A R D S

Benj. Church Eſqr;

By *T. C.*

B O S T O N: Printed by *B. Green*, in the Year, 1 7 1 6.

TO THE

READER

THE *subject of this following Narrative offering itself to your friendly Perusal; relates to the Former and Later Wars of* New-England, *which I my self was not a little concerned in : For in the Year,* 1675. *that unhappy and bloody* Indian *War broke out in* Plymouth *Colony, where I was then building, and beginning a Plantation, at a Place called by the* Indians Sekonit; *and since by the* Englifh, Little Compton. I *was the first* Englifh Man *that built upon that Neck, which was full of* Indians. *My head and hands were full about Settling a New Plantation, where nothing was brought to ; no preparation of Dwelling Houfe, or Out-Houfing or Fencing made. Horfes and Cattel were to be provided, Ground to be clear'd and broken up ; and the utter-*

moft

TO THE READER.

most caution to be used, to keep my self free from offending my Indian *Neighbours all round about me. While I was thus busily Employed, and all my Time and Strength laid out in this Laborious Undertaking; I Received a Commission from the Government to engage in their Defence. And with my Commission I receiv'd another heart inclining me to put forth my Strength in Military Service. And through the Grace of* G O D *I was Spirited for that work, and Direction in it was renewed to me day by day. And altho' many of the Actions that I was concerned in, were very Difficult and Dangerous; yet my self and those that went with me Voluntarily in the Service, had our Lives, for the most part, wonderfully preserved, by the over-ruling Hand of the Almighty, from first to last; which doth aloud bespeak our Praises: And to declare His Wonderful Works, is our Indispensible Duty. I was ever very sensible of my own Littleness and Unfitness, to be imployed in such Great Services; but calling to mind that* G O D *is* STRONG, *I Endeavoured to put all my Confidence in Him, and by His Almighty Power was carried through every difficult Action: and my desire is that His Name may have the Praise.*

It was ever my Intent having laid my self under a Solemn promise, that the many and Repeated Favours of G O D *to my self, and those with me in the Service, might be published for Generations to come. And now my great Age requiring my Dismission from Service in the Militia, and to put off my Armour; I am willing that the Great and Glorious works*

of

of Almighty G O D , to us Children of Men, should appear to the World; and having my Minutes by me; my Son has taken the care and pains to Collect from them the Insuing Narrative of many passages relating to the Former and Later Wars; which I have had the perusal of, and find nothing a-miss, as to the Truth of it; and with as little Reflection upon any particular person as might be, either alive or dead.

And seeing every particle of historical Truth is precious; I hope the Reader will pass a favourable Censure upon an Old Souldier, telling of the many Ran-Counters he has had, and yet is come off alive. It is a pleasure to Remember what a great Number of Families in this and the Neighbouring Provinces in New-England *did during the War, enjoy a great measure of Liberty and Peace by the hazardous Sta-*tions *and* Marches *of those Engaged in Military Exercises, who were a Wall unto them on this side and on that side. I desire Prayers that I may be enabled Well to accomplish my Spiritual Warfare, and that I may be more than Conquer-our through JESUS CHRIST loving of me.*

Benjamin Church.

Entertaining Paſſages

Relating to

𝕻𝖍𝖎𝖑𝖎𝖕'𝖘 WAR[1] which began in the Year, 1675.

With the Proceedings of

Benj. Church Eſqr;

I N the Year 1674, Mr. *Benjamin Church* of *Duxbury*[2] being providentially at *Plymouth* in the time of the Court,[3] fell into acquaintance with Capt. *John Almy*[4] of *Rhode-Iſland*. Capt. *Almy* with great importunity invited him to ride with him, and view that part of *Plymouth* Colony that lay next to *Rhode-Iſland*,

[1] See Introduction, for ſome account of the origin of this ſtruggle.

[2] See Introductory Memoir, for facts in the early life of Mr. Church.

[3] The "Court of His Majeſtie" met at Plymouth 4 March, 3 June, 7 July, and 27 October, in 1674. [*Plymouth Colony Records*, vol. v.]

[4] John Almy was in Plymouth, in 1643; married Mary, daughter of James Cole; removed to Portſmouth, R.-I.; loſt a horſe in the ſervice of the Rhode-Iſland Colony by "making great expedition" in watching a Dutch man-of-war, for which in 1666 he was paid £7; 23 July, 1667, was appointed "Lieftenant" of a "troope of horſe"; 24 July, 1671, was a witneſs of the articles of agreement made between the Court of New Plymouth and Awaſhonks, Squaw-Sachem of Sogkonate; 14 June, 1676, was appointed, with Mr. Thomas Borden, to take an inventory of goods of Thomas Lawton; died before Nov. 1676, at which time Plymouth Court gave his widow power to adminiſter on his eſtate within the Colony juriſdiction. [Savage's *Gen. Dict.* i: 45; *Rhode-Iſland Colonial Records*, ii: 184, 214, 544; *Plym. Col. Rec.* v: 75, 212.]

known then by their Indian Names of *Pocaſſet*[5] & *Sogkonate*.[6] Among other arguments to perſwade him, he told him, the Soil was very rich, and the Situation pleaſant. Perſwades him by all means, to purchaſe of the Company ſome of the Court grant rights.[7] He accepted his invitation, views the

[5] Now mainly Tiverton, R.-I.; including the eaſtern ſhore of Mount-Hope bay from *Quequechan* river (Fall River) on the north to Pachet brook on the ſouth. As to the meaning of the name *Pocaſſet*, Mr. Trumbull ſays, "A half-dozen good enough etymologies preſent themſelves; but as I do not know which is right, and have not much confidence in either, I let the name paſs."

[6] Extending from Pachet brook to the ocean; now mainly Little Compton, R.-I. Dr. Uſher Parſons ſays the word *Sogkonate* is compounded of *Seki*, "black," *konk*, "gooſe," and the ſyllable *et* as a locative; thus *Seki-konk-et*, *Seconknet*, *Seconet*, — equivalent to "black-goofe-place." [*Indian Names of Places in R.-I.* p. 5.] But Mr. Trumbull ſays : — "If *honck* means gooſe, why ſhould an Indian prefix the adjective *black*, as deſcriptive of the only gooſe he knew anything about? Then *Sucki* does not mean 'black,' but 'purple,' *i. e.*, black inclining to blue, as we ſee it in the inner margin of a quahaug ſhell. Then, again, the Indian never made uſe of what we call names of places, but *deſcribed* his localities; never calling a given ſituation 'black-fiſh' or 'black-goofe,' and muſt have violated the genius of his language to have done ſo. Then,

further, *Sucki-honck*, or its plural, *Sucki-honck-aog*, (for it is hardly probable that *one* black goofe would defignate the place,) can hardly have been twiſted into *Sogkonate* or *Saconet*, or (as Preſident Stiles writes and marks the name in 1760) *Saucōnet*." "As to the real meaning of the word," Mr. T. adds, "I am troubled by the *embarras de richeſſes*. It *might* mean *Sohkauün-et*, — 'the conquered territory'; or *Sowan-ohquan-et*, — 'at the ſouth point'; or *Sowanohkit* [*Eliot*, Gen. xxiv. 62; Joſh. xv. 19], — 'the ſouth country'; either of which might eaſily be corrupted into *Saucōnet*. And ſo on."

[7] It was a common proviſion in the indentures of ſervants in the Plymouth Colony, that they ſhould have land aſſigned them when their term of ſervice expired. In 1633-4, land for ſuch uſe was ſet apart in Scituate. In 1636 the amount of five acres was fixed upon as that which they were to receive. 4 June, 1661, liberty was granted to thoſe who were formerly ſervants, who have land due them by covenant, to nominate ſome perſons to be deputed in their behalf to purchaſe a parcel of land for their accommodation at Saconet. Further order to ſecure the right of theſe perſons to take up land at Saconet was made by the Court, 7 June, 1665. 4 July, 1673, the following Court order was

Country, & was pleafed with it; makes a purchafe,[8] fettled

paffed: — "Whereas there is a tracte of land graunted to the old fervants, or fuch of them as are not elfewhere fupplyed, lying att Saconett, the Court doe determine the bounds thereof to be from the bounds of the graunt made to Plymouth att Punckateefett and the bounds of Dartmouth, and foe all lands foutherly lying between that and the fea; the Court haue likewife giuen them order, or fuch as they fhall appoint, to make purchafe thereof in theire behalfe as occation fhall require, and that all fuch p'fons as haue right vuto the faid graunt as old fervants att Saconett fhall make their appeerance att Plymouth on the twenty fecond of this p'fent July, then and theire to make out theire right, and alfoe pay fuch disburfments as fhall neffefarily be required, or otherwife loofe theire right."

Agreeably to this order the following 29 perfons appeared at Plymouth, on faid 22 July, viz: Jofiah Winflow, Efq.; Mr. Conftant Southworth; Daniel Willcox; Hugh Cole (in right of James Cole, fen.); Nicolas Wade and John Cufhing, both in right of faid Nicolas Wade; Thomas Williams; *Benjamin Church* (in right of Richard Bifhop and alfo in right of Richard Beare); John Roufe, jr. (in right of Samuel Chandler); William Sherman, fen.; Jofeph Church (in right of John Smalley, and alfo in right of George Vicory); John Rogers, jun. (in right of William Tubbs); William Merrick; Martha Dean (in right of Joseph Beedle); Simon Roufe (in right of John Roufe, fen.); William Pabodie (in right of Abraham Samfon); Edward Fobes (in right of John Fobes); John Irifh, jun. (in right of John Irifh, fen.); Peter Colomore; Daniel Hayward (in right of John Hayward, fen.); Jofiah Cook; John Wafhburne, fen., "as a

---

[8] Firft iffued in 1716, and probably dictated by Col. Church to his fon Thomas not long before that time, it will not feem furprifing that flight inaccuracies fhould occafionally be found in this narrative of what took place more than 40 years before. There is fome evident confufion here. The original MS. Proprietors' Records prove that Church had bought the rights of Richard Bifhop and Richard Beare to Saconet previous to 22 July, 1673; a courfe which he here feems to reprefent himfelf as taking in the following year, on Capt. Almy's urgency. Unlefs the meeting of court to which he refers (fee note 3) was the firft for that year, he muft not only have purchafed thefe rights, but have received his affignment of lots No. 19 and No. 29, before the viewing the country here referred to. I think, in point of fact, he bought the rights on fpeculation, and went down with Capt. Almy to look at his two lots, and liked them fo well as to conclude to fettle upon them; but became confufed in his memory of the order of events.

a Farm, found the Gentlemen of the Iſland⁹ very Civil &
obliging. And being himſelf a Perſon of uncommon

freeman"; Thomas Pope; John Richmond (in right of John Price); Walter
Woodworth (in right of Thomas Si-
mons); Nathaniel Thomas (in right of
Nicolas Preſlong); Ephraim Tinkham;
Thomas Pinſon; and William Shirt-
life. They "proved their rights," and
agreed, —

1. That all were equal proprietors
of the granted premiſes, "that is to ſay,
to have and pay alike, according to
each man's proportion."

2. That all lands on their grant at
Saconet that ſhall any way become
alienated from the Indians, and appropriated to the Engliſh, "ſhall belong and
be to the aforeſaid proprietors."

3. That one equal ſhare ſhall be appropriated "to the uſe of the miniſtry,
and ſo to remain ſucceſſively forever"

4. That no perſon ſhall appropriate
to himſelf more than *two ſhares* at Saconet, on penalty of forfeiture to the
company of all ſuch overplus.

5. That no proprietor ſhall alienate
any of his land to one "not related to
him by affinity or blood," without con-
ſent of the major part of the company,
or their committee.

6. That any proprietor not paying,
by the laſt of October next, for his part
of what might have been purchaſed by
the laſt of September next, with his
proportion of charges, ſhall forfeit his
ſhare to the other proprietors.

7. That at any meeting of the company duly warned, the major part of
them that ſhall appear ſhall have full
power to act for all, except to diſpoſe
of any of the lands.

8. That William Pabodie ſhall be
their clerk.

9. That Mr. Conſtant Southworth,
William Pabodie, and Nathaniel Thomas, ſhall be a committee to act for them
in purchaſing of the Indians, calling
meetings, "and ſuch other occaſions as
may concern."

Having now authority to extinguiſh
the Indians' titles at Saconet, the Committee proceeded to the work; 31 July,
purchaſing of Awaſhonks, Squaw-Sachem, for £75, the land from Pachet
brook on the north, to a landing-place
called *Toothos*, and a white-oak tree in
Tompe ſwamp (in the range of what is
now called Taylor's Lane — ſee map),
on the fouth; with a depth, from the bay
on the weſt, of one mile inland. There
ſeems, however, to have been a queſtion
of ownerſhip long unſettled among the
Indians; for in 1662 [*Plym. Col. Rec.* iv:
16] Tatacomuncah, and a Squaw-Sachem called Namumpam (Weetamoe,
of Pocaſſet) came to Plymouth with
complaints againſt Wamſutta, for felling Saconet neck, which was claimed
by them. So, to make a ſure thing of
it, the Committee, 1 Nov. 1673, re-
purchaſed of Mamanuah (who could

---

⁹ The iſland of Rhode-Iſland; in plain ſight acroſs the "Eaſt Paſſage."

Activity and Induſtry, he ſoon erected two buildings upon his Farm, and gain'd a good acquaintance with the Natives: got much into their favour, and was in a little time in great eſteem among them.

The next Spring advancing,[10] while Mr. *Church* was diligently Settling his new Farm, ſtocking, leaſing & diſpoſing of his Affairs, and had a fine proſpect of doing no ſmall things; and hoping that his good ſuccefs would be inviting unto other good Men to become his Neighbours; Behold! the rumour of a War between the *Engliſh* and the Natives gave check to his projects. People began to be very jealous of the *Indians,* and indeed they had no ſmall reaſon to ſuſpect that they had form'd a deſign of War upon the *Engliſh.*[11] Mr. *Church* had it daily ſuggeſted to him that the Indians were plotting a bloody deſign. That *Philip* the great *Mount-hope* Sachem was Leader therein: and ſo it prov'd, he was ſending his Meſſengers to all [2] the

---

ſhow an agreement, of date 11 Mar. 1672, from his brothers Oſomehew and Poſotoquo, and from Pacuſtcheſt, Numpouce, and Joham, who were "nearly related," empowering him to ſell), Oſomehew, Suckqua, and Anumpaſh, for £35, the ſame territory, with a ſmall addition.

10 April, 1674, the company met at Duxbury, divided this land into 32 ſhares, and drew lots for them. There were 29 proprietors; Benjamin Church and his brother Joſeph had each a double right, and the 10th lot was agreed upon as to be "the miniſter's lot"; making the whole number. Benjamin Church drew Nos. 19 and 29. [*Plym. Col. Rec.* i: 23, 44; iii: 216; iv: 97; v: 125. *Original MS. Records of the Proprietors of Saconet.*]

[10] The ſpring of 1675, ſoon after the murder of Saſſamon.

[11] The many friendly and Chriſtian Indians in their intercourſe with their ſavage acquaintances came to the knowledge of many ſuſpicious circumſtances, and it was their teſtimony as well as what the ſettlers themſelves obſerved, which now began to excite their ſolicitude for the future.

Neighbouring Sachems, to ingage them in a Confederacy with him in the War.

Among the reſt he ſent Six Men to *Awaſhonks* Squaw-Sachem of the *Sogkonate* Indians,[12] to engage her in his Intereſts: *Awaſhonks* ſo far liſtened unto them as to call her Subjeƈts together, to make a great Dance, which is the cuſtom of that Nation when they adviſe about Mo mentous Affairs. But what does *Awaſhonks* do, but ſends away two of her Men that well underſtood the *Engliſh* Language (*Saſſamon* and *George*[13] by Name) to invite Mr.

---

[12] *Awaſhonks* firſt appears 24 July, 1671, when ſhe agrees with Plymouth Court to ſubmit herſelf and her people, and to give up their arms. In Auguſt following ſhe affixed her mark to a letter written to Gov. Prince in reference to this agreement. 20 June, 1672, ſhe agreed to ſet off ſome land in mortgage to Plymouth Court, in ſatisfaƈtion of a debt due to Mr. John Almy. 7 May, 1673, ſhe is named among Sachems to be treated with by the Rhode-Iſland Aſſembly "to conſult and agree of ſome way to prevent the extreme exceſs of the Indians' drunkenneſs." 31 July, 1673, ſhe ſold a large portion of the ter-ritory claimed by her, to the committee of Saconet proprietors. 7 July, 1674, ſhe is complained of at Plymouth Court by Mamanuah, "Chieffe propriator of the lands of Saconett," for "forcably detaining" ſome of his land, and hinder-ing him from giving poſſeſſion of it to the Engliſh to whom he had ſold the fame; and their reſpeƈtive rights to the land were made the ſubjeƈt of jury trial, to her diſcomfiture. 29 May, 1675, ſhe had three quarters of a mile ſquare ſet off to her by the Saconet proprietors, on the ſhore immediately ſouth of the fouth line of their firſt purchaſe. In July, 1683, ſhe, her daughter Betty, and her ſon Peter, were examined at Plym-outh Court on ſuſpicion of having murdered a child of ſaid Betty; but were diſmiſſed for want of proof. Her husband's name was *Wewayewitt*. She had, beſides Peter and Betty above named, a ſon, *William Mommynewit*, who "was put to Grammar ſchool and learned Latin, deſigned for college, but was ſeized with the palſy." [Drake's *Book of the Indians*, 250; 1 *Maſs. Hiſt. Coll.* x: 114; *R.-I. Col. Rec.* ii: 487; *Plym. Col. Rec.* v: 75; vi: 113; vii: 191. *MS. Rec. Prop. Saconet.*]

[13] *Saſſamon* (*Sauſaman*) was one of the forty-two Saconet Indians, who, 24 July, 1671, ſigned a paper approving the ſubmiſſion which *Awaſhonks* had made. George proved himſelf a friend to the Engliſh. [Drake's *Indian Biog.*, 250.]

Church to the Dance. Mr. *Church* upon the Invitation, immediately[14] takes with him *Charles Hazelton*[15] his Tennants Son, who well underſtood the *Indian* Language, and rid down to the Place appointed: Where they found hundreds of *Indians* gathered together from all Parts of her Dominion. *Awaſhonks* her ſelf in a foaming Sweat was leading the Dance. But ſhe was no ſooner ſenſible of Mr. *Churches* arrival, but ſhe broke off, ſat down, calls her Nobles round her, orders Mr. *Church* to be invited into her preſence. Complements being paſt, and each one taking Seats. She told him, King *Philip* had ſent Six Men of his with two of her People that had been over at *Mount-hope*,[16] to draw her into a confederacy with him in

[14] It would ſeem to be ſettled by what follows, that this was in the early part of the week preceding the firſt outbreak, which would aſſign it to 14-17 June, 1675. Bliſs [*Hiſt. Rehoboth,* 75] ſays it was on the 15th.

[15] I find no trace of this name in the Plymouth Colony at this date. There was a Charles Hazelton at Ipſwich, 1661-6. Probably this "Tennant" might have come from Rhode-Iſland. A "Charles Haſtleton" was Grand Juror at a Quarter Seſſions held at Rocheſter, for Rhode-Iſland and Providence Plantations, in September, 1688. [Savage's *Gen. Dict.* ii: 395; *R.-I. Col. Rec.* iii: 243.]

[16] Mount-Hope was the eaſy and inevitable Angliciſm of *Montop* (*Montaup*), which was the Indian name of the hill on the eaſtern ſhore of what is now Briſtol, R.-I., fronting Tiverton.

Mount-Hope neck included the land running down into the bay, ſhaped by Kikemuit river on the eaſt and north, and Warren (or *Sowams*) river on the weſt; being ſome nine miles in length by from two miles to one in width, including the preſent towns of Warren and Briſtol, R.-I. On this neck were then three Indian villages, — *Montaup*, near the hill; *Kikemuit*, around the ſpring of that name; and *Sowams*, on the ſpot where the village of Warren now ſtands. *Sowams* was the chief ſeat of Maſſaſoit; Philip ſeems to have more identified himſelf with *Montaup*. [Feſſenden's *Warren, R.-I.* 13, 27, 65.]

The name *Montop* (*Montaup* is better Indian), Mr. Trumbull ſays, has poſſibly loſt an initial ſyllable. *Ontop*, or *Ontaup*, in compound words, means "head," "ſummit." If the name, as

a War with the *Englifh*. Defiring him to give her his advice in the cafe, and to tell her the Truth whether the *Umpame*[17] Men (as *Philip* had told her) were gathering a great Army to invade *Philips* Country. He affured her he would tell her the Truth, and give her his beft advice. Then he told her twas but a few days fince he came from *Plymouth*, and the *Englifh* were then making no Preparations for War; That he was in Company with the Principal Gentlemen of the Government, who had no Difcourfe at all about War; and he believ'd no tho'ts about it.[18] He afk'd her whether fhe tho't he would have brought up his Goods to Settle in that Place, if he apprehended an entering into War with fo near a Neighbour. She feem'd to be fome-what convin'd by his talk, and faid fhe believ'd he fpoke the Truth.

Then fhe called for the *Mount-hope* Men: Who made a formidable appearance, with their Faces Painted, and their Hair Trim'd up in Comb-fafhion, with their Powder-

written, nearly reprefents the Indian, it is unqueftionably derived from *mooi*, "black" (or dark-colored), and *ontup*, "head"; *moo-ontop*, "black head";— as *wompont-up* (ufed by Eliot, with the participial affix, as in *Levit.* xix. 32), for "white head," "hoary head." One may readily fuppofe that, when this beautiful fummit was thickly wooded, this name would be a natural one among the Indians for it.

[17] "*Umpame*, written *Apaum* in the Colony Records, is the name of Plymouth in Church's Hiftory; and fo it is called ftill by the natives of *Maffapee*." [2 *Mafs. Hift. Coll.* iii : 175.]

[18] This was true. The authorities were very flow to believe in the danger of an Indian uprifing, even after they had been warned by friendly Indians, and were witnefs to fome of Philip's fufpicious movements. The Governor ordered a military watch to be kept up in every town, but took no other notice of the conduct of the Indians, hoping that the ftorm would blow over, as it had feveral times done before. [*Governors of New Plymouth*, 182.]

horns, and Shot-bags at their backs; which among that Nation is the poſture and figure of preparedneſs for War. She told Mr. *Church*, theſe were the Perſons that had brought her the Report of the *Engliſh* preparation for War: And then told them what Mr. *Church* had ſaid in anſwer to it.

Upon this began a warm talk among the Indians, but 'twas ſoon quaſh'd, and *Awaſhonks* proceeded to tell Mr. *Church*, that *Philips* Meſſage to her was, that unleſs ſhe would forth-with enter into a confederacy with him in a War againſt the *Engliſh*, he would ſend his Men over privately, to kill the *Engliſh* Cattel, and burn their Houſes on that ſide the River, which would provoke the *Engliſh* to fall upon her, whom they would without doubt ſup- [3] poſe the author of the Miſchief. Mr. *Church* told her he was ſorry to ſee ſo threatning an aſpect of Affairs; and ſteping to the *Mount-hopes*, he felt of their bags, and finding them filled with Bullets, ask'd them what thoſe Bullets were for: They ſcoffingly reply'd to ſhoot *Pigeons* with.

Then Mr. *Church* turn'd to *Awaſhonks*, and told her, if *Philip* were reſolv'd to make War, her beſt way would be to knock thoſe Six *Mount-hopes* on the head, and ſhelter her ſelf under the Protection of the *Engliſh*: upon which the *Mount-hopes* were for the preſent Dumb. But thoſe two of *Awaſhonks* Men who had been at *Mount-hope* ex-preſs'd themſelves in a furious manner againſt his advice.

And *Little Eyes*[19] one of the Queens Council joyn'd with them, and urged Mr. *Church* to go aside with him among the bushes that he might have some private Discourse with him, which other Indians immediately forbid being sensible of his ill design: but the Indians began to side and grow very warm. Mr. *Church* with undaunted Courage told the *Mount-hopes* they were bloody wretches, and thirsted after the blood of their *English* Neighbours, who had never injur'd them, but had always abounded in their kindness to them. That for his own part, tho' he desired nothing more than Peace, yet if nothing but War would satisfie them, he believed he should prove a sharp thorne in their sides; Bid the Company observe those Men that were of such bloody dispositions, whether Providence would suffer them to Live to fee the event of the War, which others more Peaceably disposed might do.

Then he told *Awashonks* he thought it might be most advisable for her to send to the Governour of *Plymouth*,[20] and shelter her self, and People under his Protection. She lik'd his advice, and desired him to go on her behalf to the *Plymouth* Government, which he consented to: And at

---

[19] *Little Eyes* with his family deserted the Saconets when they made friends with Plymouth. He was taken prisoner during the progress of the war, when Capt. Church was urged to take revenge for the hostility here displayed, but replied that " it was not Englishmen's fashion to seek revenge," and gave him the same good quarter with the rest.

[20] Gov. Prince died in the spring of 1673, and Josias Winslow was chosen his successor in the following June. He was the only son of the first Governor Winslow by his second marriage; in 1652, had military command in Marshfield; 1658, was Major, then Commander; 1675, General - in - Chief against Philip. [*Govs. New Plym.* 175-196; *N. E. Hist. and Gen. Reg.* iv: 297.]

parting advifed her what ever fhe did, not to defert the
Englifh Intereft, to joyn with her Neighbours in a Rebel
lion which would certainly prove fatal to her. [He
mov'd none of his Goods from his Houfe that there might
not be the leaft umbrage from fuch an Action.] She
thank'd him for his advice, and fent two of her Men to
guard him to his Houfe;[21] which when they came there,
urged him to take care to fecure his Goods, which he re-
fufed for the reafons before mentioned. But defired the
Indians, that if what they feared, fhould happen, they
would take care of what he left, and directed them to a
Place in the woods where they fhould difpofe them;
which they faithfully obferved.

He took his leave of his guard, and bid them tell their
Miftrefs, if fhe continued fteady in her dependence on the
Englifh, and kept within her own limits of *Sogkonate*,[22] he
would fee her again quickly; and then haftned away to
Pocaffet, where he met with *Peter Nunnuit*,[23] the Husband

[21] Situated on lot No. 19, which was
629 rods fouth of Pachet brook; being the farm in Little Compton now
owned and occupied by Mr. John B.
Howland, on the weft fide of the road,
—oppofite to the fchool-houfe,—nearly
two miles fouth of the prefent Tiverton
line.

[22] It is difficult to make out the exact limits of the fmall Sachemdoms
which divided between them what is
now Little Compton and Tiverton,
R.-I. It is doubtful if thofe limits were
ever very well defined. But from an

examination of the Proprietors' and
early town records, and of the original
deeds from the Indians, I think that
Awafhonks's territories centered about
Tompe fwamp, — lying along the weftern fhore of the peninfula of Saconet,
from the fouth fide of "Windmill hill"
to what is now the Breakwater.

[23] This Indian's name was *Petonowowet*, or *Pe-tan-a-nuet*, which the Englifh corrupted eafily into *Peter Nunnuit*.
8 May, 1673, he, with two other Indians, fold a lot of land in Swanfey to
Nathaniel Paine and Hugh Cole, for

of the Queen of *Pocaſſet*,[24] who was juſt then come over in a Canoo from *Mount-hope*. *Peter* told him that there would certainly be War; for *Philip* had held a [4] Dance of ſeveral Weeks continuance, and had entertain'd the Young Men from all Parts of the Country: And added that *Philip* expected to be ſent for to *Plymouth* to be exam ined about *Saſamon*'s[25] death, who was Murder'd at *Aſſa-*

£35 5*s*. He was, about the ſame time, a witneſs in regard to a land caſe on Taunton river. In Philip's war he for-ſook his wife and fought with the Eng-liſh. In 1676 (ordered by the Council, 22 July, and confirmed by the Court, 1 November) he, with Numpas and Iſacke, was made inſpector of Indian priſoners who had applied "for accept-ence to mercye" from "the weſtermoſt ſyde of Sepecan Riuer, and ſoe weſt-ward to Dartmouth bounds." He was then ſtyled Sachem *Ben Petananuett.* [Drake's *Book of Ind.* 188; *Plym. Col. Rec.* v: 210, 215.]

[24] This was *Weetamoe*, (or *Namum-pam*), who had been the wife of Philip's elder brother *Wamſutta*, or *Alexander*. The author of the *Old Indian Chron-icle* [p. 8] intimates that ſhe believed her husband had been poiſoned by the Engliſh, and that this made her more willing to liſten to Philip. In October, 1659, ſhe was at Plymouth to ſecure the third part of the pay for ſome land which Alexander had ſold; and acknowledged the receipt of the ſame. 3 June, 1662, ſhe complained, at Plymouth, of ſome infringement on her rights in Wamſut-ta's ſale of Saconet. At the ſame time advice was given to her and her huſ-band, Alexander, (here called *Quique-quanchett*,) in reference to difficulties exiſting between them and Philip in regard to the entertaining of ſome Nar-raganſett Indians againſt Philip's good-will. Weetamoe did not follow her ſec-ond husband, as he appears to have ex-pected ſhe would, to the Engliſh. She united her fortunes to thoſe of Philip, and miſerably periſhed, when her head was cut off and ſet on a pole at Taun-ton. [Drake's *Book of Ind.* 187; *Plym. Col. Rec.* iv: 17, 24, 186.]

[25] *Saſſamon* (or *Wuſſauſmon*) was born in the neighborhood of Dorcheſter, be-came a convert and was educated, and employed as a ſchoolmaſter at Natick, and is ſaid to have aided John Eliot in tranſlating the Indian Bible. After a time he left the Engliſh and became Philip's ſecretary, and, as ſuch, privy to his deſigns. Subſequently he returned to his Chriſtian faith, and became teach-er to the Nemaskets, whoſe chief, *Wa-tuſpaquin*, gave him a houſe-lot in Aſ-ſawompſett neck (Middleborough), with one alſo to his ſon-in-law. He revealed Philip's plot to the government at Plym-outh, and not long after (29 Jan. 1674–5) was found dead, under the ice on Aſſawompſett pond, with marks of

womſet-Ponds;[26] knowing himſelf guilty of contriving that
Murder. The fame *Peter* told him that he faw Mr. *James
Brown*[27] of *Swanzey*,[28] and Mr. *Samuel Gorton*[29] who was
an Interpreter, and two other Men who brought a Letter
from the Governour of *Plymouth* to *Philip*. He obſerv'd
to him further, that the Young Men were very eager to
begin the War, and would fain have kill'd Mr. *Brown*, but
Philip prevented it; telling them, that his Father had
charged him to ſhew kindneſs to Mr. *Brown*.[30] In ſhort,

violence. Three Indians were tried and
executed for his murder, there being
little doubt that it had occurred by
Philip's command. [Mather's *Relation*,
74; Hubbard's *Narrative*, 14; *N. E.
Hiſt. and Gen. Reg.* xv: 43, 149.]

[26] *Aſſawompſett* (*Sowampſit, Sowam-
ſet*) *pond* is, with its connecting ponds,
the largeſt ſheet of water in Plymouth
County not merely, but in Maſſachu-
fetts; being ſome fix miles long by a
width varying from four miles to a few
rods. It lies partly in Rocheſter, more in
Middleborough, moſt in the new town
of Lakeville. Preſident Stiles, on the
authority of "Jonathan Butterworth, *æt.*
63, of Rehoboth," in 1762, ſays that
"Aſſawampſett is ſo called from a place
or patch of beech-trees, called in Indian
ſawamps; so *Aſſawampſett, Sawamp-
ſett*, both names of the ſame place."
But he adds, "*Sowampſit* ſignifies '*a
ſmall pond encompaſſed with trees*';
ſowamps, '*beech-trees*'; and putting both
together, ſignifies *a pond of water with
beech-trees growing around it*." Mr.
Trumbull comments, "I don't believe
a word of this; but as Preſident Stiles is

reſpectable authority, and Butterworth
can't be impeached, I give it, for what
it is worth. *Sowams, Sowamps* ('*Saw-
hames bay*.' Winthrop's *Journal*, ii:
121, note) is the fignificant word; the
et marking the locative."

[27] James Brown was born probably in
England; was the ſon of John, eminent
in the Colony, being ſeventeen years
Aſſiſtant and many years Commiſſioner
of the United Colonies. James was alſo
Aſſiſtant in various years from 1665 to
1684. He died at *Wannamoiſett*, in
Swanſey, 29 Oct. 1710, aged 87, leaving two ſons, James and Jabez, and one
daughter, Dorothy Kent. [Baylies's
Plym. Col. iv: 18; Bliſs's *Rehoboth*,
53, 75, 78.]

[28] *Swanſey* then included Somerſet,
Maſs., and Barrington, R.-I., with a
portion of Warren, R.-I., beſides the
preſent town of Swanſey. [Bliſs's *Rehoboth*, I.]

[29] The man of that name famous in
the early controverſies of New England.

[30] Mr. John Brown, father of this
Mr. Brown, was a man of great kind-

Philip was forc'd to promife them that on the next Lords Day when the *Englifh* were gone to Meeting they fhould rifle their Houfes, and from that time forward kill their Cattel.

Peter defir'd Mr. *Church* to go and fee his Wife, who was but up the hill;[31] he went and found but few of her People with her. She faid they were all gone, againft her Will to the Dances; and fhe much fear'd there would be a War. Mr. *Church* advis'd her to go to the Ifland[32] and fecure her felf, and thofe that were with her; and fend to the Governour of *Plymouth* who fhe knew was her friend; and fo left her, refolving to haften to *Plymouth*, and wait on the Governour: and he was fo expeditious that he was with the Governour early next Morning,[33] tho' he waited on fome of the Magiftrates by the way, who were of the Council of War,[34] and alfo met him at the

nefs of heart, a friend of toleration, and the firft of the Plymouth magif- trates who doubted the expediency of coercing the people to fupport the min- iftry. Thefe qualities would naturally endear him to Maffafoit, to whom he was a neighbor, and lead that good old chief to give the charge which Philip mentions, in reference to his family. Mr. James Brown, indeed, feems to have inherited his father's difpofition, and it was at his urgent folicitation that this letter was fent to promote peace. [Blifs's *Rehoboth*, 75.]

[31] Tiverton heights, which the upper road to Fall River climbs almoft imme- diately after leaving the Stone bridge.

[32] Rhode-Ifland.

[33] The diftance — making allowance for the indirectnefs of the Indian paths — could not have been lefs, probably, than forty-two miles from Pocaffet, and nearly fifty from Church's houfe at Saconet. The date of his arrival was Wednefday, 16 June, 1675. [*N. E. Hift. and Gen. Reg.* xv: 260.]

[34] The Council of War was a body which was empowered to act fpecially on military queftions, and was compofed of the Governor and Affiftants *ex officio*, and of others fpecially appointed. The laft record of election previous to Phil- ip's war was, 7 July, 1671, when Capt. Mathew Fuller, Leift. Ephraim Mor-

Governours. He gave them an account of his obferva-
tions and difcoveries, which confirmed their former intel
ligences, and haftned their preparation for Defence.

Philip according to his promife to his People, permitted
them to March out of the Neck[35] on the next Lords-
Day,[36] when they plundred the neareft Houfes[37] that the
Inhabitants had deferted:[38] but as yet offer'd no violence
to the People, at left none were killed. However the
alarm was given by their Numbers, and hoftile-Equipage,
and by the Prey they made of what they could find in the
forfaken Houfes.

An exprefs came the fame day[39] to the Governour, who
immediately gave orders to the Captains of the Towns to

---

ton, Enfign Mark Eames, Cornett Rob-
ert Studfon, Mr. Jofias Winflow, fen.,
Sec. Nathaniel Morton, and Meffrs.
James Walker, Thomas Huckens, and
Ifacke Chettenden, were chofen by the
Court, and fworn. [*Plym. Col. Rec.* v :
73.]

[35] The narrow ftrip between Kikemuit and Warren rivers, by which the
peninfula of Mount-Hope, or Pock-
anocket, was joined to the main-land
at Swanfey.

[36] 20 June, 1675. [Trumbull's *Hift.
Conn.* 1 : 327]

[37] Thefe were probably the houfes
which Judge Davis refers to where he
fays, "There was a fettlement within
Mount-Hope neck appertaining to
Swanfey. It contained eighteen houfes,
all deftroyed." [Davis's *Morton's Memorial,* 463.] This was in the northern part of what is now Warren, R.-I.

[38] "Tenantlefs for the time, in con-
fequence of their occupants being ab-
fent at church." [Feffenden's *Warren,*
66.] Mr. Drake fuggefts [*Notes on the
Indian Wars in N. E.,* in *N. E. Hift.
and Gen. Reg.* xv : 154], on the authority of Winflow's and Hinckley's *Narrative of the Beginning and Progrefs
of the Prefent Troubles,* that the people
had deferted them through fear.

[39] The meffenger reached Plymouth
at "break of day," Monday morning.
[Barry's *Mafs.* i : 410.] Befides fending expreffes to the Captains of the
towns, the Court, on Tuefday, iffued a
proclamation for a faft on the next
Thurfday. That proclamation was as
follows [Blifs's *Rehoboth,* 79]:

"The Council of this Colony, taking
"into their ferious confideration the awe-
"ful hand of God upon us, in permitting
"the heathen to carry it with infolency

March the greateſt Part of their Companies, and to randezvous at *Taunton* on *Monday* Night, where Major *Brad-*
ʒford[40] was to receive them, and diſpoſe them under Capt.
(now made Major) *Cutworth*[41] of *Situate.* The Govern

"and rage againſt us, appearing in their
"great hoſtile preparations, and alſo
"ſome outrageous carriages, as at other
"times, ſo in ſpecial, the laſt Lord's
"day to ſome of our neighbours at
"Swanſey, to the apparent hazard if
"not real loſs of the lives of ſome al-
"ready; do therefore judge it a ſolemn
"duty, incumbent upon us all, to lay to
"heart this diſpenſation of God, and
"do therefore commend it to all the
"churches, miniſters, and people of this
"colony to ſet apart the 24th day of this
"inſtant, June, which is the 5th day of
"this week, wherein to humble our
"ſelves before the Lord for all thoſe
"ſins whereby we have provoked our
"good God ſadly to interrupt our peace
"and comfort, and alſo humbly to ſeek
"his face and favour in the gracious
"continuance of our peace and privi-
"leges, and that the Lord would be en-
"treated to go forth with our forces,
"and bleſs, ſucceed and proſper them,
"delivering them from the hands of his
"and our enemies, ſubduing the heathen
"before them, and returning them all
"in ſafety to their families and relations
"again; and that God would prepare
"all our hearts humbly to ſubmit to his
"good pleaſure concerning us.

"By orders of the Court of N. P.

"Nathaniel Morton, Secretary.
"Plymouth, June 22, 1675."

Beſides the 12 churches and miniſters of the "Standing Order," there
was then one Baptiſt church, formed in
Rehoboth in 1663, of which Rev. John
Myles was Paſtor, to accommodate
which with a place "where they might
not prejudice any exiſting church,"
they had been incorporated, in 1667, as
the town of Swanſey. This, of courſe,
was the neareſt church to the ſcene of
the breaking out of Philip's war, and it
was, doubtleſs, to their meeting-houſe
—which ſtood a few rods ſouth of the
ſouth line of Rehoboth, on the road
leading to the houſe of the late Mr.
Squire Allen, about fifteen or twenty
rods from the main road leading from
Warren to Seekonk and Providence —
that the ſettlers had gone, on Lord's Day,
June 20, when their houſes were plun-
dered by the Indians in the firſt aſſault.
[*Baptiſt Memorial*, iv: 227.]

[40] *William Bradford*, ſecond ſon of
Gov. William, of imperiſhable memory, was born 17 June, 1624, and was,
next to Miles Standiſh, a chief ſoldier of
the Colony. He was Aſſiſtant Treaſurer
and Deputy Governor from 1682 to
1686, and from 1689 to 1691, and in the
latter year one of the Council of Maſſachuſetts. He married (1) Alice Richards, (2) Widow Wiſwall, (3) Widow
Holmes; lived in what is now Kingſton,
on the ſouth ſide of Jones's river, and
died 20 Feb. 1703–4, aged nearly 80.
[*N. E. Hiſt. and Gen. Reg.* iv: 45.]

[41] *James Cudworth* was in Scituate
in 1634, lived for a time in Barnſtable,

our defired Mr. *Church* to give them his Company, and to ufe his intereft in their behalf with the Gentlemen of *Rhode-Ifland*.[42] He comply'd with it, and they March'd the next day.[43] Major *Bradford* defired Mr. *Church* with a commanded party confifting of *Englifh* and fome *Friend-Indians*, to March in the Front at fome diftance from the Main body. Their orders were to keep fo far before, as not be in fight of the Army. And fo they did, for by the way, they killed a Deer, [5] flead, roafted, and eat the moft of him before the Army came up with them. But the *Plymouth* Forces foon arriv'd at *Swanzey*, and were

---

but returned to Scituate; was Deputy for feveral years; Captain of the militia, 1652; Affiftant, 1656-8; was deprived of his command and offices and diffranchifed, 1658-73, being a friend of toleration, and fo judged an "oppofer of the Government." In 1674 he was chofen Affiftant, and in 1675 "General and Commander in Chief" for Philip's war. In 1682 he went to England for the Colony, to obtain a new Charter, where he took the fmall-pox and died. He was "paft feventy" when he took the field at this time againft Philip. [Deane's *Scituate*, 245-251.]

[42] To underftand this expreffion it is needful to remember that Rhode-Ifland had been excluded from the Confederacy of the Colonies formed for mutual defence in 1643: "on account of her heretical toleration of religious freedom, and her open advocacy of liberty of confcience," fays the Editor of Eafton's *Narrative;* "upon grounds which re-

flect no credit upon the Puritan confederates," says Arnold; "becaufe they had not been able to inftitute a government, fuch as could be relied on for the fulfilment of the ftipulations mutually made by the Four Colonies," with more juftice, fays Palfrey. Thus ftanding by themfelves, no *claim* for aid could be made upon her citizens, while the fact that their interefts were, in the refpects now involved, one with thofe of the Confederacy, made it probable, that, if fuitably approached — by one of their friends, as Church was — they would furnifh fuch aid as might be in their power. Eafton fays that the Governor of Plymouth wrote them at this juncture, "to defier our Help with fum Boats if they had fuch Ocation, and for us to looke to our felfs." [Eafton's *Narrative*, vi, 16; Arnold's *Hift. Rhode-Ifland*, i: 115; Palfrey's *Hift. New England*, i: 629.]

[43] Tuefday, 22 June, 1675.

pofted at Major *Browns* and Mr. *Miles*'s Garrifons[44] chiefly; and were there foon joyned[45] with thofe that came from *Maffachufetts*,[46] who had entred into a Confederacy with their *Plymouth* Brethren, againft the Perfidious Heathen.

The Enemy who began their Hoftilities with plundring and deftroying Cattel, did not long content themfelves with that game. They thirfted for *Englifh* blood, and they foon broach'd it;[47] killing two Men in the way not far

[44] *Myles's Garrifon* was the fortified houfe of the Rev. John Myles, paftor of the Baptift Church in Swanfey [fee note 39, *ante*], which is fuppofed to have ftood in what is now Barneyville, about 75 rods a little north of due weft from Miles's bridge, which croffes Palmer (or Warren) river about three miles north of Warren, R.-I. Mr. Myles was put to fo much expenfe by the war, that, 25 Feb. 1679, it was voted by the town that " Mr. John Myles fhall have the houfe built for him to indemnify him for debts due him in the time of the Indian war, in full of his demands," etc. [*MS. Haile Records*, 42.] The pofition of Maj. Brown's [fee note 27, *ante*] garrifon has not been exactly identified, but it is fuppofed to have been in the fame part of Swanfey with Myles's garrifon.

[45] The Plymouth forces probably reached Swanfey on the afternoon of Tuefday, 22 June, or, at furtheft, on Wednefday, 23 June; while the firft of the Maffachufetts forces left Bofton on Saturday, 26 June, and all of them arrived at Swanfey on Monday, 28 June. [Feffenden's *Warren*, 66, 69.]

[46] The Maffachufetts forces, on this occafion, confifted of a troop of horfe under Capt. Thomas Prentice, one of foot under Capt. Daniel Henchman, and one hundred and ten " volunteers " under Capt. Samuel Mofley. Mofley had been a " Privateer at Jamaica," and his " volunteers " included ten or twelve pirates under fentence of death, who were taken out of jail to join the command, and promifed life on good behavior. Three Chriftian Indians — James and Thomas *Quannapohutt* and *Zechary Abram* — were attached to Capt. Prentice's troop as guides. Several dogs — to be ufed in hunting the Indians — were with Mofley's company. [Drake's *Hift. of Bofton*, i : 402 ; *N. E. Hift. and Gen. Reg.* xv : 262 ; *Tranfactions Amer. Antiquarian Society*, ii : 441.]

[47] It is very difficult to harmonize the various conflicting authorities fo as to be certain when, or in what manner, the firft blood was drawn. Rev. Abiel Fifher, in his hiftory of the Firft Baptift Church in Swanfey, fays that Eldad Kingfley — one of its members — was the firft man flain, on Faft-day, the 24th, at Swanfey. The *Breiff Narratiue*

from Mr. *Miles*'s Garriſon. And ſoon after, eight more at *Mattapoiſet*:[48] Upon whoſe bodies they exerciſed more than brutiſh barbarities; beheading, diſ-membring and mangling them, and expoſing them in the moſt inhumane manner, which gaſh'd and ghoſtly objeɗs ſtruck a damp on all beholders.

The Enemy fluſh'd with theſe exploits, grew yet bolder, and skulking every where in the buſhes, ſhot at all Paſſengers, and kill'd many that ventured abroad. They came ſo near as to ſhoot down two Sentinels at Mr. *Miles*'s

---

preſented by the Plymouth Colony to the "Commiſſioners of the United Colonies," which ſeems to have been prepared with minute care, mentions as the firſt perſon killed, "on the 24th Thomas layton was ſlaine att the fall Riuer." Hubbard and moſt writers name the 24th, — Thurſday, the day of Faſt. But the anonymous author of the *Preſent State of New England with reſpeɗ to the Indian War* [p. 5] ſays that "the firſt that was killed was June 23[d]"; while Baylies [*Hiſt. New Plym. Col.* iii: 33] ſeems to ſpecify the 22d. [See Bliſs's *Rehoboth*, 80-84; *Baptiſt Memorial*, iv: 232; Feſſenden's *Warren*, 68, 69; Eaſton's *Narrative*, 17; *Plym. Col. Rec.* x: 364; Drake's *Notes on the Indian Wars*, in *N. E. Hiſt. and Gen. Reg.* xv: 156, etc., for various particulars bearing on the queſtion.] Niles [*Hiſt. of Indian and French Wars*, 3 *Maſs. Hiſt. Coll.* vi: 178, etc.] careleſſly deſcribes all theſe occurrences as being in 1674, inſtead of 1675.

[48] *Mattapoiſet* (*Mattapoyſett, Meta-poiſet, Matapuyſt, Mattapoiſe*), was the ſmall peninſula running into Mount-Hope bay oppoſite the ſouthweſtern extremity of Somerſet, having Cole's river on the weſt, and Lee's river on the eaſt; now called Gardner's neck. Parſons [*Indian Names of Places in R.-I.* 16] ſays the word means "crying chief." Trumbull ſays "it does not mean 'crying chief.' The Indians never gave names of *perſons*, or *animate objeɗs* to *places*, unleſs with an adjeɗive or verb compounded, to mark the relation of perſon to thing, *e. g.* a pond might be called 'a fiſhing-place for pickerel,' or a hill 'the camping place of Sofo,' but never 'pickerel,' or 'Sofo.' *Metapoiſet*, or *Matapyſt*, ſeems to be identical with *Matabeſet* (*Mattapeaſet, Mattabeſick*), the name of Middletown, Conn. This name *looks* like a derivative of *mattappu*, 'he ſits down' or 'reſts,' and I know of no other word from which it can be derived. But I am by no means confident that it is from this."

Garrifon, under the very Nofes of moft of our Forces. Thefe provocations drew out the refentments of fome[49] of Capt. *Prentices*[50] Troop, who defired they might have liberty to go out and feek the Enemy in their own quarters. Quarter Mafters *Gill*[51] & *Belcher*[52] commanded the Parties drawn out, who earneftly defired Mr. *Churches* company: They provided him a Horfe and Furniture (his own being out of the way) he readily comply'd with their defires, and was foon Mounted.

This party were no fooner over *Miles*'s Bridge, but were fired on by an Ambufcado of about a dozen *Indians*, as they were afterwards difcovered to be. When they drew off, the Pilot[53] was Mortally wounded, Mr. *Belcher*

[49] Hubbard fays "*twelve* of the Troop." [*Narrative*, 18.] He fixes the time alfo as on the day of the arrival of the troop, viz: Monday, 28 June.

[50] *Capt. Thomas Prentice* was born in England in 1620-1; came over, 1648-9; fettled in the eafterly part of Cambridge; was chofen Lieut. of Troopers in 1656, and in 1662 Captain; was Deputy, 1672; was appointed to remove the Natick Indians to Deer Ifland, which he did; fucceeded Maj. Gookin as magiftrate to advife the Chriftian Indians; died 6 July, 1710. There is a tradition that he ferved under Cromwell. [Jackfon's *Hift. of Newton*, 389, 469-475.]

[51] Mr. Drake fuppofes his Chriftian name to have been John. [*Hift. Boft.* i: 403.] In which cafe he was probably that John who lived on Milton hill, who joined the church in Dorchefter,

1640, and petitioned for the incorporation of Milton in 1662. He died in 1678, and left a daughter, who married Rev. Jofeph Belcher, third minifter of Dedham. [*Hift. of Dorchefter*, 120.]

[52] Mr. Drake [*Hift. Boft.* i: 403] fuppofes this to be Andrew Belcher (father of Gov. Jonathan), who was now a little more than 28 years of age.

[53] Hubbard fays, "killing one *William Hammond*." [*Narrative*, 18.] This was probably "Wm. Hammon," whofe mark was affixed as a witnefs to Philip's quitclaim of the "eight miles fquare" purchafe in Rehoboth, of date 30 March, 1668; who was doubtlefs the fame "William Hamon" who had a daughter Elizabeth born at Rehoboth, 24 Sept. 1661. Savage doubts, becaufe "this man was of the troop of Capt. Prentifs, which muft, we fuppofe, have chiefly been compofed of volun-

received a fhot in his knee, and his Horfe was kill'd under him, Mr. *Gill* was ftruck with a Musket-ball on the fide of his belly; but being clad with a buff Coat[54] and fome thicknefs of Paper under it, it never broke his skin. The Troopers were furprized to fee both their Commanders wounded, and wheel'd off. But Mr. *Church* perfwaded, at length ftorm'd and ftampt, and told them 'twas a fhame to run, and leave a wounded Man there to become a Prey to the barbarous Enemy. For the Pilot yet fat his Horfe, tho' fo maz'd with the Shot, as not to have fenfe to guide him. Mr. *Gill* feconded him, and offer'd, tho' much dif-enabled, to affift in bringing him off. Mr. *Church* asked a Stranger who gave them his company in that action, if he would go with him and fetch off the wounded Man: He readily confented, they with Mr. *Gill* went, but the wounded Man fainted and fell off his Horfe before they came to him; but Mr. *Church* and the Stranger difmounted, took up the Man dead, and laid him before Mr. *Gill* on

teers of Cambridge, and the neighboring town of Dedham." But Jackfon [*Hift. Newt.* 471] fays this Hammond, here killed, was "not of Cambridge," and Church fays he was the "pilot" of the party, (Mather [*Brief Hiftory*, 4] fays "the Indians fhot the Pilot who was directing our Souldiers in their way to Philip's Country,") who would moft naturally be not of the troop, but a refident of the neighborhood, familiar with the wood-paths and the enemy. Savage further fuggefts that the ftory of "William Hamman of the Bay," mentioned in Gardener's *Pequot Warres* as killed in that war, was an anachroniftic rendering of this occurrence. But Gardener wrote in 1660, — fifteen years before this Swanfey skirmifh. [Blifs's *Rehoboth*, 66; *Plym. Col. Rec.* viii: 52; *Gen. Dict.* ii: 348; 3 *Mafs. Hift. Coll.* iii: 130, 157.]

[54] "A clofe military outer garment, with fhort fleeves, and laced tightly over the cheft, made of *buffalo*-skin, or other thick and elaftic material, worn by foldiers in the feventeenth century as a defenfive covering." — *Webfter.*

his Horfe. Mr. *Church* told the other two, if they would take care of the dead Man, he would go and fetch his Horfe back, which was going off the Caffey[55] toward [6] the Enemy; but before he got over the Caffey he faw the Enemy run to the right into the Neck. He brought back the Horfe, and call'd earneftly and repeatedly to the Army to come over & fight the Enemy; and while he ftood calling & perfwading, the skulking Enemy return'd to their old ftand, and all difcharged their Guns at him at one clap, tho' every fhot mifs'd *him*; yet one of the Army on the other fide of the river received one of the balls in his foot. Mr. *Church* now began (no fuccour coming to him) to think it time to retreat: Saying, *The Lord have Mercy on us*, if fuch a handful of Indians fhall thus dare fuch an Army![56]

Upon this 'twas immediately refolv'd,[57] and orders were given to March down into the Neck, and having paffed

---

[55] This is a truer fpelling than the modern "caufeway," fince the word came into our language from the French *chauffée*, a way paved with limeftone. The road adjacent to the bridge was here evidently banked up to give dry paffage over the marfh skirting the ftream.

[56] Mather fays "a Souldier (a ftout man) who was fent from *Water-town*, feeing the *Englifh Guide* flain, and hearing many profane oaths among fome of our Souldiers (namely thofe Priva- teers, who were alfo Volunteers) and confidéring the unfeafonablenefs of the

weather was fuch, as that nothing could be done againft the enemy; this man was poffeffed with a ftrong conceit, that God was againft the *Englifh*; where- upon he immediately ran diftracted, and fo was returned home a lamentable Spectacle." [*Brief Hiftory*, 4.] Mr. Drake, in his late valuable reprint of Mather, makes it probable that this man's name was William Sherman, jr. [p. 58.]

[57] Hubbard fays "the next morn- ing"; which would be Tuefday, 29 June. [*Narrative*, 18.]

the Bridge, and Caſſey, the direction was to extend both wings, which being not well headed, by thoſe that remain'd in the Center, ſome of them miſtook their Friends for their Enemies, and made a fire upon them on the right wing, and wounded that noble Heroick Youth Enſign *Savage*[58] in the thigh; but it happily prov'd but a fleſh wound. They Marched[59] until they came to the narrow of the Neck, at a Place called *Keekkamuit*,[60] where they

[58] *Perez Savage*, fourth ſon of Thomas, who came in the Planter from London, April, 1635, was born 17 Feb. 1652, and was now, therefore, in his 24th year, though Hubbard calls him "that young Martial Spark ſcarce twenty years of age." He was wounded again in the "ſwamp fight" in the following December, when he was Lieut. of the ſame corps. He went to London in 1690, to carry on trade with Spain; was taken captive by the Turks and died at Mequinez, in Barbary, during 1694. Some curious particulars about his wills are mentioned by Savage. [*Gen. Dict.* iv: 25, 26.] Hubbard [*Narrative*, 19] ſays he had "one bullet lodged in his Thigh, another ſhot through the brim of his hat, by ten or twelve of the Enemy diſcharging upon him together, while he boldly held up his Colors in the Front of his Company." Church, as on the ground, — though dictating this account forty years after the occurrence, — is the more truſtworthy authority as to the ſource of the wound, and the fact of the blunder, which he alone narrates.

[59] Church's language would lead one to ſuppoſe that they *immediately* continued their march. But Hubbard ſays, "the weather not ſuffering any further action at that time, thoſe that were thus far advanced, were compelled to retreat back to the main Guard"; and adds that Major Savage, Commander-in-Chief of the Maſſachuſetts forces, arrived that night, and the next day the whole body intended to march into Mount-Hope, "but the weather being doubtful, our Forces did not march till near noon." This interpoſes more than twenty-four hours between the skirmiſh in which Enſign Savage was wounded, and what Church next proceeds to narrate. [*Narrative*, 19.] So that the actual march into the neck was on Wedneſday, 30 June.

[60] The narroweſt part of the neck between Warren and Kikemuit rivers is a little north of the line which divides Briſtol from Warren. The name *Keekkamuit* was appropriated to an Indian village that ſtood around a ſpring of that name, in this "narrow of the neck." This is ſome four miles from Miles's bridge. This accords with what Hubbard ſays: "After they had marched

23

took down the heads of Eight *Englifh* Men that were kill'd at the head of *Metapoifet*-Neck, and fet upon Polls, after the barbarous manner of thofe Salvages. There *Philip* had ftaved all his Drums,[61] and conveyed all his Canoo's to the Eaft-fide of *Metapoifet*-River.[62] Hence it was concluded by thofe that were acquainted with the Motions of thofe People, that they had quitted the Neck. Mr. *Church* told 'em that *Philip* was doubtlefs gone ever[63] to *Pecaffet* fide, to ingage thofe Indians in Rebellion with him: which

ahout a mile & a half, they paffed by fome Houfes newly burned, &c.; two or three miles further they came up with fome Heads, Scalps and Hands cut off from the bodys of fome of the Englifh, and ftuck upon Poles near the Highway, in that barbarous and inhumane manner bidding us Defyance." [*Narrative*, 19.]

Parfons [*Indian Names*, etc. 14] fays *Kikemuit* means "a back river." Mr. Trumbull fays "no; it has loft an initial fyllable. *Tŏ-kĕkommu-it* (*Tohke-kom*, Eliot) fignifies 'at the fpring,' or 'water-fource.' This name agrees with Rev. Samuel Deane's 'clear fpring' [2 *Mafs. Hift. Coll.* x: 174], though it has nothing to do with '*Kike-gat* = day, or clearnefs.' Another derivation is poffible: *Nkĕke* (Nĕkik) fignifies 'otter' [*R.-I. Hift Coll.* i: 95], and *may* = 'path'; whence *Nkĕke-may-it* would mean 'the otter path.' The former derivation is the more probable. Many Indian names have, in like manner fuffered mutilation."

[61] Roger Williams faid, in 1643, that the New England Indians originally had no drums or trumpets, though he had known a native make a very good drum in imitation of the Englifh. [*R.-I. Hift. Coll.* i: 38, 149.] The North American Indians, in general, however, appear to have ufed the drum (and without any hint that it was borrowed from the whites) in their religious dances, and in their ceremonies when beating up recruits for war. [De Foreft's *Hift. Indians of Conn.* 29; Schoolcraft's *Hift. of Indian Tribes*, ii: 60; alfo *Ibid.* plate 75, where reprefentations of Indian drums are given. See alfo, i: 425, and plate 68.] Philip had probably employed their aid in raifing volunteers, and as his tactics now led him to defert his own village, and he did not wifh to encumber himfelf with them in actual warfare, he "ftaved" and threw them away here.

[62] Now known as Lee's river; feparating Gardner's neck from the fouthern extremity of Somerfet.

[63] Mifprint for "over," as "Pecaffet" is for "Pocaffet."

they foon found to be true. The Enemy were not really beaten out of *Mount-hope* Neck, tho' 'twas true they fled from thence; yet it was before any purfu'd them. 'Twas but to ftrengthen themfelves, and to gain a more advantagious Poft. However, fome and not a few pleafed themfelves with the fancy of a Mighty Conqueft.[64]

A grand Council was held, and a Refolve paft, to build a Fort there to maintain the firft ground they had gain'd, by the Indians leaving it to them.[65] And to fpeak the Truth, it muft be faid, That as they gain'd not that Field, by their Sword, nor their Bow; fo 'twas rather their fear than their courage, that oblig'd them to fet up the marks of their Con queft. Mr. *Church* look'd upon it, and talk of it with contempt, and urged hard the purfuing the Enemy on *Pocaffet* fide, and with the greater earneftnefs, becaufe of his promife made to *Awafhonks*, before mentioned.[66] The Council adjourned themfelves from *Mount-hope* to *Rehoboth*,[67] where Mr. Treafurer *Southworth*[68] being weary

---

[64] Hubbard and Mather fo thought. [*Narrative*, 19; *Magnalia*, (ed. 1853,) ii : 562.)

[65] The fite of this fort has been identified by Mr. Feffenden as being oppofite the narrow entrance to Kikemuit river from Mount-Hope bay, on the top of the moft fouthweftern of feveral hills on the north fide of a cove. The hill is faft wearing away by the action of the water at its bafe, fo that the charcoal and fcorched ftones from the fireplace of the fort are often falling down the declivity toward the water. [*Hift. Warren, R.-I.* 71.]

[66] See page 11, *ante*.

[67] Hubbard fays " *Seaconke*, or *Rehoboth*, a town within fix miles of *Swanzy*." [*Narrative*, 20.] The exact locality referred to here would feem to be one of the "three houfes" which were ufed as garrifons by the inhabitants of Rehoboth and Swanfey during Philip's war, viz: that which ftood on the fouth end of Seekonk plain, on the fpot lately occupied by the houfe of Mr. Phanuel Bifhop, on the foutheaft fide of the Common. [Blifs's *Rehoboth*, 78.]

[68] *Conftant Southworth* was a fon of Edward Southworth (Savage wrongly

4

of his charge of Commiſſary General, (Proviſion being ſearce & difficult to be obtained, for the Army, that now lay ſtill to Cover the People from no body, while they were building a Fort for nothing) retired, and the Power & Trouble of that Poſt was left with Mr. *Church*, who ſtill urged the Commanding Officers to move over to *Pocaſſet* ſide, to purſue the Enemy, [7] and kill *Philip*, which would in his opinion be more probable to keep poſſeſſion of the Neck, than to tarry to build a Fort. He was ſtill reſtleſs on that ſide of the River, and the rather becauſe of his promiſe to the *Squaw Sachem* of *Sogkonate*. And Capt. *Fuller*[69] alſo urged the ſame, until at length there came fur-

ſays " *Conſtant*, or *Thomas* " [*Gen. Dict.* iv : 143]) and Alice Carpenter (who, after her firſt huſband's death, became the ſecond wife of Gov. Bradford); ſeems to have come over in 1628 [3 *Maſs. Hiſt. Coll.* i : 199]; was made freeman in 1637; married Elizabeth Collier, 2 Nov. 1637; was Deputy in 1647 and 22 years following, and Treaſ-urer from 1659 to 1678; was often Aſſiſtant, once Commiſſioner for the United Colonies, and acted as Com-miſſary-General in Philip's war; died 11 March, 1679. He left three ſons, and five daughters, — the ſecond of whom had married Church, 26 Dec. 1667. This relationſhip by marriage explains his here throwing off "the Power & Trouble" of his poſt on his ſon-in-law. [Winſor's *Hiſt. Duxbury*, 68; *Plym. Col. Rec.* i : 68, 74; ii : 117; iii : 8, 138, 153, 162; iv : 14, 37; v : 17, 34, etc.]

[69] *Matthew Fuller* was ſon of Ed-ward (who was brother of the famous Dr. Samuel); was at Plymouth in 1642; went to Barnſtable in 1652, and was the firſt phyſician there. He was Lieut. of Barnſtable company in 1652; Deputy from Barnſtable in 1653; went Lieut. to Miles Standiſh in the Dutch expedi-tion in 1654; was fined 50s. for "ſpeak-ing reproachfully of the Court, etc.," in 1658; was appointed on the Council of War the ſame year; is ſpoken of as Captain in 1670; was choſen "Surjean general" for the Dutch expedition in 1673; and evidently was with this ex-pedition in the ſame capacity, as, at the October Court following theſe firſt con-flicts in Philip's war, there was allowed "to Capt. Mathew Fuller, as ſurjean generall of the forces of this collonie, and *for other good ſervice, p'formed in the countryes behalfe againſt the enemie, in the late expeditions*, or

ther order concerning the Fort. And with all, an order for Capt. *Fuller* with Six files to crofs the River to the fide fo much infifted on, and to try if he could get Speech with any of the *Pocaffet* or *Sogkonate* Indians, and that Mr. *Church* fhould go his Second. Upon the Captains receiving his orders, he ask'd Mr. *Church* whither he was willing to engage in this interprize: To whom 'twas indeed too agreeable to be declined; tho' he thought the enterprize was hazardous enough, for them to have more Men affign'd them. Capt. *Fuller* told him that for his own part he was grown Ancient and heavy, he feared the travel and fatigue would be too much for him. But Mr. *Church* urged him, and told him, he would chearfully excufe him, his hardfhip and travel, and take that part to himfelf, if he might but go; for he had rather do any thing in the World than ftay there to build the Fort.

Then they drew out the Number affigned them and March'd the fame Night[70] to the Ferry,[71] and were tranf-ported to *Rhode-Ifland*, from whence the next Night they

which may be done for the future, as occation may require, the Court alloweth him 4s. a day." He died in 1678. [Freeman's *Hift. Cape Cod*, ii : 324; Savage's *Gen. Dict.* ii : 217; *Plym. Col. Rec.* ii : 37, 45, 50; iii : 17, 24, 55, 150, 153; v : 48, 136, 175.]

[70] Hubbard [*Narrative*, 24] fays, "Upon thurfday July 7" [7 July was *Wednefday*] Captain *Fuller*, with Captain *Church*, went into Pocaffet to feck after the enemy," etc. It is doubtful whether he means, by this date, to

indicate the day of their departure from the fort on this expedition, or the day of their arrival at Pocaffet; probably the former (as moft likely to be noted and reported by the general company). If fo, then the little band left the fort 7 July, and got acrofs the ferry into Pocaffet on the night of *Thurfday*, 8 July. This would fix the date of the Punkatees fight as Friday, 9 July.

[71] Briftol ferry; from the lower end of Mount-Hope neck to Rhode-Ifland, then commonly called Tripp's ferry.

got a paffage over to *Pocaffet*-fide[72] in *Rhode-Ifland* Boats, and concluded there to difpofe themfelves in two Ambuf-cado's before day, hoping to furprize fome of the Enemy by their falling into one or other of their Ambufments. But Capt. *Fullers* party being troubled with the Epide-mical plague of luft after Tobacco, muft needs ftrike fire to Smoke it;[73] and thereby difcovered themfelves to a party of the Enemy coming up to them, who immediately fled with great precipitation.

This Ambufcado drew off about break of day, perceiv-ing they were difcover'd, the other continued in their Poft until the time affigned them, and the light and heat of the Sun rendred their Station both infignificant and trouble-fome, and then return'd, unto the place of Randezvous, where they were acquainted with the other parties difap-pointment, and the occafion of it. Mr. *Church* calls for the breakfaft he had ordered to be brought over in the Boat: but the Man that had the charge of it confeffed that he was a-fleep when the Boats-men called him, and in hafte came away and never thought of it. It happened that Mr. *Church* had a few Cakes of Rusk in his Pocket, that Madam *Cranfton* (the Governour of *Rhode-Ifland's* Lady[74]) gave him, when he came off the Ifland, which he

[72] Doubtlefs the croffing was done at what was then a ferry, — fince known as " Howland's ferry," — where the Stone bridge now ftands; the narrow-eft point of the " Eaft Paffage," or Nar-raganfett river.

[73] " To fmoke it " was, in my child-hood, a common phrafe in the Old Col-ony for the act of ufing tobacco by the pipe.

[74] *Gov. John Cranfton* feems to make his firft appearance upon record as appointed *drummer* by the General Court at Newport, 14 March, 1644,

divided among the Company, which was all the Provifions they had.

Mr. *Church* after their flender breakfaft propofed to Capt. *Fuller,* That he would March in queft of the Enemy, with fuch of the Company as would be willing to March with him; which he complyed with, tho' with a great deal of fcruple, becaufe of his fmall Number, & the extream hazard he forefaw muft attend them.[75] [8]

But fome of the Company had reflected upon Mr. *Church,* that notwithftanding his talk on the other fide of the River, he had not fhown them any *Indians* fince they came over. Which now mov'd him to tell them, That if it was their defire to fee *Indians,* he believ'd he fhould now foon fhew them what they fhould fay was enough.

The Number allow'd him foon drew off to him, which could not be many, becaufe their whole Company con-

when he muft have been 18; was among freemen in 1655; was licenfed to practife phyfic, and *had the degree of M.D. conferred on him by the General Affembly* in 1664; was chofen Deputy Govcruor in 1672, and ferved alfo in 1673, '76, '77, and '78, in which year Gov. Arnold died, and he was chofen Govcruor; ferved as Governor till 12 March, 1680, when he died in office, aged 54. He was the firft who ever held the place of Major-General in Rhode-Ifland. He married Mary, daughter of Dr. Jeremiah Clark of Newport; who after his death married John Stanton, and who died 7 April, 1711. Gov. Samuel Cranfton was his fon. He had only

reached the rank of Deputy Governor at the date fpoken of in the text, but Church, dictating forty years after, refers to him under the title by which he was afterwards beft known. [*R.I. Col. Rec.* i: 127, 301; ii: 33, 451, 481, 541, 565; iii: 3, 4, 24; Arnold's *Hift. R.-I.* i: 459; Savage's *Gen. Dict.* i: 472.]

[75] Hubbard's account would indicate that a day and night had been fpent on the Pocaffet fide, before this propofition of Church's took place. [*Narrative,* 24.] Probably he confounded this with the time fpent on Rhode-Ifland. Church, as a participant, is, of courfe, the beft witnefs.

fifted of no more than Thirty Six.[76]   They mov'd towards *Sogkonate*, until they came to the brook that runs into *Nun naquohqut* Neck,[77] where they difcovered a frefh and plain Track, which they concluded to be from the great Pine Swamp[78] about a Mile from the Road that leads to *Sogkonet*.   Now fays Mr. *Church* to his Men, If we follow this Track no doubt but we fhall foon fee *Indians* enough; they exprefs'd their willingnefs to follow the Track, and mov'd in it, but had not gone far before one of them narrowly efcaped being bit with a *Rattle-fnake*:[79] And the

[76] "There being not above fifteen with Church." [Hubbard, *Narrative*, 24.] This would leave twenty-one with Capt. Fuller. But Church afterwards fays there were *nineteen* with him befides his "pilot"; which would indicate a nearly equal divifion of the little force.

[77] Mr. Drake's note would fix the rivulet referred to as "that which empties into the bay nearly a mile fouthward from Howland's ferry"; now, for fome reafon which I have never heard, bearing the ftrange name of "Sin and Flefh brook." I am perfuaded, however, that Nanaquaket brook, which croffes the road to Little Compton, fay a mile and a half further fouth, juft before you reach the fchool-houfe, is that of which Church fpeaks. That "runs in" juft in the angle where Nanaquaket neck is joined to the main land, and therefore feems more exactly defignated by the phrase "that runs into *Nunnaquohqut* Neck" than one fo much further removed, emptying into the cove.

Moreover, its relative bearing to the fwamp of which Church proceeds to fpeak is nearer to the demand of the text than that of the other.

This neck is that promontory in Tiverton which flopes up northward and weftward toward the ifland of Rhode-Ifland, next fouth of the Stone bridge. The name (*Nunnaquahqatt*, *Nonequacket*, *Nanaquaket*, *Quacut*, etc.) may have this fenfe: *Nunnukque* means "dangerous," "unfafe"; whence *Nunnukqueohke* (contracted *Nunnukquok*) would be "an unfafe or dangerous place." The final *et* is locative, "at" or "in."

[78] Still there, and diftant about a mile due eaft from the fpot which I fuppofe Church to have now reached.

[79] Rattlefnakes were formerly abundant in New England. Prince fays, (14 Aug. 1632,) "this fummer is very wet and cold, except now and then a hot day or two, which caufes great ftore of musketoes and rattlefnakes." [Ed. 1852, 400.]

Woods that the Track lead them through was haunted much with thofe Snakes which the little Company feem'd more to be afraid of than the black Serpents they were in queft of, and therefore bent their courfe another way; to a Place where they thought it probable to find fome of the Enemy. Had they kept the Track to the Pine Swamp they had been certain of meeting *Indians* enough; but not fo certain that any of them fhould have return'd to give account how many.

Now they pafs'd down into *Punkatees*[80] Neck; and in their March difcocovered a large Wigwam full of *Indian* Truck, which the Souldiers were for loading themfelves with; until Mr. *Church* forbid it; telling them they might expect foon to have their hands full, and bufinefs without caring for Plunder. Then croffing the head of the Creek into the Neck, they again difcovered frefh, Indian Tracks, very lately pafs'd before them into the Neck. They then got privately and undifcovered, unto the Fence of Capt. *Almy*'s Peafe-field,[81] and divided into two Parties, Mr. *Church* keeping the one Party with himfelf, fent the other with *Lake*[82] that was acquainted with the ground, on the

---

[80] *Punkatees* neck — fome two miles in length and one mile in extreme width — fhoots out from the main land of Tiverton fouthward and weftward, much as *Nunnaquohqut* neck turns up northward and weftward. It was alfo called Pocaffet neck. The entrance to it is directly weft from the fmall village of Tiverton Four Corners. The deriva-tion or fignification of the name has not been fuggefted.

[81] See note 4. At leaft four fami-lies of Almys now own and till many of the fertile acres of this beautiful promontory.

[82] *David Lake*, or *Leake*, volun-teered 10 Aug. 1667, in a troop of horfe upon Rhode Ifland. If this were

other fide. Two *Indians* were foon difcovered coming
out of the Peafe-field towards them: When Mr. *Church*
& thofe that were with him concealed themfelves from
them, by falling flat on the ground: but the other divifion
not ufing the fame caution were feen by the Enemy, which
occafioned them to run; which when Mr. *Church* per-
ceiv'd, he fhew'd himfelf to them, and call'd, telling them
he defired but to fpeak with them, and would not hurt
them. But they run, and *Church* purfued. The *Indians*
clim'd over a Fence and one of them facing about difcharged his Piece, but without effect on the *Englifh*: One
of the *Englifh* Souldiers ran up to the Fence and fir'd upon
him that had difcharged his Piece; and they concluded by
the yelling they heard that the *Indian* was wounded; but
the *Indians* foon got into the thickets, whence they faw
them no more for the prefent. [9]

Mr. *Church* then Marching over a plain piece of Ground
where the Woods were very thick on one fide; order'd his
little Company to March at double diftance, to make as
big a fhow (if they fhould be difcovered) as might be.
But before they faw any body, they were Saluted with a

the fame man, he probably — as a refident of the ifland and familiar with the
neighboring localities — accompanied
this expedition as the " pilot," of whom
Church fpeaks further on. [*R.-I. Col.
Rec.* ii. 218.) Plymouth Colony the
next year granted to David Lake "three-
fcore acrees" of land eaftward from
Punchateefet pond and north of Saconet line, (which would be in what is
now Tiverton, where men of the fame
name now live, upon it,) becaufe he had
" bin very ufefull and ferviceable to the
country in the late warr." Thomas
Lake — whether his brother, or not, I
cannot fay — had a fimilar grant, at the
fame time, of forty acres. [*R.-I. Col.
Rec.* ii: 218; *Plym. Col. Rec.* v: 214.]

Volly of fifty or fixty Guns; fome Bullets came very fur-
prizingly near Mr. *Church*, who ftarting, look'd behind
him, to fee what was become of his Men, expecting to
have feen half of them dead, but feeing them all upon
their Leggs and briskly firing at the Smokes of the Enemies Guns, (for that was all that was then to be feen) *He
Blefs'd God, and called to his Men not to difcharge all
their Guns at once, left the Enemy fhould take the advantage of fuch an opportunity to run upon them with their
Hatches.*[83]

Their next Motion was immediately into the Peafe-field.
When they came to the Fence Mr. *Church* bid as many as
had not difcharg'd their Guns, to clap under the Fence,
and lye clofe, while the other at fome diftance in the
Field ftood to charge; hoping that if the Enemy fhould
creep to the Fence to gain a fhot at thofe that were charg-
ing their Guns, they might be furprized by thofe that lay
under the Fence. But cafting his Eyes to the fide of the
Hill above them;[84] the hill feem'd to move, being covered
over with *Indians*, with their bright Guns glittering in the
Sun, and running in a circumference with a defign to furround them.

Seeing fuch Multitudes furrounding him and his little
Company; it put him upon thinking what was become of
the Boats that were ordered to attend him: And looking

---

[83] Hatchets, or tomahawks.

[84] The bluff above them; the peafe-
field being near the fhore, and the land
rifing abruptly toward the ridge of the
promontory. The hill is not very high,
yet the flope is fteep.

up, he fpy'd them a fhore at *Sandy-point*[85] on the Ifland fide
of the River, with a number of Horfe and Foot by them,
and wondred what fhould be the occafion; until he was
afterwards informed, That the Boats had been over that
Morning from the Ifland, and had landed a Party of Men
at *Fogland*,[86] that were defign'd in *Punkatees* Neck to fetch
off fome Cattel and Horfes, but were Ambufcado'd, and
many of them wounded by the Enemy.[87]

Now our Gentlemans Courage and Conduct were both
put to the Teft, he incourages his Men; and orders fome
to run and take a Wall to fhelter before the Enemy gain'd
it. Twas time for them now to think of efcaping if they
knew which way. Mr. *Church* orders his Men to ftrip to
their white Shirts, that the *Iflanders* might difcover them
to be Englifh Men; & then orders Three Guns to be fired
diftinct, hoping it might be obferv'd by their friends on
the oppofite Shore.[88] The Men that were ordered to take

[85] Probably what is now defignated
as "McCarry's point," on the Portfmouth fhore, rather than that now called
"Sandy point," which is a mile and a
half further fouth.

[86] *Fogland* point is a fpur of land
projecting from the weftern fhore of
Punkatees neck, and reaching a third
of the way acrofs Narraganfett river
toward Portfmouth on the ifland of
Rhode-Ifland.

[87] Hubbard fays: "It feems in the
former part of the fame day, five men
coming from *Road-Ifland*, to look up
their Cattle upon *Pocaffet Neck*, were

affaulted by the fame *Indians*, and one
of the five was Capt. *Churches* Servant,
who had his Leg broke in the Skirmifh,
the reft hardly efcaping with their lives:
this was the firft time that ever any
mifchief was done by the *Indians* upon
Pocaffet Neck. Thofe of *Road-Ifland*
were hereby Alarmed to look to themfelves, as well as the reft of the Englifh
of *Plimouth*, or the *Maffachufets Colony*." [*Narrative*, 25.]

[88] It was probably not over a mile
and a half in a ftraight line, from the
fcene of this fkirmifh to the point acrofs
the water where their friends were.

the Wall, being very hungry, ſtop'd a while among the Peaſe to gather a few, being about four Rod from the Wall; the Enemy from behind it hail'd them with a Shower of Bullets; but ſoon all but one came tumbling over an old hedge down the bank where Mr. *Church* and the reſt were, and told him that his Brother *B. Southworth*,[89] who was the Man that was miſſing, was kill'd, that they ſaw him fall; and ſo they did indeed ſee him fall, but 'twas without a [10] Shot, and lay no longer than till he had opportunity to clap a Bullet into one of the Enemies Fore head, and then came running to his Company. The mean-neſs[90] of the *Engliſh*'s Powder was now their greateſt mis-

[89] Either this record is wrong in this initial, or Conſtant Southworth (note 68) had a ſon not down on the records. Savage, Winſor, and Mitchell agree that he had only three ſons, (*Edward, Nathaniel,* and *William,*) and four daughters, beſides Alice, who married Church. The earlieſt Benjamin on the record of the family was Benjamin, ſon of Edward (Conſtant's eldeſt ſon), who was born in 1680, five years after this fight. Edward's age at this date is not known, but, as he had been married in 1669, he may perhaps have been near 30; Nathaniel was 27, and William only 16. It ſeems clear that the perſon here alluded to was one of Church's brothers-in-law, and it is more probable that the initial "W" or "N" was miſprinted "B," and the blunder paſſed uncorrect-ed, than that there was any "B. South-worth," ſon of Conſtant, elſewhere un-recorded. [*Gen. Dict.* iv: 143; *Hiſt.*

Duxbury, 314; *Hiſt. Bridgewater,* 304.]

[90] Church ſeems here to uſe the word "meanneſs" as equivalent to ſcantineſs, — with reference to the quantity rather than the quality. There is no hint in the account of the action but that the powder which they had was good enough, but they were evidently re-duced to a very ſhort allowance. Up to this date the powder of the Coloniſts appears to have been Engliſh made. The firſt powder-mill on this ſide was juſt in proceſs of preparation; Rev. John Oxenbridge, Rev. James Allen, Dea. Robert Sanderſon, (all of the firſt church in Boſton,) with Capt. John Hall and Freegrace Bendall, merchants of Boſton, 22 Aug. 1673, having pur-chaſed of John Gill, of Milton, a privi-lege on Neponſet river, and having entered into articles of agreement, 16 July, 1675, to erect a building and "im-

fortune; when they were immediately upon this befet with Multitudes of *Indians,* who poffeffed themfelves of every Rock, Stump, Tree, or Fence that was in fight, firing upon them without ceafing; while they had no other fhelter but a fmall bank & bit of a water Fence. And yet to add to the difadvantage of this little handful of diftreffed Men; The *Indians* alfo poffeffed themfelves of the Ruines of a Stone-houfe that over look'd them, and of the black Rocks to the Southward of them;[91] fo that now they had no way to prevent lying quite open to fome, or other of the

prove a powder mill" at faid Neponfet. The fafety of this mill was a fubject of legiflation, in October and November following. [*Hift. of Dorchefter,* 607, 609.]

[91] In the fecond edition of this narrative [*Newport, R.-I.* 1772], Southwick's compofitor here carelefsly dropped out the words "and of the black Rocks to the Southward of them," and Dr. Stiles did not difcover the omiffion; fo that, as all the fubfequent editions have been reprints of Southwick's, and not of the original, the hint of exact locality which they furnifh has hitherto been overlooked. On recently vifiting Punkatees neck and going carefully over it in order to identify, if poffible, the exact fpot where this peafe-field was fituated, I found on the edge of the fhore the remains of an outcropping ledge of foft black flaty rock, which differs fo decidedly from any other rocks in the vicinity, and which — making allowance for the wear of the waves for near 200 years — anfwers fo well to the demand of the text, as to incline me to the judgment that they may identify the fpot. If this be fo, the peafe-field muft have been on the weftern fhore of Punkatees neck, a little north of the juncture of Fogland point with the main promontory, and almoft due eaft of the northern extremity of Fogland point, — which runs up northerly and wefterly as it pufhes over toward Rhode-Ifland; lying a little north of the range of the Almy burying-ground, which is in the rear of the prefent refidence of Mr. Horace Almy. Whether this be a correct fuppofition or not, the near neighborhood of what is ftill called Church's well — a fpring ftoned round like a well, and fending a tiny rivulet down to the fea, a few rods fouth of thefe remains of what were once "black rocks," and almoft oppofite the prefent refidence of Mr. Samuel Almy, at the terminus of the road leading to Fogland ferry — fixes the fcene of the fight with fufficient accuracy, as being near the juncture of Fogland point with Punkatees neck.

Enemy, but to heap up Stones before them, as they did, and ftill bravely and wonderfully defended themfelves againft all the numbers of the Enemy. At length came over one of the Boats from the Ifland Shore, but the Enemy ply'd their Shot fo warmly to her as made her keep at fome diftance; Mr. *Church* defired them to fend their Canoo a-fhore to fetch them on board; but no perfwafions, nor arguments could prevail with them to bring their Canoo to fhore. Which fome of Mr. *Churches* Men perceiving, began to cry out, *For God's fake to take them off, for their Ammunition was fpent*, &c. Mr. *Church* being fenfible of the danger of the Enemies hearing their Complaints, and being made acquainted with the weaknefs and fcan tinefs of their Ammunition, fiercely called to the Boats mafter, and bid either fend his Canoo a-fhore, or elfe be gone prefently, or he would fire upon him.

Away goes the Boat and leaves them ftill to fhift for themfelves. But then another difficulty arofe; the Enemy feeing the Boat leave them, were reanimated & fired thicker & fafter than ever; Upon which fome of the Men that were lighteft of foot, began to talk of attempting an efcape by flight: until Mr. *Church* follidly convinc'd them of the impraĉticablenefs of it; and incouraged them yet, told them, *That he had obferv'd fo much of the remarkable and wonderful Providence of God hitherto preferving them, that incouraged him to believe with much confidence that God would yet preferve them; that not a hair of their head fhould fall to the ground; bid them be Patient, Couragious and Prudently*

37

sparing of their Ammunition, and he made no doubt but they should come well off yet, &c. until his little Army, again re-solve one and all to stay with, and stick by him. One of them by Mr. *Churches* order was pitching a flat Stone up an end before him in the Sand, when a Bullet from the Enemy with a full force stroke the Stone while he was pitching it an end; which put the poor fellow to a miser-able start, till Mr. *Church* call'd upon him to observe, *How God directed the Bullets that the Enemy could not hit him when in the same place, yet could hit the Stone as it was erected.*

While they were thus making the best defence they could against their numerous Enemies that made the Woods ring with their constant yelling [11] and shout-ing: And Night coming on, some body told Mr. *Church*, they spy'd a Sloop up the River as far as *Gold-Island*,[92] that seemed to be coming down towards them: He look'd up and told them *Succour was now coming, for he believ'd it was Capt.* Golding,[93] *whom he knew to be a Man for busi-*

---

[92] *Gould Island* is a small rocky island, perhaps three quarters of a mile due south of the Stone bridge. It was purchased of the Indians, 28 Mar. 1657, by Thomas Gould, of Newport, and took its name from him, and not, as has been sometimes stated, from the occur-rence here narrated. [Arnold's *Hist. R.-I.* i: 266; Fowler's *Hist. Sketch of Fall River,* 9.]

[93] *Capt. Roger Golding* (*Golden, Goulden*) was captain of a vessel, and seems to have lived in Portsmouth, R.-

I.; at any rate he is dubiously referred to in that connection in the *R.-I. Colonial Records* for 6 Nov. 1672. He was present at the killing of Philip. He married Penelope, daughter of the first Benedict Arnold. Plymouth Colony, 1 Nov. 1676, gave Capt. Golding one hundred acres of land, because he "hath approued himselfe to be our constant, reall frind in the late warr, and very of-ficious and healpfull as occation hath bine, when as our armies and souldiers haue bin in those p'tes, and haue had

nefs; and would certainly fetch them off, if he came: the Wind being fair, the Veffel was foon with them; and Capt. *Golding* it was. Mr. *Church* (as foon as they came to Speak one with another) defired him *to come to Anchor at fuch a diftance ?from the Shore that he might veer out his Cable and ride a float, and let flip his Canoo that it might drive afhore*; which directions Capt. *Golding* obferv'd; but the Enemy gave him fuch a warm Salute, that his Sails, Colour, and Stern were full of Bullet holes.

The Canoo came afhore,[94] but was fo fmall that fhe would not bare above two Men at a time; and when two were got aboard, they turn'd her loofe to drive afhore for two more: and the Sloops company kept the *Indians* in play the while. But when at laft it came to Mr. *Churches* turn to go aboard, he had left his Hat and Cutlafh at the Well[95] where he went to drink, when he firft came down; he told his Company, *He would never go off and leave his Hat and Cutlafh for the* Indians; *they fhould never have that to reflect upon him.* Tho' he was much diffwaded from it, yet he would go fetch them. He put all the Powder he had left into his Gun (and a poor charge it was) and went

---

neffefitie of the tranfportation of our men to the faid iland [Rhode-Ifland] and otherwife very reddy to doe vs good." This land adjoined that of the Lakes (note 82, *ante*). [*R.-I. Col. Rec.* ii: 480; Savage, *Gen. Dict.* ii. 287; *Plym. Col. Rec.* v: 214. See alfo *Plym. Col. Rec.* v: 242, and vi: 120, for further facts concerning Capt. G.]

[94] The wind was probably northweft-erly, as it is apt to be there on a pleaf-ant day, which would be exactly "fair" for Capt. Golding in running down, as narrated; and which would foon drift a light canoe on fhore.

[95] See note 91, *ante*. I fee no reafon to doubt the truftworthinefs of the tra-dition identifying this well.

prefenting his Gun at the Enemy, until he took up what he went for; at his return he difcharged his Gun at the Enemy to bid them farewel, for that time; but had not Powder enough to carry the Bullet half way to them.

Two Bullets from the Enemy ftuck the Canoo as he went on Board, one grazed the hair of his Head a little before; another ftruck in a fmall Stake that ftood right againft the middle of his Breaft.

Now this Gentleman with his Army, making in all 20 Men, himfelf, and his Pilot being numbred with them, got all fafe aboard after Six hours ingagement with 300 *Indians*; whofe Number we were told afterwards by fome of themfelves. *A deliverance which that good Gentleman often mentions to the Glory of God, and His Protecting Providence.* The next day[96] meeting with the reft of their little Company, whom he had left at *Pocaffet*, (that had alfo a fmall skirmifh with the *Indians*, and had two Men Wounded)[97] they return'd to the *Mount-hope* Garrifon; which Mr. *Church* us'd to call the loofing Fort. Mr. *Church* then returning to the Ifland[98] to feek Provifion for the Army, meets with *Alderman*,[99] a noted *Indian* that

[96] Friday, 9 July, 1675.

[97] Capt. Fuller "either faw or heard too many Indians for himfelf and his Company to deal with, which made him and them betake themfelves to an Houfe near the Water-fide, from whence they were fetched off by a floop before night to *Road-Ifland*." [Hubbard's *Narrative*, 24.]

[98] Rhode Ifland.

[99] *Alderman* was a fubject of *Weetamoe* (note 24), but at the commencement of the war went to the Governor of Plymouth, and defired to remain at peace with the Englifh; and now left Pocaffet for Rhode Ifland in that intent. It was his bullet that eventually killed Philip. [Drake's *Book of the Ind.* 226.]

was juſt come over from the *Squaw Sachem's* Cape of *Pocaſſet,* having deſerted from her, and had brought over his Family: Who gave him an account of the State of the *Indians,* and where each of the *Sagamores* head quarters were. Mr. *Church* then diſcours'd with ſome who knew the Spot well where the *Indians* ſaid *Weetamores* head quarters were, and offered their Service to Pilot him. With this News he [12] haſtned to the *Mount-hope* Gar-riſon. The Army expreſs'd their readineſs to imbrace ſuch an opportunity.

All the ableſt Souldiers were now immediately drawn off equip'd & diſpatch'd upon this deſign, under the Com mand of a certain Officer:[100] and having March'd about two Miles, *viz.* until they came to the Cove[101] that lyes *S.W.* from the Mount, where orders was given for an halt. The Commander in Chief told them he thought it proper to take advice before he went any further; called Mr. *Church* and the Pilot, and aſk'd them, *How they knew that* Philip *and all his Men were not by that time got to* Weeta-mores *Camp; or that all her own Men were not by that time return'd to her again?* With many more frightful queſtions. Mr. *Church* told him, *they had acquainted him with as much as they knew, and that for his part he could*

---

[100] Hubbard ſays, Church borrowed "three files of Men of Capt. *Henchman* with his Lieutenant:" this Lieutenant was doubtleſs, then, the officer in command. Fortunately for his memory his name was not deſignated. [*Narrative,* 25.]

[101] Now called *Mount Cove.* They were, no doubt, on their way to Briſtol ferry — then called Tripp's ferry [*R.-I. Col. Rec.* iii: 535] — to croſs to Rhode-Iſland, and thence, over Howland's fer-ry, to Pocaſſet, whence it would be a little over ſix miles to "the Fall River."

difcover nothing that need to difcourage them ?from Proceed-
ing, that he thought it fo practicable, that he with the Pilot
would willingly lead the way to the Spot and hazard the
brunt. But the Chief Commander infifted on this, *That*
the Enemies number were fo great, and he did not know
what numbers more might be added unto them by that time:
And his Company fo fmall, that he could not think it practi-
cable to attack them. Added moreover, *That if he was*
?fure of killing all the Enemy, and knew that he muft lofe the
Life of one of his Men in the action, he would not attempt
it. Pray Sir, then (Reply'd Mr. *Church) Pleafe to lead*[102]
your Company to yonder Windmill on Rhode-Ifland, *and*
there they will be out of danger of being kill'd by the Enemy,
and we fhall have lefs trouble to fupply them with Provifions
But return he would, and did, unto the Garrifon until
more ftrength came to them: And a Sloop to tranfport
them to the Fall River,[103] in order to vifit *Weetamores*

[102] The abfence of water power on the Ifland led, as early as 1663, to the erection of windmills for grinding corn; and feveral eminences in the town of Portfmouth are now crowned with them, which may be feen from far. [Arnold's *Hift. R.-I.* i: 370.]

[103] *Quequechan* River — the outlet of Watuppa Pond — was about two miles long and lefs than one rod in width, and when within 150 rods of tide-water it fuddenly defcended 132 feet to meet it. It took naturally, therefore, the name of "the fall of the river," or *Fall River.* The various factories have now abforbed this fall; fo that the vifitor muft fearch for what was once the moft prominent feature of the locality. Fowler fays, the word *Quequechan* fignifies "falling water," or "quick-running water;" but Mr. Trumbull fays, "*Chĕkee*, or *Chĕche*, alone, or in compofition, means 'violent,' 'forcible,' and is fometimes applied to running water, as it is to 'that which fweeps away,' e. g. *chekhihunk*, 'a broom' or 'befom,' and *chék-efu* 'the northweft wind.' I do not think, however, that it is found in *Quequechan*, and clearly not unlefs the laft part of the name —

Camp. Mr. *Church*, one *Baxter*[104] and Capt. *Hunter*[105] an Indian profer'd to go out on the difcovery on the left Wing; which was accepted; they had not March'd above a quarter of a Mile before they ftarted Three of the Enemy. Capt. *Hunter* wounded one of them in his knee, whom when he came up he difcovered to be his near kinfman; the Captive defired favour for his *Squaw*, if fhe fhould fall into their hands, but afk'd none for himfelf, excepting the liberty of taking a Whiff of Tobacco, and while he was taking his Whiff, his kinfman with one blow of his Hatchet difpatch'd him. Proceeding to *Weetamores* Camp,[106] they were difcover'd by one of the Enemy, who

fignifying 'water,' 'ftream,' or fomething of the kind—has been loft." [Fowler's *Hift. Sketch, Fall River*, 27.]

[104] *Thomas Baxter*, bricklayer, of Yarmouth, 5 March, 1671-2, was accufed of "mifdemeanor att the meeting-houfe att Yarmouth;" and, again, of entering Edward Sturgis's houfe on Lord's Day, 11 April, 1675, and ftealing from the fame; but was cleared on both charges: he was alfo one of 30 foldiers "that were preffed into the country's fervice, and went to Mount-Hope againft our enemies the Indians, in the year 1675, and took their firft march June 24." He was wounded in the war, and £20 were allowed him by the Plymouth Court, 10 July, 1677, as a "maimed fouldier, whoe hath loft the vfe of one of his hands in the time hee was in the countryes fervice." I have met with no record of any other of the name as being in this war, and prefume this reference to be to him. [*Plym. Col. Rec.* v: 87, 168, 239; Freeman's *Hift. Cape Cod*, ii: 193.]

[105] *Capt. Hunter* appears to have been a Chriftianized *Nipmuk* Indian. On the 6th of July—two days before the fight in Almy's peafe-field—Capt. Johnfon, on the order of the Governor and Council of Maffachufetts, had conducted a body of "about 52" Praying Indians (being one-third part of their able-bodied men) to the army at Mount-Hope. Among them was *John Hunter*, who, on his return, had a reward given him for his faithfulnefs; he bringing back with him a fcalp; that, no doubt, of the Indian referred to in the text. [*Tranfactions Amer. Antiquarian Society*, ii: 442, 444.]

[106] This feems to have been fituated on the northern fide of what is now called Pocaffet Cedar Swamp; perhaps two miles and a half fouth of the city

ran in and gave Information; upon which a lufty Young Fellow left his Meat upon his Spit, running haftily out told his companions, *he would kill an Englifh man before he eat his dinner*: but fail'd of his defign, being no fooner out but fhot down. The Enemies fires, and what fhelter they had was by the Edge of a thick Cedar Swamp, into which on this Alarm they betook themfelves; and the Englifh as nimbly purfued; but were foon commanded back by their Chieftain after they were come within hearing of the Crys of their Women, and Children, and fo ended that Exploit.[107] But returning to their Sloop the Enemy purfued them and wounded two of their Men. The next day return'd to the *Mount-hope* Garrifon. [13]

Soon after this,[108] was *Philips* head Quarters vifited by fome other *Englifh* Forces; but *Philip* and his gang had the very fortune to efcape that *Weetamore* and hers (but now mentioned) had: they took into a Swamp and their purfuers were commanded back. After this[109] *Dart-*

of Fall River, and lying between South Watuppa Pond and the hights which look down on Mount-Hope Bay.

[107] Hubbard fays, "wherein fome few of them [the Indians] fourteen or fifteen were flain." [*Narrative*, 25.]

[108] Hubbard fays that our forces went to Rehoboth on Friday, 15 July (15 July was *Thurfday*), next day to Mattapoifett, and next day to Taunton. July 18 (Hubbard calls it "Munday," but the 18th was *Sunday;* fo that they probably ftarted on the 19th) they marched 18 miles, and attacked Philip "in the great fwampe upon *Pocaffet* neck, of feven miles long." They

thought they had him hemmed in there, and fo the Plymouth forces and Capt. Henchman with 100 foot, were left to "attend the Enemies motion, being judged fufficient for that end." One night, however, "in the end of *July*," Philip and his warriors either waded acrofs Taunton river, at a very low tide, or got over on rafts, and efcaped to the *Nipmuk* Country. [*Narrative*, 25–27.] Fowler [*Hift. Sketch, Fall River*, 10] fays they croffed juft above where Fall River now ftands.

[109] Dartmouth feems to have been deftroyed by the Indians in the latter half of July.

mouths diftreffes required Succour, great Part of the Town
being laid defolate, and many of the Inhabitants kill'd; the
moft of *Plymouth* Forces were order'd thither: And coming to *Ruffels* Garrifon at *Poneganfet*,[110] they met with a
Number of the Enemy that had furrendred themfelves
Prifoners on terms promifed by Capt. *Eels*[111] of the Garrifon; and *Ralph Earl*[112] that perfwaded them (by a friend
Indian he had employed) to come in. And had their
promifes to the *Indians* been kept, and the *Indians* farely
treated, 'tis probable that moft if not all the *Indians* in
thofe Parts, had foon followed the Example of thofe that
had now furrendred themfelves; which would have been
a good ftep towards finifhing the War. But in fpite of all
that Capt. *Eels, Church,* or *Earl* could fay, argue, plead, or
beg, fome body elfe that had more Power in their hands

[110] The *Apponeganfett* River (or
cove) is the fecond cove making up
from Buzzard's Bay weft and fouth of
New-Bedford harbor. Faint traces
of the cellar of this garrifon-houfe
might lately be feen, near a fpring on
the eaft bank of this river, about a mile
from its mouth. John Ruffell was one
of the earlieft fettlers of Dartmouth.
[Ricketfon's *Hift. New Bedford*, 15,
35, 154.]

[111] *Capt. Samuel Eells* feems to have
been the fon of John, of Dorchefter.
He was baptized at Dorchefter, 3 May,
1640. He "commanded a garrifon at
Dartmouth, Mafs., in Philip's war,"
married Anna, daughter of Rev. Robert
Lenthal of Weymouth, and died in
Hingham in 1709; leaving, among

eight children, Rev. Nathaniel, of Scituate. [*Hift. Dorchefter*, 51; Deane's
Scituate, 197; Barry's *Hanover*, 301.]

[112] *Ralph Earl* appears to have been
fon of Ralph, of Portfmouth, R.-I., and
to have removed to Dartmouth in con-
fequence of the gift to him of "half a
fhare in Coaxit and Acufhnet" by
Francis Sprague of Duxbury, who calls
him "fon-in-law." He was fined, 29
Oct. 1668, 5 s, for "affronting the conftable" of Dartmouth. He was himfelf
conftable in 1670. I am forry to add
that a perfon of that name was fined
20 s, at Plymouth, 5 Oct., 1663, for
"drawing his wife in an vnciuell man-
or on the fnow." [Savage's *Gen. Dict.*
ii: 91; *Plym. Col. Rec.* iv: 47; v: 10,
36.]

improv'd it; and without any regard to the promifes made them on their furrendring themfelves, they were carry'd away to *Plymouth*, there fold, and tranfported out of the Country; being about Eight-fcore Perfons.[113]   An action fo

[113] The following I take to be the order of the Council of war upon this cafe, 4 Aug., 1675, which hints the light in which the government viewed the matter.

"In reference vnto a companie of "natiues now in coftody, brought in to "Plymouth, being men, weomen, and "children, in number one hundred and "twelue, vpon ferioufe and deliberate "confideration and agitation conferning "them, the conclufion is as followeth: "that wheras, vpon examination, it is "found that feuerall of them haue bine "actors in the late rifing and warr of "the Indians againft vs, and the reft "complyers with them therein, which "they haue done contrary to engage-"ment and couenant made and plighted "with this collonie, which they haue "p'fidioufly broken, as appeereth fur-"ther alfoe in that they did not dif-"couer that p'nifious plott which Phillip, "with others, completed againft vs, "which hath caufed the deftruction of "feuerall of vs, by loffe of liues and "eftates, and ftill held in danger "therby, the p'mifes confidered as "aforefaid, the councell adjudged them "to be fold, and deuoted vnto fervi-"tude, excepting fome few of them, "which, vpon fpeciall confideration, "are to be otherwife difpofed of, and "the Treafurer is appointed by the "councell to make fale of them in the "countryes behalfe."

On the fecond of September follow-ing, fimilar action was taken in the cafe of "a certaine p'fell of Indians lately come in to Sandwich in a fub-miffiue way to this collonie." They were adjudged to be "in the fame con-dition of rebellion," and "condemned vnto p'petuall fervitude." There were 57 of thefe, which, added to the former 112, made 169; not far from Church's eight fcore. Thacher, under date of Oct. 4, 1765, fays, "one hundred and feventy-eight [Indians] had recently been shipped on board of Captain Sprague, for Cadiz"; unqueftionably referring to this fame melancholy mif-judgment. It is effential to the proper underftanding of fuch a tranfaction as this, that the general cuftom and feeling of the time fhould be confidered. A very curious document has been pre-ferved, of date 14 Aug., 1676, fhowing that Roger Williams was chairman of a committee in Rhode-Ifland to difpofe of fome Indian captives whom *they* had taken. All under 5 years of age were fold to ferve till they were 30; all be-tween 5 and 10, till 28; all between 10 and 15, till 27; all between 15 and 20, till 26; all between 20 and 30 were to ferve 8 years; all above 30, 7 years. Judge Staples fays that, in moft in-ftances, Indian prifoners "were fent out of the country and fold for flaves for life." [*Plym. Col. Rec.* v: 173, 174; *Hift. Plym.* 136; *R.-I. Hift. Coll.* v: 170.]

hateful to Mr. *Church*, that he oppof'd it to the lofs of the good Will and Refpeᶜts of fome that before were his good Friends. But while thefe things were aᶜting at *Dartmouth*, *Philip* made his efcape, leaving his Country, fled over *Taunton*-River, and *Rehoboth*-Plain,[114] and *Petuxet*-River,[115] where Capt. *Edmunds* of *Providence*[116] made fome fpoil upon; and had probably done more, but was prevented by the coming up of a Superiour Officer,[117] that put him by. And now another Fort was built at *Pocaſſet*,[118]

[114] Seekonk Plain.

[115] See note 108, *ante*. Pawtucket and Pawtuxet should not be confounded, as they are different names. *Pautuck-et* is "at the falls of the river;" *Pautuxet* (*Pautuck-efe-et*) introduces a diminutive, i. e. "at the *little* falls of the river." The river referred to in the text is now called the Blackſtone.

[116] *Capt. Andrew Edmunds* (*Edmonds or Edmands*) was of Providence, and married Mary, dau, of Benj. Herendean, 14 Oᶜt., 1675; 7 Aug., 1676 the R.-I. Aſſembly voted him and his company one-half of the money accruing from the fale of 35 Indians "brought in by them;" 17 June, 1684 he ferved on a Coroner's Jury on the death of John Miller of Rehoboth; 25 Dec., 1689 Plymouth Court ordered him 20s. a week for his fervice in the Eaſtern Expedition, and, by vote of 3 March, 1690, the Rhode-Iſland Aſſembly added £6 to it. He died previous to 1696, having had five children. His widow was allowed to keep the ferry over Seekonk river. [Savage's *Gen. Diᶜt.* ii: 101; *R.-I. Col. Rec.* ii: 549; iii: 263,

277, 280, 313; *Plym. Col. Rec.* vi: 143, 229.]

[117] Hubbard names Capt. *Henchman* in this conneᶜtion, and adds "what the reafon was why Philip was followed no further, it is better to fufpend, then too critically to inquire." The inference, taken with what Church fays, is that Henchman was the man on whom the blame refted. [*Narrative*, 28.] The Rev. Noah Newman of Rehoboth was very efficient and ufeful in this affault on the retreating Philip. [Blifs's *Rehoboth*, 87.]

[118] Capt. Cudworth urged this. He wrote to Gov. Winſlow, 20 July, 1675, from Mount-Hope Neck, faying "Now that which we confider to be beſt, is to maintain our garrifon, though but with twenty men, and that there be another garrifon at *Pocaſſet;* and to have a flying army, to be in motion" (doubtleſs with thefe points as its bafe) "to keep the Indians from deſtroying our cattle, and fetching in fupply of food; which being attended, will bring them to great ſtraights, &c." [1 *Maſs. Hiſt. Coll.* vi: 85.] I have not been able to identify

that prov'd as troublefome and chargeable as that at
Mount-hope; and the remainder of the Summer was improv'd in providing for the Forts and Forces there main-
tained, while our Enemies were fled fome hundreds of
Miles into the Country, near as far as *Albany*. And now
ftrong Sufpicions began to arife of the *Narraganfet Indians*,[119] that they were ill affected, and defigned mifchief;
and fo the event foon difcovered. The next Winter they
began their Hoftilities, upon the *Englifh*.[120] The United
Colonies then agreed to fent an Army to fupprefs them:[121]

the fite of this Pocaffet garrifon, but
fuppofe it to have been within the prefent city-limits of Fall River.

[119] The *Narraganfett Indians* may be
generally defcribed as having occupied
the lower half of what is now the main
land of the State of Rhode-Ifland, including the whole of Wafhington, with
the lower portion of Kent Counties.
[Gookin, 1 *Mafs. Hift. Coll.* i: 147; *R.-
I. Hift. Coll.* iii: 1.] With regard to
the fignificance of this name, concerning which various fuggeftions have
been made, (Drake's *Book of the Indians*, 87, *note*,) Mr. Trumbull quotes
Roger Williams: "I was within a pole
of it, but could not learn why it was
called *Nahiganfet*," and fays, "to whom
I have nothing to add."

[120] From the date of Philip's efcape
acrofs Taunton River (1 Aug.), hoftilities
had been in progrefs. Mendon fettlers
fell firft. Early in Auguft, *Quaboag*
(Brookfield) was deftroyed. About the
firft of September, Deerfield was burned.
Soon after, *Squakeag* (Northfield) was

affaulted, and the majority of Capt
Beers's party, going to its relief, killed.
Early in October, Springfield was attacked, and 32 houfes fired. A few days
later, 19 Oct., Hatfield was affailed.
The Narraganfetts fheltered the women
of the warrior Indians, and guns were
found among them which had been
taken from Beers's men; fo that they
were judged to be in complicity with
Philip. [Hubbard's *Narrative*, 32–42,
48; Holmes's *Annals*, i: 372–375; Hoyt's
Indian Wars, 99–112.]

[121] The Commiffioners of the United
Colonies wrote from Bofton, 12 Nov.,
1675, to Rhode-Ifland, on this fubject, as
follows: "Findeing that yᵉ Narrigan-
fets under pretence of freindfhip haue
bine and are very fals and perfideoufe,
holdeing as is reported to us great Cor-
rifpondency with the Enemy that are
in more open hoftillity receiveing,
releeving, and Contrary to their Covenant detayneing many of the Enemy
men, women, and children to their
great advantage and our prejudife, and

Governour *Winflow*[122] to command the Army.   He undertaking the Expedition invited Mr. *Church* to command a Company in the Expedition; which he declin'd, craving excufe from taking Commiffion, he promifed to wait upon him as a *Reformado*[123] thro' the Expedition.   Having rid with the General to *Bofton*,[124] and from thence to *Reho both*.   Upon the Generals requeft he went thence the neareft way over the Ferries, with Major *Smith*[125] to his

by many other infolenceys declaering their Enmity, and that indeed they are and are like to bee the very randivoufe, and feat of the warr, it hath drawne us to refolue to rayfe 1000 men in the Confœderate Coloneys befides them alredy in paye, to bee improved there or as the providence of God may direct to reduce them to reafon; And therefore judge it neceffary to advife you of our intents in that refpect, to intent that you may not only take cair of your fronteer places, but afforde fo[me] addition to our numbers, and giue us fuch afiftance by your floopes and veffells as wee may ftand in need of, &c." The new levy was proportioned thus: Mafs. 527, Plym. 158, Conn. 315 = 1000. The actual attendance of troops feems to have been, as follows: from Mafs. 465 foot (in fix companies) and 75 horfe = 540 men; from Plymouth 158 men (in two companies); from Conn. 450 men (in five companies); making a total of 1148 men from the Confederate Colonies. Befides thefe, a "confidcrable number" of recruits joined the expedition from the Rhode-Ifland Colony.   The Army was under command of Gen. Jofias Winflow.   The Mafs.

troops were officered by Maj. Appleton and Capts. Mofely, Davenport, Gardner, Oliver, Johnfon, and Prentice; the Plymouth, by Maj. Bradford and Capt. Gorham; and the Conn. by Maj. Treat and Capts. Seely, Gallup, Mafon, Watts, and Marfhall. A partial lift of the names of the Mafs. men has been publifhed. [*Plym. Col. Rec.* x: 365, 458; Barry's *Hift. Mafs.* i: 426; Trumbull's *Hift. Conn.* i: 337; Arnold's *Hift. R.-I.* i: 403; *N. E. Gen. Reg.* viii: 241.]

[122] See note 20, *ante*.

[123] "*Reformado*, a reformed Officer, or one whofe Company, or Troop, is fuppreffed in a Reform, and he continued either in whole, or half Pay, he doing Duty in the Regiment. In a fhip of war, a Gentleman who ferves as a Voluntier, in order to gain Experience, and fucceed the principal Officers." [Bailey.]

[124] As Church's home at Saconet was temporarily broken up, he would feem to have been, in this interval, with his friends at Plymouth, or Duxbury.

[125] *Richard Smith, jr.*, was the fon of Richard, "who left faire Poffeffions in Glofter Shire" Eng., and was one

Garriſon in the *Narraganſet Country*,[126] to prepare and provide for the coming of General *Winſlow*; who March'd round thro' the Country with his Army, propoſing by Night to ſurprize *Pumham* (a certain *Narraganſet* Sachem) and his Town;[127] but being aware of the approach of [14] our

of the firſt ſettlers of Taunton, and went to Wickford, R.-I., about 1641, "for his conſcience ſake (many differences ariſing)"; where he built a block-houſe on the great Pequot road, on the ſite where the Updike houſe ſtands, or lately ſtood, a little to the north of Wickford Hill, in No. Kingſtown, R.-I. He was mixed up in the conflict of juriſdiction between Rhode-Iſland and Connecticut, and was appointed Conſtable of Wickford by Conn. in 1663; was put under bonds in £400 to anſwer to R.-I. in 1664; 28 Dec., 1665 appears as witneſs in the Warwick "acquittance"; is ſaid to have been one of Andros's Council in 1686; was appointed by Andros in that year Juſtice of the Peace and "Sergeant-major and chief Commander of his Majeſty's militia both of horſe and foot within the Narraganſett Country, or Province, and all the Iſlands"; died before 1692, when his will was proved, mentioning no wife nor children. Church calls him "Major" now, although he does not appear to have been ſo until ſome years after this date. [*R.-I. Hiſt. Coll.* iii: 32, 166, 271; *R.-I. Col. Rec.* iii: 198; Arnold's *Hiſt. R.-I.* i: 283, 305, 307, 484.]

[126] Aſſuming that by "Rehoboth" here is meant Myles's Garriſon (ſee note 44, *ante*), the "neareſt way over the Ferries" thence to Smith's block-

houſe, would ſeem to have been through Mount-hope neck to Briſtol ferry, thence down Rhode-Iſland to Newport, thence over by ferry to Conanicut, and thence by ſtill another ferry to Wickford;—a diſtance which I eſtimate as a little over 30 miles. The ferries from Newport to Jameſtown and from Jameſtown to Narraganſett were not indeed formally eſtabliſhed by the Aſſembly until 1700, but they had doubtleſs been running for many years as an irreſponſible individual enterpriſe. It is poſſible that this diſtance might, at the date to which the text refers, have been materially ſhortened by a route from Briſtol Ferry to Prudence, and from thence to Wickford; the latter a diſtance of 5 or 6 miles by water. The remark about "fair winds" which follows, perhaps favors this latter ſuppoſition; and, at any rate, ſeems to ſettle it that Church did not go round by Seekonk, Providence, Pawtuxet and Apponaug Ferries,—neither of which was wide enough to make a fair wind of much conſequence in croſſing. This latter was clearly however the route of the army, who made a detour from it in the vain hope of catching Pumham at his village in Warwick. [*R.-I. Col. Rec.* iii: 406, 415.]

[127] *Pumham* (*Pomham*) was Sachem of *Shawomet* (*Shaomet*), the neck that

Army made their efcape into the defarts. But Mr. *Church* meeting with fair Winds arriv'd fafe at the Major's Garrifon in the evening.[128] And foon began to inquire after the Enemies Reforts, Wigwams or Sleeping Places; and having gain'd fome intelligence, he propofed to the *Eldriges*,[129] and fome other brisk hands, that he met with, to attempt the Surprizing of fome of the Enemy to make a Prefent of to the General, when he fhould arrive: which might advantage his defign; being brisk blades, they readily comply'd with the motion, and were foon upon their March. The Night was very cold, but blefs'd with the *Moon*; before the day broke they effected their exploit, and by the rifing of the Sun arrived at the Major's Garrifon, where they met the General and prefented him with Eighteen of the Enemy, they had Captiv'd. The General

projects into Narraganfett Bay, having Providence River on the eaft, and Cowcfet Bay on the fouth and weft, it being the eaftern portion of the town of Warwick, R.-I. The name is perhaps from *pummu*, "he fhoots"; *pumwaen, pummuaen*, "one who fhoots." With reduplicative — *pé-pumwaen*, "an archer" (Eliot). Or perhaps, from *pummŏhham*, "he goes by water" (goes in boats). Eliot ufes the derivative, *pummohhamwaenuog* (pl.) for "mariners" (Jonah, i: 5.). The pofition of the Shaomet or Warwick Indians favors this etymology.

[128] The evening of Saturday, 11 Dec., 1675. [*R.-I. Hift. Coll.* iii: 83.]

[129] There were three *Eldridges* (or *Eldreds*), Samuel, James, and Thomas, in Wickford, R.-I., in 1670; as is proven by their names attached to a coroner's jury verdict, dated July 14, of that year. In 1679, the names of John and Samuel are attached to a petition to the king. In 1692, Thomas was *Lieut.*, and John, *Enfign;* and in 1702, Daniel was *Captain.* Samuel was Conftable under appointment of Conn. in the boundary troubles of 1670, and thereabouts, and was committed to jail by the R.-I. authorities for attempting to act for Conn. in an arreft for murder. Savage fuggefts that Samuel (of Cambridge in 1646) was the father of at leaft fome of them, adding that Samuel (the fon) was at Rochefter in 1688. [*R.-I. Col. Rec.* ii: 344; iii: 60, 287, 461; *R.-I. Hift. Coll.* iii: 73. *Gen. Dict.* ii: 107.]

pleas'd with the exploit, gave them thanks, particularly to Mr. *Church*, the mover and chief actor of the bufinefs; and fending two of them (likely Boys) a prefent to *Bofton*; fmiling on Mr. *Church*, told him, *That he made no doubt but his Faculty would fupply them with* Indian Boys *enough before the War was ended.*

Their next move[130] was to a Swamp which the *Indians* had Fortifyed with a Fort.[131] Mr. *Church* rid in the Gen-

[130] Other authorities fhow that a week elapfed between the evening of the exploit above related and the fwamp fight to which Church now refers. The Mafs. and Plym. troops arrived on the evening of the 12th. On the 14th, two forays were made upon the enemy, and nine Indians were killed, twelve captured, and 150 wigwams burned. On the 15th, feveral ftragglers from the main body of the Englifh were cut off. On the 16th, Capt. Prentice with his troop of horfe went to Bull's Garrifon at *Pettaquamfcut* (on Tower Hill, in So. Kingftown, R.-I.), and returned with the news that the Indians had burned it, and killed 10 men and 5 women and children. On the 17th, the Connecticut troops arrived at Bull's. On the 18th, the Mafs. and Plym. forces joined them at *Pettaquamfcut* at 5 P.M. They all then marched forward in the fnow, and camped out that night; ftarting again at break of day on Sunday the 19th, and about 1 P.M. reached the edge of the fwamp in which was the Indian fort. [Hubbard's *Narrative*, 50; *R.-I. Hift. Coll.* iii : 83.]

[131] This fwamp is fituated in the north-weft portion of the t⸱ ⸱f South Kingf-

town, R.-I., very near the line of Richmond, — lefs than a mile north-weft from the track of the Providence and Stonington R.R., — on the farm of J. G. Clarke, Efq., and not far from the houfe of Judge W. Marchant. Dr. Stiles ftates that it "is about feven miles nearly due weft from Narraganfet South Ferry." On this, Judge Davis comments : " It is apprehended there is an error in the ftatement of the diftance of the fort from the South Ferry. *Seventeen* miles, inftead of *feven*, would be more confiftent with the accounts given of the marches of the army, by cotemporary hiftorians." But the identification of the locality is complete, and by the road it is nearly *ten* miles from the Ferry. The explanation of the diftance named by cotemporaries is partly that the return route lay not to the Ferry, but to Smith's garrifon in Wickford, the fite of which is diftant (by way of Bull's on Tower Hill,) fcarcely lefs than feventeen miles, by the prefent roads, from the fwamp; and more, that the journey followed the winding Indian paths, and was accomplifhed through deep fnow and in a night of intenfe cold. The fort was a ftockade enclofing

erals guard when the bloudy ingagement began; but being impatient of being out of the heat of the action, importunately beg'd leave of the General that he might run down to the affiftance of his friends, the General yielded to his requeft, provided he could rally fome hands to go with him. Thirty Men immediately drew out and followed him: They entred the Swamp and paffed over the Log, that was the paffage into the Fort, where they faw many Men and feveral Valiant Captains lye flain:[132] Mr. *Church* fpying Capt. *Gardner*[133] of *Salem* amidft the Wigwams in

five or fix acres of upland in the middle of the fwamp by a palifade, which was defended by a hedge "of almoft a rod thicknefs through which there was no paffing, unlefs they could have fired a way through, which then they had no time to doe." The only regular entrances were along a log which bridged a fpace of water, and over another log which was defended by a block-house. [Hubbard's *Narrative*, 52; *R.-I. Hift. Coll.* iii : 85; Stiles's ed. *Church*, 29; Davis's *Morton's Memorial*, 433.]

[132] The accounts vary very much as to the number of killed and wounded. A letter — fuppofed by Hutchinfon to be by Maj. Bradford, but fhown by Mr. Drake [*Book of the Indians*, 219] to be by Capt. James Oliver — written a fhort time after, from the field, and which the writer fays he has verified by reading to the officers in his tent, would feem to have the beft elements of reliablenefs. It fays 8 were left dead in the fort, 12 were carried away dead, and many died by the way, or as foon as brought in; fo that they buried the next

day (20 Dec.) 34, the next day 4, and the next day 2. Eight died on Rhode-Ifland (whither moft of the wounded were carried, for care), 1 at *Pettaquamf-cut*, and 2 were loft in the woods. He makes the total "about 68" who died, and 150 wounded who recovered. Capts. Johnfon, Davenport, Gardner, Seely, Gallup, Marfhall, and Mafon were killed, or died of their wounds. [Hutchinfon's *Hift. Mafs.*, (ed. 1795), i : 272.] See Drake's *Hift. Bofton* [i : 414] for a lift of the killed and wounded of the Mafs. quota.

[133] *Capt. Jofeph Gardner* was fon of the firft Thomas, of Salem; married Ann, dau. of Emanuel Downing, in 1656; was freeman in 1672; captain of one Salem company in 1674. He owned the fine old houfe in Salem — ftanding until 1750 (of which Felt gives an engraving) — known afterward as the "Bradftreet Manfion"; his widow marrying Simon (afterwards Gov.) Bradftreet. [Savage's *Gen. Dict.* ii : 228; Felt's *Annals of Salem*, i : 412; ii : 497.]

the Eaſt end of the Fort, made towards him, but on a ſudden, while they were looking each other in the Face, Capt. *Gardner* ſettled down, Mr. *Church* ſtep'd to him and ſeeing the blood run down his cheek, lifted up his Cap, and calling him by his Name; he look'd up in his Face, but ſpoke not a Word, being Mortally Shot thro' the head; and obſerving his Wound, Mr. *Church* found the ball entred his head on the ſide that was next the Up-land, where the *Engliſh* entred the Swamp. Upon which, having ordered ſome care to be taken of the Captain, he diſpatch'd information to the General that the beſt and for-wardeſt of his Army that hazarded their lives to enter the Fort, upon the muzzle of the Enemies Guns, were Shot in their backs, and kill'd by them that lay behind. Mr. *Church* with his ſmall Company haſten'd out of the Fort (that the *Engliſh* were now poſſeſſed of) to get a Shot at the *Indians* that were in the Swamp, & kept firing upon them. He ſoon met with a broad bloody track, where the Enemy had fled with their Wounded men; following hard in the traɑ, he ſoon ſpy'd one of the Enemy, who clap'd his Gun a-croſs his breaſt, made towards Mr. *Church*, and beckned to him with his hand; Mr. *Church* immediately commanded [15] no Man to hurt him, hoping by him to have gain'd ſome intelligence of the Enemy, that might be of advantage; but it unhappily fell out that a Fellow that had lag'd behind coming up, ſhot down the *Indian*, to Mr. *Church*'s great grief and diſappointment. But immedi-ately they heard a great ſhout of the Enemy, which ſeem'd to be behind them, or between them and the Fort; and diſcover'd them running from tree to tree to gain advantages of firing upon the *Engliſh* that were in the Fort. Mr. *Churches* great difficulty now was how to diſcover himſelf to his Friends in the Fort, uſing ſeveral inventions, till at length gain'd an opportunity to call to, and inform a Serjeant in the Fort, that he was there, and might be expoſed to their Shots, unleſs they obſerv'd it. By this time he diſcovered a number of the Enemy almoſt within Shot of him, making towards the Fort; Mr. *Church* and his Company were favoured by a heap of bruſh that was between them and the Enemy, and prevented their being diſcover'd to them. Mr. *Church* had given his Men their particular orders for firing upon the Enemy; and as they were riſing up to make their Shot, the afore-mentioned Serjeant in the Fort called out to them, *for God's ſake not to fire, for he believed they were ſome of their* Friend Indians;[134] They clap'd down again, but were ſoon ſenſible of the Serjeants miſtake. The Enemy got to the top of the Tree, the body

---

[134] One hundred and fifty Mohegans and Pequots formed a part of the Conn. forces. Capt. Oliver (note 132, *ante*) does not ſpeak well of them. He ſays: "Monhegins and Pequods proved very falſe, fired into the air, and ſent word before they came they would do ſo, but got much plunder, guns and kettles." So Joſhua Tiſt, a renegade Engliſhman, who had married an Indian wife, and was active in this fight, but was afterwards taken, examined, condemned, and executed; teſtified, according to Roger Williams's record, " if the Monhiggins & Pequts had bene true, they might haue deſtroyed moſt of the Nahiggonſiks; but the Nahigonſiks parlied with them in the beginning of the fight, ſo that they promiſed to ſhoote high, which they did, & kild not one Nahigonſik man, except againſt thejr wills." [Trumbull's *Hiſt. Conn.* i: 337; Hutchinſon's *Hiſt. Maſs.* (ed. 1795,) i: 273; 4 *Maſs. Hiſt. Coll.* vi: 308.]

whereof the Serjeant ftood upon, and there clap'd down out of fight of the Fort, but all this while never difcovered Mr. *Church*, who obferved them to keep gathering unto that Place, until there feem'd to be a formidable black heap of them. *Now brave boys* (faid Mr. *Church* to his Men) *if we mind our hits, we may have a brave Shot, and let our fign for firing on them, be their rifing up to fire into the Fort.* It was not long before the *Indians* rifing up as one body, defigning to pour a Volley into the Fort. When our *Church* nimbly ftarted up and gave them fuch a round Volley, and unexpected clap on their backs, that they who efcaped with their Lives, were fo- furprized, that they fcampered, they knew not whether themfelves; about a dozen of them ran right over the Log into the Fort, and took into a fort of a Hovel that was build with Poles, after the manner of a corn crib. Mr. *Church*'s Men having their Catteridges fix'd, were foon ready to obey his order, which was immediately to charge and run on upon the Hovel, and over-fet it, calling as he run on to fome that were in the Fort to affift him in over-fetting of it; they no fooner came to Face the Enemies fhelter, but Mr. *Church* difcover'd that one of them had found a hole to point his Gun through, right at him; but however incouraged his Company, and ran right on, till he was ftruck with Three Bullets, one in his Thigh, which was near half of it cut off as it glanced on the joynt of the Hip-bone; another thro' the gatherings of his Breeches and Draws, with a fmall flefh Wound; a third peirced his Pocket, and

56

wounded a pair of Mittins, that he had borrowed of Capt. *Prentice*; being wrap'd up together had the mif- [16] fortune of having many holes cut thro' them with one Bullet: But however he made fhift to keep on his Legs, and nimbly difcharged his Gun at them that wounded him: being difinabled now to go a ftep, his Men would have carried him off, but he forbid their touching of him, until they had perfeated their projeat of over-fetting the Enemies fhelter; bid them run, *for now the Indians had no Guns charged.* While he was urging them to run on, the *Indians* began to fhoot Arrows, and with one peirc'd thro' the Arm of an *Englifh* Man that had hold of Mr. *Churches* Arm to fupport him. The *Englifh*, in fhort, were difcourag'd, and drew back. And by this time the *Englifh People* in the Fort had began to fet fire to the *Wigwams & Houfes* in the Fort, which Mr. *Church* laboured hard to prevent; they told him, *They had orders? from the General to burn them*; he beg'd them to forbear until he had difcours'd the General; and haftning to him, *he beg'd to fpare the Wigwams, &c. in the Fort? from fire,* told him, *The Wigwams were Mufket=proof being all lin'd with Bafkets and Tubbs of Grain, and other Provifions, fuf-ficient to fupply the whole Army, until the Spring of the Year;*[135] *and every wounded Man might have a good warm Houfe to lodge in, which other-ways would neceffarily perifh with the Storms and Cold. And more-over, that the Army*

---

[135] Church's paft experience in the commiffary department had been of a nature to urge this confideration upon his mind with great force.

*had no other Provifion to truft unto or depend upon; that he
knew that* Plymouth *Forces had not fo much as one Bifcake
left, for he had feen their laft dealt out,* &c. The General
advifing a few Words with the Gentlemen that were about
him, Mov'd towards the Fort, defigning to ride in himfelf,
and bring in the whole Army. But juft as he was entring
the Swamp, one of his Captains[136] meet him, and asked
him, *Whither he was going?* He told him into the Fort;
the Captain laid hold of his Horfe, and told him, *His Life
was worth an hundred of theirs, and he fhould not expofe
himfelf.* The General told him, *That he fuppofed the
brunt was over, and that Mr.* Church *had inform'd him
that the Fort was taken,* &c. *And as the cafe was circum-
ftanced he was of the Mind, that it was moft practicable for
him, and his Army to fhelter themfelves in the Fort.* The
Captain in a great heat, reply'd, *That Church ly'd*; and
told the General, *That if he mov'd another ftep towards the
Fort he would fhoot his Horfe under him.* Then brufled
up another Gentleman, a certain Doctor,[137] and oppofs'd
Mr. *Church's* advice, and faid, *If it were comply'd with, it*

---

[136] Likely to be Captain Mofely, who
was a " rough and fanguinary foldier,"
and whom Hubbard names as very
active and ferviceable in the fight.
[*Narrative*, 54.]

[137] Church's reticence in regard to
names, where cenfure is implied, is no-
ticeable. No record of the furgeons
accompanying this expedition has met
my eye. Trumbull fays, " the beft furgeons which the country could furnifh,

were provided." Dr. John Clark, apparently fon of Dr. John, who came to
Bofton from Newbury, and whofe pic-
ture hangs in the rooms of the Mafs.
Hift. Soc., was appointed by the Mafs.
Court, on the 25th Feb. following,
" chirurgion for yᵉ fervice." Dr.
Matthew Fuller (fee note 69, *ante*) was,
no doubt, ftill furgeon-general of the
Plymouth troops. [*Hift. Conn.* i: 340,
note; Mafs. Col. Rec. v: 75.]

would kill more Men than the Enemy had killed; for (ſaid he) *by to Morrow the wounded Men will be ſo ſtiff that there will be no moving of them*: And looking upon Mr. *Church*, and ſeeing the blood flowing a pace from his Wounds, told him, *That if he gave?ſuch advice as that was, he ſhould bleed to Death like a Dog, before they would endeavour to ſtench his blood.* Though after they had prevailed againſt his advice, they were ſufficiently kind to him. And burning up all the Houſes and Proviſions in the Fort; the Army return'd the ſame Night in the Storm and Cold: And I Suppoſe every one that is acquainted with the circumſtances of that Nights March, deeply laments the miſeries that attended them, eſpecially the [17] wounded & dying Men. But it mercifully came to paſs that Capt. *Andrew Belcher*[138] arrived at Mr. *Smiths* that very Night from *Boſton*, with a Veſſel loaden with Proviſions for the Army, who muſt otherwiſe have periſh'd for want. Some of the Enemy that were then in the Fort have ſince inform'd us, that near a third of the *Indians* belonging to all that *Narraganſet Country* were killed by the *Engliſh*, and by the Cold that Night,[139] that they fled

[138] See note 52, *ante.* Smith's blockhouſe ſtood on the cove making up north-weſterly from the entrance of what is now called Wickford harbor.

[139] Hubbard ſays, on the ſtory of one *Potock*, afterwards taken, that the Indians loſt 700 warriors killed, beſides 300, moſt of whom died of their wounds and of expoſure, with a number of old men, women, and children, which they could not eſtimate. Capt. Oliver ſays, 300 warriors were ſlain, and about 350 were taken, with above 300 women and children. The *Conn.* Council wrote to Andros (13 Jan., 1675-6), "about 600 of the Indians, men, women, & children, as is ſaid, are ſlaine." Roger Williams, in his account of the examination of Joſhua Tift, ſays, he ſaid that the Indians "found 97 ſlaine & 48 wounded, beſide

out of their Fort fo haftily that they carried nothing with them: that if the *Englifh* had kept in the Fort, the *Indians* had certainly been neceffitated, either to furrender themfelves to them, or to have perifhed by Hunger, and the feverity of the Seafon. Some time after this Fort-fight a certain *Sogkonate Indian* hearing Mr. *Church* relate the manner of his being wounded, told him, *That he did not know but he himfelf was the* Indian *that wounded him, for that he was one of that company of* Indians *that Mr.* Church *made a Shot upon when they were rifing up to make a Shot into the Fort; they were in number about* 60 *or* 70, *that juft then came down ?from* Pumhams *Town, and never before then fired a Gun againft the* Englifh; *that when Mr.* Church *fired upon them he killed* 14 *dead in the Spot, and wounded a greater number than he killed, many of which dyed afterwards with their wounds, in the Cold and Storm the following Night.*

Mr. *Church* was mov'd with other wounded men over to *Rhode-Ifland*, where in about a Months time[140] he was in fome good meafure recovered of his Wounds, and the Fever that attended them. And then went over to the General to take his leave of him, with a defign to return home.

what flaughter was made in the howfes & by the burning of the howfes, all of which he fajth were burnt except 5 or 6 thereabouts." [*Narrative*, 54; Hutchinfon's *Hift. Mafs.* (ed. 1795), i: 273, *note; Col. Rec. of Conn.* ii: 398; 4 *Mafs. Hift. Coll.* vi: 309.]

[140] Southwick's compofitors, in copy-ing the firft edition, made here the curious blunder of fubftituting "three months time" for "*a* months time," as originally fet down; and Dr. Stiles did not correct their error, which has been perpetuated in all the editions fince, and which led Mr. Drake, in his fecond edition, quite naturally to fup

But the Generals great importunity again perfwaded him, to accompany him in a long March, into the *Nipmuck* Country,[141] tho' he had then Tents in his Wounds, and fo Lame as not able to Mount his Horfe without two Mens affiftance.

In this March the firft thing remarkable was, they came to an *Indian* Town,[142] where there were many *Wigwams*

pofe that Church here refers to an expedition into the Nipmuck country in *March*, 1676, which no other chronicler had noticed. As Church dictated his narrative, the chronology was correct. The fight was on the 19th of December. It was probably feveral days after that date before Church, with the wounded, was got over to Rhode-Ifland. The Conn. forces foon went home to recruit, but the Maff. and Plym. troops remained in garrifon at Wickford, and were re-enforced from Bofton, Jan. 10. The Conn. forces (fee Maj. Palmes's letter, *Conn. Col. Rec.* ii: 402) appear to have reached Wickford again, 27 Jan., when the whole army feems to have ftarted for the Nipmuck country (whither the enemy were underftood to have fled), 1600 ftrong. This correfponds, very accurately, with the month's interval of which Church fpeaks, if he accompanied Gov. Winflow on this firft march, in force, from Wickford. Hubbard's account implies that our men ftarted from Wickford, 27 Jan. [Hubbard's *Narrative*, 58, 60; Arnold's *Hift. R.-I.* i: 406; Drake's *Church*, 65.]

[141] *Nipmuck* [*Nipnet*] was a name given to the petty tribes, or clans, of inland Indians fcattered over a large extent of country, in Windham and Tolland Counties in Connecticut, Worcefter and Hampden Counties in Maffachufetts, and the northern part of Rhode-Ifland; but their principal feat was at, or near, the great ponds in Oxford (Webfter), Maff. From thefe ponds they probably derived their name of "Pond" or "Frefh-water" (*nippe*, *nip*) Indians. If the two names, or forms of the name, are not identical in origin, *Nipnet* belongs to the territory, i.e. "at the frefh-water pond"; *Nipmuck*, to the tribe, (*nip-amaug*) "they fifh in frefh water"; but poffibly "a frefh water fifhing-place." This diftinguifhed them from the *Shore* Indians, and the *River* Indians of the Connecticut Valley; their neighbors on the weft. *Snipfic* (corrupted from *Mifhenipf-et*) Pond, in Ellington, Conn., was the bound where the country of the Nipmucks joined that of the *River Indians* on the weft, and the *Mohegan* north-weft angle.

[142] Suppofed to be Pumham's town (fee note 127, *ante*) in a rocky fwamp in Warwick, R.-I., — Warwick then embracing moft of what is now Warwick and Coventry. The diftance is ftated as 20 miles from Smith's. [Baylies' *Mem. Plym. Col.* iii: 104.]

in fight, but an Icy Swamp lying between them and the *Wigwams*, prevented their running at once upon it as they intended: there was much firing upon each fide before they pafs'd the Swamp. But at length the Enemy all fled, and a certain *Moohegan* that was a friend *Indian*, purfued and feiz'd one of the Enemy that had a fmall wound in his Leg, and brought him before the General, where he was examined. Some were for torturing of him to bring him to a more ample confeffion, of what he knew concerning his Country-men. Mr. *Church* verily believing he had been ingenious in his confeffion, interceeded and prevailed for his efcaping torture. But the Army being bound forward in their March, and the *Indians* wound fomewhat difinabling him for Travelling, 'twas concluded he fhould be knock'd on the Head: Accordingly he was brought before a great fire, and the *Moohegan* that took him was allowed, as he defired, to be the Executiner. Mr. *Church* taking no delight [18] in the Sport, fram'd an arrant at fome diftance among the baggage Horfes, and when he had got fome Ten Rods, or thereabouts from the fire, the Executioner fetching a blow with his Hatchet at the head of the Prifoner, he being aware of the blow, dodged his afide, and the Executioner miffing his ftroke the Hatchet flew out of his hand, and had like to have done execution where 'twas not defign'd. The Prifoner upon his narrow efcape broke from them that held him, and notwithftanding his Wound made ufe of his Legs, and hap'd to run right upon Mr. *Church*, who laid hold on him, and a clofe skuffle they had, but the *Indian* having no Clothes on flip'd from him, and ran again, and Mr. *Church* purfued the *Indian*, altho' being Lame, there was no great odds in the Race, until the *Indian* ftumbled and fell, and they clofed again, skuffled and fought pretty fmartly, until the *Indian* by the advantage of his nakednefs flip'd from his hold again, and fet out on his third Race, with Mr. *Church* clofe at his heels, endeavouring to lay hold on the hair of his Head, which was all the hold could be taken of him; and running thro' a Swamp that was covered with hollow Ice, it made fo loud a noife that Mr. *Church* expected (but in vain) that fome of his *Englifh* friends would follow the noife, and come to his affiftance. But the *Indian* hap'd to run a-thwart a mighty Tree that lay fallen near breaft-high, where he ftop'd and cry'd out a loud for help; but Mr. *Church* being foon upon him again, the *Indian* feized him faft by the hair of his Head, and endeavouring by twifting to break his Neck; but tho' Mr. *Churches* wounds had fome-what weakned him, and the *Indian* a ftout fel low, yet he held him well in play, and twifted the *Indians* Neck as well, and took the advantage of many opportu nities, while they hung by each others hair gave him notorious bunts in the face with his head. But in the heat of this skuffle they heard the Ice break with fome bodies coming a-pace to them, which when they heard, *Church* concluded there was help for one or other of them, but was doubtful which of them muft now receive the fatal ftroke; anon fome body comes up to them, who prov'd to be the Indian that had firſt taken the Priſoner. Without ſpeaking a word, he felt them out (for 'twas ſo dark he could not diſtinguiſh them by fight) the one being clothed, and the other naked, he felt where Mr. *Churches* hands were faſtned in the Netops[143] hair, and with one blow fettled his Hatchet in between them, and ended the ſtrife. He then ſpoke to Mr. *Church* and hugg'd him in his Arms, and thank'd him abundantly for catching his Priſoner; and cut off the head of his Victim, and carried it to the Camp, and giving an account to the reſt of the friend Indians in the Camp, how Mr. *Church* had ſeized his Priſoner, &c. they all joyn'd a mighty ſhout.

Proceeding in this March, they had the ſucceſs of killing many of the Enemy: until at length their Proviſion failing, they return'd home.[144]

King *Philip* (as was before hinted) was fled to a Place called *Scattacook*, [19] between *York* and *Albany*,[145] where

---

[143] *Netop* means "friend"; (plu.) *Netompaûog*, "friends." The *n'* is the pronoun of the firſt perſon; the *o* is naſal. Eliot writes *netomp*, as (Matt. xxvi: 50) *netomp, tohwuchpeyauan?* "Friend, why art thou come hither?" The general uſe of the word by the Engliſh was to deſignate a friendly Indian, an ally. From its couſtant employment (Roger Williams, [*Key, chap*. 1, *R.-I. Hiſt. Coll.* i: 27] ſays "What cheere, *Netop?*" is the general ſalutation of all Engliſh to the Indians) in addreſs, *Netop* came to be uſed as an appellative for any Indian man, juſt as *Monſieur* for a Frenchman, or *Hans* or *Mynheer*

for a Dutchman. In this looſer ſenſe it is uſed here.

[144] Hubbard ſays, "our Forces, having purſued them into the woods between *Marlberough* and *Brookfield* in the Road toward *Conneꝗicut*, were conſtrained to turn down to *Boſton*, in the beginning of *February*, for want of proviſion, both for themſelves and their horſes." Mather ſays, "So then, February 5' the Army returned to *Boſton*, not having obtained the end of their going forth." [*Narrative*, 60; *Brief Hiſt.* 22.]

[145] *Schaghticoke* is on the Hoofic and Hudſon Rivers, 12 miles from Troy.

the *Moohags*[146] made a defcent upon him and killed many of his Men, which moved him from thence.

His next kennelling Place was at the falls of Connecti-cut River,[147] where fometime after Capt. *Turner*[148] found him, came upon him by Night, kill'd him a great many

The Pincheon papers fay "the Scata-kook or River Indians, moft of them, were fugitives from New England in the time of Philip's war." [2 *Mafs. Hift. Coll.* viii : 244.]

[146] Increafe Mather fays, "We hear that *Philip* being this winter enter-tained in the *Mohawks* Country, Made it his defign to breed a quarrel between the *Englifh* and them; to effect which, divers of our returned Captives do re-port that he refolved to kill fome fcat-tering *Mohawks*, & then to fay that the *Englifh* had done it; but one of thofe whom he thought to have killed was only wounded, and got away to his Country men, giving them to under-ftand that not the *Englifh* but *Philip* had killed the Men that were Murdered, fo that inftead of bringing the *Mohawks* upon the *Englifh*, he brought them upon himfelf." Judd fays this "does not deferve the leaft credit." [*Brief Hif-tory*, 38; *Hift. Hadley*, 182.]

[147] The great falls in the Connecticut River, near where the towns of Mon-tague, Gill, and Greenfield meet, which Dr. Hitchcock thought the fineft in New England. Unable to plant as ufual, the Indians were driven to avail themfelves more of fifh; and no fpot in the country offered fuch fhad-fifhing as this. [*Geology of Mafs.* 275; Hoyt's *Antiq. Refearches*, 127.]

[148] *William Turner*, of Dartmouth, Eng., then of Dorchefter, 1642, free-man, 10 May, 1643, removed to Bof-ton, was "by trade a tailor," and was one of the founders of the firft Bap-tift Church in 1665. Early in Phil-ip's war, "he gathered a company of volunteers, but was denied a commif-fion, and difcouraged becaufe the chief of the company were Anabaptifts. After-wards, when the war grew more general and diftructive, and the country in very great diftrefs, having divers towns burnt, and many men flain, then he was defired to accept a commiffion. He complained it was too late, his men on whom he could confide being fcat-tered; however was moved to accept." He marched "as Captain, under Maj. Savage as chief commander," to relieve the weftern towns. 19 May, 1676, with 180 men, he furprifed the Indians at thefe falls and killed from 130 to 180, but on his return was killed, with 38 of his men. He married Mary, widow of Key Alfop; though he feems to have had another wife — perhaps named Frances. His will, dated 10 Feb., 1676, mentions children. [Savage's *Gen. Dict.* iv : 348; Backus's *Hift. New Eng.* i : 423; Hoyt's *Antiq. Refearches*, 128. Holland's *Hift. Weftern Mafs.* i : 121; Judd's *Hift. Hadley*, 163, 171; Bene-dict's *Hift. Bapt.* i : 384.]

9

Men, and frighted many more into the River, that were hurl'd down the falls and drowned.

Philip got over the River, and on the back fide of the *Wetufet-hills* [149] meets with all the Remnants of the *Narraganfet* and *Nipmuck Indians,* that were there gathered together, and became very numerous; and made their defcent on *Sudbury,* and the Adjacent Parts of the Country, where they met with and fwallowed up Valiant Capt. *Wadfworth* [150] and his Company, and many other doleful defolations, in thofe Parts [151] The News whereof coming to *Plymouth,* and they expecting probably the Enemy would foon return again into their Colony: The Council of War were called together; [152] and Mr. *Church* was fent

[149] Wachufett (*Watchofuck*) Mountain in Princeton, Mafs. The word means " [the country] about the mountain."

[150] *Samuel Wadfworth,* youngeft fon of Chriftopher, of Duxbury, was born about 1630; was freeman 1668; married Abigail, dau. of James Lindall of Marfhfield, and was father of Benjamin, Minifter of the Firft Church, Bofton, and ninth Prefident of Harvard College; he was the firft Captain of militia in Milton, was diftinguifhed in Philip's war, and was cut off, with his Lieut. and " about thirty" of his men, in this Sudbury fight. The portion of Sudbury which was attacked is now Wayland. See the *New-England Hift. and Gen. Regifter,* vii : 221, and Hudfon's *Hift. Marlborough,* 75, for a difcuffion of the true date of this ftruggle. [Savage's *Gen. Dict.* iv : 380.]

[151] Col. Church was here obvioufly confufed in his order of remembrance of events which had become diftant when he dictated this narrative. The attack on Sudbury took place, and Capt. Wadfworth and his company were " fwallowed up" on the 21ft of April, 1676, nearly a month before the Falls fight, while the Plymouth Council of War — which, by what follows, affembled before Rehoboth fell, on the 26th and 28th March, of the fame year — muft have been called together more than a month before the Sudbury maffacre. The tidings which alarmed the Colonifts and convoked the Council, muft evidently have been thofe of the furprife of Lancafter on the 10th, and of the burning of Medfield on the 21ft of February.

[152] By the records, it appears that the Plymouth Council of War met on the 29th Feb. and the 7th and 10th March.

for to them, being obferved by the whole Colony to be a Perfon extraordinarily qualify'd for and adapted to the Affairs of War. Twas propofed in Council that leaft the Enemy in their return fhould fall on *Rehoboth,* or fome other of their Out-Towns, a Company confifting of 60 or 70 Men fhould be fent in to thofe Parts; and Mr. *Church* invited to take the Command of them. He told them, *That if the Enemy returned into that Colony again, they might reafonably expect that they would come very numerous; and that if he fhould take the Command of Men, he fhould not lye in any Town or Garrifon with them, but would lye in the Woods as the Enemy did: And that to fend out fuch fmall Companies againft fuch Multitudes of the Enemy that were now Muftered together, would be but to deliver fo many Men into their hands, to be deftroyed, as the Worthy Capt.* Wadf-worth *and his Company were.* His advice upon the whole was, That if they fent out any Forces, to fend not lefs than 300 Souldiers; and that the other Colonies fhould be ask'd to fend out their *Quota's* alfo; adding, *That if they intended to make an end of the War, by fubduing the En-*

The meeting of the 29th Feb. was at Marfhfield, and would appear to be that of which Church here fpeaks. My reafon for fixing upon that of this date is, that this is the neareft date to the Medfield alarm, and that one conclu-fion at which this feffion arrived was to order "20 or 30 of the Southern In-dians" to go forth "with the other (i.e. white Colonifts) whoe are under preffe" under the command of Capt. Michael Pierce and Lieut. Samuell Ful-ler. Had it been *already* determined by the Council to fend out friend Indians, they would hardly have "thought it no wayes advifable," as Church fays they did when he talked with them. It is more likely that his arguments on this occafion led them to change their form-er policy in that refpect, and pafs this vote before they feparated. [*Prym. Col. Rec.* v: 187.]

emy, they must make a business of the War, as the Enemy did; and that for his own part, he had wholly laid aside all his own private business and concerns, ever since the War broke out. He told them, *That if they would send forth such Forces as he should direct to, he would go with them for Six weeks March, which was long enough for Men to be kept in the Woods at once; and if they might be 'sure of Liberty to return in such a space, Men would go out chearfully. And he would engage* 150 *of the best Souldiers should immediately List Voluntarily to go with him, if they would please to add* 50 *more; and* 100 *of the Friend Indians; and with such an Army he made no doubt but he might do good Service; but on other terms he did not incline to be concern'd.*

Their reply was, That they were already in debt, and so big an Army would bring such charge upon them, that they should never be able to pay.[153] And as for sending

---

[153] The Council, at its 10th March session, assigned lands at *Showamett* (Warwick, R.-I.) to the supposed value of £500, at *Assonett* neck (Freetown) to the value of £200, at *Assawampsett* (around the pond in Middleborough) to the value of £200, and about *Agawam* and *Sepecan* (in Wareham, and what is now Marion) to the value of £100, to be divided to the soldiers; "*noe way att p'sent appeering to raise moncys.*" They, at the same time, further laid a rate of £1000. upon the eleven towns of the Colony, "to be payed in clothing, provisions, or cattle, att mony prise; an indifferent good, ordinary cow being to be vallued at 45 s. and other cattle according to that proportion, for the payment of such of the souldiers whose needy condition may call for other supplyes more suitable for their families then lands," &c. The following list of the proportions of the several towns in this rate has interest as indicating their then relative size. I add their several proportions of a "presse" of 300 men, on the 29th March following.

	£	s.	d.	Men.
Plymouth .	. 99 :	03 :	06 .	30
Duxbury .	46 :	11 :	10	16
Bridgewater	46 :	11 :	10	16
Scituate .	. 165 :	09 :	00 .	50
Taunton .	. 92 :	13 :	06 .	30

out *Indians*, they thought it no wayes advifable, and in fhort, none of his advice practicable. [20]

Now Mr. *Churches* Confort, and his then only Son were till this time remaining at *Duxborough*, and his fearing their fafety there (unlefs the War were more vigoroufly ingaged in) refolved to move to *Rhode-Ifland*;[154] tho' it was much oppofed both by the Government, and by Relations. But at length, the Governour confidering that he might be no lefs Serviceable by being on that fide of the Colony, gave his permit,[155] and wifh'd he had Twenty more as good Men to fend with him.

Then preparing for his Removal, he went with his fmall Family to *Plymouth* to take leave of their Friends; where

	£	s.	d.	Men.
Sandwich	.	92 : 13 : 06		28
Yarmouth	.	74 : 15 : 06	.	26
Barnftable	.	99 : 03 : 06	. .	30
Marfhfield		75 : 08 : 00		26
Rehoboth	.	136 : 19 : 00	. .	30
Eaftham		66 : 16 : 06		18

Rehoboth was probably lightly rated in foldiers on account of the loffes which it had met with, after this affeff-ment of money and before the "preffe" for men. [*Plym. Col. Rec.* v : 191-3.]

[154] At firft glance it feems ftrange to think of removing from the very heart of the old fettlements to a poft then fur-rounded by hoftile Indians, for greater fafety. But it muft be remembered that the infular pofition of Rhode-Ifland rendered it comparatively fecure; in addition to which that Colony employed four row-boats (Arnold fays *floops*), to be conftantly on the lookout, on every fide, to prevent any invafion from the main. [*R.-I. Hift. Coll.* v : 165; *R.-I. Col. Rec.* ii : 535; Arnold's *Hift. R.-I.* i : 409.]

[155] The Plymouth Council of War, at the feffion of 29 Feb., 1675-6, paffed an order that "whereas great damage and prejudice may acrew, &c. all the inhabitants feated in this gou'ment fhall and doe abide in each towne of this col-lonie to which hee belongs, and not de-part the fame on p'ill of forfeiting the whole p'fonall eftate of each one that ·fhall foe doe to the collonies vfe, except it be by the fpeciall order or allowance of the Gou', or any two of the other maj-eftrates, &c." This was to prevent the inhabitants of the Colony from remov-ing for prefent fafety to places from which they might not afterward return; to the Colony's detriment. [*Plym. Col. Rec.* v : 185.]

they met with his Wives Parents, who much perfwaded that She might be left at Mr. *Clarks* Garrifon,[156] (which they fuppofed to be a mighty fafe Place) or at leaft that She might be there until her foon expected lying-inn was over (being near her time.) Mr. *Church* no ways inclining to venture her any longer in thofe Parts, and no arguments prevailing with him, he refolutely fet out for *Taunton*, and many of their Friends accompanyed them. There they found Capt. *Peirce*,[157] with a commanded Party, who offered Mr. *Church* to fend a Relation of his with fome others to guard him to *Rhode-Ifland*. But Mr. *Church* thank'd him for his Refpectful offer, but for fome good reafons refus'd to accept it. In fhort, they got fafe

---

[156] *Clark's Garrifon* was fituated about three miles fouth-eaft from the village of Plymouth, on the weft bank of the Eel River, almoft againft the point of junction of Plymouth Beach with the main land, and, perhaps three-quarters of a mile inland from that junction; very near to the fite of the houfe for many years occupied by the late Rev. B. Whitmore. It was deftroyed on Sunday, 12 March, 1676; "Miftris Sarah Clarke" and ten other perfons being killed. The outrage was committed by Tatofon and ten other Indians, of whom five were brought in and executed at Plymouth. [*Plym. Col. Rec.* v: 204-6.] This was the only ferious attack made on Plymouth by the natives.

[157] *Capt. Michael Pierce* was at Hingham in 1646; in 1647 purchafed lands in the Conihaffet grant (Scituate); was in the Narraganfett fight, previous to which, he made his will, beginning thus: "Being, by the appointment of God, going out to war againft the Indians, I do ordain this my laft will, &c."; was put in command, early in 1676, of 63 Englifhmen and 20 friendly Indians. They were to rendezvous at Plymouth, on Wednefday, the 8th March, and probably reached Taunton on the afternoon of the next day, March 9th, where Mr. Church now found him. On the 26th of the fame month he was killed, with 51 of his Englifh, and 11 of his Indian foldiers, at Rehoboth, by an overwhelming force of the enemy. He had had two wives, and ten children. [Deane's *Hift. Scit.* 325; *Plym. Col. Rec.* v: 187; Blifs's *Hift. Rehoboth*, 91.]

to Capt. *John Almy*'s houfe[158] upon *Rhode-Ifland*, where
they met with friends and good entertainment. But by
the way, let me not forget this remarkable Providence.
viz. That within Twenty-four hours, or there abouts,[159]
after their arrival at *Rhode-Ifland*, Mr. *Clarks* Garrifon
that Mr. *Church* was fo much importuned to leave his
Wife and Child at, was deftroyed by the Enemy.

Mr. *Church* being at prefent difinabled from any particular Service in the War, began to think of fome other
employ; but he no fooner took a tool to cut a fmall ftick,
but he cut off the top of his Fore finger, and the next to it,
half off; upon which he fmillingly faid, That he thought
he was out of his way, to leave the War; and refolved he
would to War again. Accordingly his Second Son[160]
being born on the 12th of *May* and his Wife & Son like to
do well, Mr. *Church* imbraces the opportunity of a paffage

[158] See note 4, *ante.* After confiderable refearch, I had failed to fecure
proof fixing the fpot of Capt. Almy's
refidence, but from all the probabilities
of the cafe had decided that he muft
have lived on the eaftern fhore of
Portfmouth, R.-I., fomewhere between
M'Carry's Point on the north and
Sandy Point on the fouth, oppofite
Punkatees neck. I have now, by the
kindnefs of Judge W. R. Staples, received, from Mr. Richard Sherman,
who was Town Clerk of Portfmouth for
nearly half a century, a note in which
he fays: "I have been informed by
old perfons now deceafed, that one
Capt. John Almy lived in a houfe near
what was called Fogland, or Codman's
ferry, and at that time kept a houfe of
entertainment, &c." This endorfes my
fuppofition, as Fogland ferry connects
Punkatees neck with Portfmouth, midway between the points above named.
(See notes 86 and 91, *ante.*)

[159] This fettles the date of this arrival as 11–13 March, 1676. Probably
Church left Plymouth with his family
on Wednefday or Thurfday, the 8th or
9th, and reached Almy's on Saturday,
the 11th, the day before Clark's Garrifon was burned.

[160] *Conftant*, who became a Captain
under his father in fome of his later
expeditions.

in a Sloop bound to *Barnftable*; who landed him at *Sogko neffet*,[161] from whence he rid to *Plymouth*; arrived there on the firft Tuefday in *June*:[162] The General Court then fitting,[163] welcom'd him, told him they were glad to fee him Alive. He reply'd, He was as glad to fee them Alive, for he had feen fo many fires and fmokes towards their fide of the Country fince he left them, that he could fcarce eat or fleep with any comfort, for fear they had been all deftroyed. For all Travelling was ftop'd, and no News had paffed for a long time together. He gave them account, that the *Indians* had made horrid defolations at *Providence, Warwick, Petuxit,* and all over the *Narraganfet* Country,[164] & that they prevailed daily againft the *Englifh* on that fide of the Country. Told them, he long'd to hear what Methods they defign'd in the War. [21] They told him, They were particularly glad that Providence had brought him there at that jun-cture: For they had concluded the very next day to fend out an Army of 200 Men, two third *Englifh*, and one third *Indians*, in fome meafure agreeable to his former propofal; expecting *Bofton* and *Connecticut*

---

[161] *Sogkoneffet* (*Sachonefit, Sugkones, Succonefit, Succonneffet, &c.*) was the general name applied to the townfhip of Falmouth, Mafs., in the early records. The word appears to be a diminutive from *Sogkonate*. The harbor where Church landed was what is now known as Wood's Hole in Falmouth. This would then be diftant probably 35 miles from Plymouth.

[162] 6 June, 1676.

[163] The "Court of Election" met at Plymouth, on Monday, 5 June, 1676.

[164] Warwick, R.-I., was burned 17 March (fo *Hubbard*, 66; *Mather*, 24; Palfrey's *Hift. N. E.* iii: 188; but *Arnold*, i: 408, fays March 16, quoting no authority.); Seekonk, or Pawtucket, March 28th, and Providence, March 30th. [See Davis's *Morton's Memorial*, 438; *R.-I. Hift. Coll.* v: 166.]

to joyn with their *Quota*'s.[165] In fhort, It was fo concluded.   And that Mr. *Church* fhould return to the *Ifland*,
and fee what he could Mufter there, of thofe that had
mov'd from *Swanzey, Dartmouth,* &c.[166] So returning the
fame way he came; when he came to *Sogkoneffet,* he had
a fham put upon him, about a Boat he had bought to go
home in; and was forced to hire two of the friend Indians
to paddle him in a Canoo from *Elfabeths*[167] to *Rhode-
Ifland.*

It fell out that as they were in their Voyage paffing by
Sogkonate-point,[168] fome of the Enemy were upon the

---

[165] The vote was thus: "Vpon confideration of the neffefitie of fending
forth fome forces, to be, by the healp
of God, a meanes of our fafety and
prefervation, the Court came to a conclufion and doe heerby voate, that one
hundred and fifty Englifh, and fifty Indians, be with the beft fpeed that may
be raifed and provided and fent forth
towards the frontiere p'tes of this collonie, to be vpon motion to fcout to and
frow for the fafty of the collonie; the
time appointed of fending forth is on
Weddenfday, the 21ft of this inftant
June, 1676." [*Plym. Col. Rec.* v:
197.]

[166] The General Affembly of R.-I.
voted, 13 March, 1675-6: "Wee finde
this Collony is not of ability to main-
taine fufficient garrifons for the fecurity
of our out Plantations. Therefore, we
thinke and judge it moft fafe for the
inhabitants to repaire to this Ifland,
which is the moft fecureift." Some of

thofe Plymouth Colonifts who refided
near, feem to have availed themfelves
of this fuggeftion, and taken refuge on
the Ifland. [*R.-I. Col. Rec.* ii: 533.]

[167] The Elizabeth Iflands, with very
narrow channels between them, ftretch
fouth-weft from Falmouth nearly feventeen miles; dividing Buzzard's Bay
above them from Vineyard Sound below them.   The diftance from Falmouth to Rhode-Ifland, following the
fouthern fhore of thefe iflands, then
bearing away for Saconet Point, and
round that ftraight to the neareft point
of Rhode-Ifland, is about 35 miles.

[168] *Saconet Point* is the fartheft
fouth-weftern extremity of Little Compton, R.-I.   The rocks on which thefe
Indians were fifhing were, moft likely,
thofe of the ledge known as "Onion
rock," a few feet off from the Point;
now acceffible at low water, and then,
doubtlefs, joined to the main by a fand-
hill fince worn away.   A canoe, pad-

Rocks a fiſhing; he bid the *Indians* that managed the Canoo to paddle ſo near to the Rocks as that he might call to thoſe *Indians*; told them, That he had a great mind ever ſince the War broke out to ſpeak with ſome of the *Sogkonate Indians,* and that they were their Relations, and therefore they need not fear their hurting of them. And he added, *That he had a mighty conceit that if he could gain a ʾfair Opportunity to diſcourſe them, that he could draw them off ʾfrom* Philip, *for he knew they never heartily loved him.* The Enemy hollowed and made ſigns for the Canoo to come to them: But when they approach'd them they skulked and hid in the clifts of the Rocks; then Mr. *Church* ordered the Canoo to be paddled off again, leaſt if he came too near they ſhould fire upon him. Then the *Indians* appearing again, beckn'd and call'd in the *Indian* Language, and bid them come a-ſhore, they wanted to ſpeak with them. The *Indians* in the Canoo anſwered them again; but they on the Rocks told them, That the

---

dling for Rhode-Iſland from the Vineyard Sound, in ſmooth water (and it could make the paſſage in no other), would head from the ſouth-weſtern extremity of Cuttyhunk obliquely acroſs the entrance of Buzzard's Bay, ſtraight toward Saconet Point, and in rounding that Point would go inſide of both Eaſt and Weſt iſlands into the "Eaſt Paſſage." This would bring it, inevitably, within a ſhort diſtance of the rocks here deſcribed. Many tautog are ſtill yearly caught from them.

Hubbard, through ignorance of the localities, has made ſome curious blunders in his verſion of this occurrence. He ſays: "It hapened that the ſaid Capt. *Church,* ſome time in *June* laſt, *viz.* of this preſent year, 1676, paſſing over in a Canoo from *Pocaſſet* to *Road-Iſland,* as he uſed frequently to do (having had much imployment upon the ſaid Neck of Land, ſo called) ſeveral Indians whom he had known before at *Lakenham* (a village on *Pocaſſet ſide*) beckned to him, as if they had a mind to ſpeak with him, &c. &c." [*Narrative,* 104.]

furff made fuch a noife againft the Rocks, they could not hear any thing they faid [169] Then Mr. *Church* by figns with his hands, gave to underftand, That he would have two of them go down upon the point of the beach (a place where a Man might fee who was near him [170]) accordingly two of them ran a-long the beach, and met him there; without their Arms, excepting that one of them had a Lance in his hand; they uged Mr. *Church* to come a-fhore for they had a great defire to have fome difcourfe with him; He told them, if he that had his weapon in his hand would carry it up fome diftance upon the beach and leave it, he would come a-fhore and difcourfe them: He did fo, and Mr. *Church* went a-fhore, halled up his Canoo, ordered one of his *Indians* to ftay by it, and the other to walk above on the beach, as a Sentinel to fee that the Coafts were clear. And when Mr. *Church* came up to the *Indians*, one of them happened to be honeft *George*, [171] one of the two that *Awafhonks* formerly fent to call him to her Dance, and was fo careful to guard him back to his Houfe again; the laft *Sogkonate Indian* he fpoke with before the War broke out; he fpoke *Englifh* very well.

[169] This is ftill the cafe, even in a calm day when there are no furface waves which would fwamp a canoe; as the northward ground-fwell rolls in here without obftruction from the broad Atlantic through the opening of near fifty miles, between Block Ifland and Martha's Vineyard. During and after a ftorm, the furf is fublime.

[170] Two or three " points " will read-ily occur to one familiar with this fpot as now fuitable for the ufe which Church here propofed; but the abrafion of the ftorms of almoft 200 years has, unqueftionably, fo changed all the con-figuration of the fand fpits, that none of them now remain exactly as then, though it has fcarcely modified the rocks them-felves.

[171] See note 13, *ante.*

[22] Mr. *Church* asked him where *Awashonks* was? he told him in a Swamp about three Miles off.[172] Mr. *Church* again asked him, What it was he wanted that he hollowed and called him a-shore? he answered, That he took him for *Church* as soon as he heard his Voice in the Canoo, and that he was very glad to see him alive, and he believed his Miſtriſs would be as glad to see him, and speak with him; he told him further, That he believed ſhe was not fond of maintaining a War with the *English*; and that ſhe had left *Philip*, and did not intend to return to him any more; he was mighty earneſt with Mr. *Church* to tarry there while he would run and call her: but he told him no; for he did not know but the *Indians* would come down and kill him before he could get back again; he said, if *Mount-hope* or *Pocaſſet Indians* could catch him, he believed they would knock him on the head: But all *Sogkonate Indians* knew him very well, and he believed would none of them hurt him. In ſhort, Mr. *Church* re fuſed then to tarry, but promiſed that he would come over again, and speak with *Awashonks*, and ſome other *Indians* that he had a mind to talk with.

Accordingly he appointed him to notifie *Awashonks*, her

---

[172] This was *Tompe* Swamp (ſo called in the Proprietors' Records) on an upland mound in which, the favorite headquarters of this Squaw-ſachem ſeem to have been. It is that ſwamp through which what is called the "ſwamp road" paſſes, in croſſing from the road from Saconet Point to Tiverton, to the road from the Town farm to the Commons. The houſe of Mr. Gray Wilbor is probably now the neareſt dwelling to the ſite of this lair of Awaſhonks. I am told that an old Indian burying-ground is ſtill traceable in that vicinity.

Son *Peter*, their Chief Captain, and one *Nompaſh*[173] (an *Indian* that Mr. *Church* had formerly a particular reſpect for) to meet him two dayes after, at a Rock at the lower end of Capt. *Richmonds* Farm; which was a very noted place;[174] and if that day ſhould prove Stormy, or Windy, they were to expect him the next moderate day.[175] Mr. *Church* telling *George*, that he would have him come with the Perſons mentioned, and no more. They giving each other their hand upon .it parted, and Mr. *Church* went home,[176] and the next Morning to *New-port*, and informed the Government, what had paſſed between him and the *Sogkonate Indians*. And deſired their permit for him and *Daniel Wilcock*,[177] (a Man that well underſtood the *Indian*

[173] *Nompaſh* (*Numpoſh*, *Numpus*, *Numpas*) was appointed by Plymouth Court, 1 Nov., 1676, with Petananuet (note 23, *ante*) and another Indian, to have the overſight of the ſubmitted Indians weſt of Sippican River; and ſerved as Captain of the Saconet Indians in the firſt Expedition to the Eaſtward, in 1689. [*Plym. C. R.* v : 215.]

[174] *John Richmond* was one of the original proprietors of Little Compton, and drew the land here referred to in the firſt diviſion by lot, 10 April, 1674. It is the farm now owned by William H. Chafe, and next north of that of Joſeph Brownell. The rock is ſtill in exiſtence, and well known in the neighborhood as "Treaty Rock." It is a dark fine-grained gneifs, lying, like an embedded bowlder, in a cultivated field, and evidently a good deal worn down by the attritions of huſbandry and the

viſits of the curious. It is ſaid that the Indians uſed to leave traces on it, but few if any of them are now diſtinguiſhable. The rock is not immediately on the ſhore, but well up the aſcent of a beautiful ſlope, not far from 500 paces from the water's edge, and ſome 30 paces north of the northern boundary of Mr. Brownell's land. The landing oppoſite to it is, perhaps, a half mile north of what is now known as Church's Point.

[175] Probably becauſe croſſing in a canoe — ſhould that be neceſſary — would be impoſſible in a day windy enough to raiſe even the moſt moderate ſwell.

[176] That is to Almy's houſe, near the Portſmouth landing of Fogland ferry. (See note 158, *ante*.)

[177] *Daniel Wilcocks* would ſeem to be a ſon of Daniel, who was choſen to the "grand inqueſt" at Newport by the inhabitants of Portſmouth, R.-I., March

Language) to go over to them. They told him, They thought he was mad, after such Service as he had done, and such dangers that he escaped, now to throw away his Life, for the Rogues would as certainly kill him, as ever he went over; and utterly refused to grant his permit, or to be willing that he should run the risque.

Mr. *Church* told them, *That it had ever been in his thoughts since the War broke out, that if he could discourse the* Sogkonate Indians, *he could draw them off from* Philip, *and employ them against him; but could, till now, never have an Opportunity to speak with any of them, and was very lothe to lose it,* &c. At length, they told him, If he would go, it should be only with the two *Indians* that came with him;[178] but they would give him no permit under their hands. He took his leave of them, Resolving to prosecute his design; they told him they were sorry to

---

13, 1643; in 1678 had £10 granted him on account of a lawsuit from Rhode-Island, by Plymouth Court; in 1679 became one of the purchasers of land at Pocasset; in 1686 (down as "of *Pankoteest*") was bound over in £500 to answer for purchasing land of an Indian contrary to law; and in 1690 was obscurely complained of, in the half-obliterated record, as making a "tumultuous opposition" to Thomas Hinckley's taking possession of a grant of land at Saconet. Whether he was the same Daniel Willcocks who married Elizabeth Cook, of Plymouth, 28 Nov., 1661; who was a proprietor at Saconet, 10 Apr., 1673; who complained of an outrage of the Sheriff of Bristol County, at Little Compton, in 1695; whose marriage in Rhode-Island, with Mary Wordell, was declared illegal, 23 March, 1696–7, and of whom Bellomont complained, in 1699, as having been convicted of high misdemeanor and fined, and as having made his escape, I cannot determine. Persons of the name still own land at *Puñkatees* neck in Tiverton, R.-I. [*R.-I. Col. Rec.* i: 76; ii: 307, 323, 393; *Plym. Col. Rec.* v: 261; vi: 30, 202, 245; viii; 23.]

[178] That is, who paddled him from Falmouth.

fee him fo Refolute, nor if he went did they ever expect to fee his face again.

He bought a Bottle of Rhum, and a fmall role of Tobacco, to carry with him, and returned to his Family. The next Morning, being the day ap[23]pointed for the Meeting, he prepared two light Canoo's for the defign, and his own Man, with the two *Indians* for his company. He ufed fuch arguments with his tender, and now almoft broken hearted Wife, from the experience of former prefervations, and the profpect of the great Service he might do, might it pleafe God to fucceed his defign, &c. that he obtained her confent to his attempt; and committing her, his Babes and himfelf to Heavens protection. He fet out, they had from the Shore about a League to paddle;[179] drawing near the place, they faw the *Indians* fetting on the bank, waiting for their coming. Mr. *Church* fent one of the *Indians* a-fhore in one of the Canoo's to fee whither it were the fame *Indians* whom he had appointed to meet him, and no more; and if fo to ftay a-fhore and fend *George* to fetch him. Accordingly *George* came and fetch'd Mr. *Church* a-fhore, while the other Canoo play'd off to fee the event, and to carry tydings if the *Indians* fhould prove falfe.

Mr. *Church* afk'd *George* whether *Awaſhonks* and the other *Indians* he appointed to meet him were there? He

---

[179] It is juft about that diftance from "Sandy Point," juft fouth of the probable fite of Almy's houfe (fee note 158, *ante*), to the fhore oppofite Treaty Rock; the courfe being very nearly S.E. by S.

anfwered they were. He then afk'd him, If there were no more than they whom he appointed to be there? To which he would give him no direct anfwer. However he went a-fhore, where he was no fooner landed, but *Awa-fhonks* and the reft that he had appointed to meet him there, rofe up and came down to meet him; and each of them fucceffively gave him their hands, and expreffed them-felves glad to fee him, and gave him thanks for expofing himfelf to vifit them. They walk'd together about a Gun-fhot from the water to a convenient place to fit down.[180] Where at once a-rofe up a great body of *Indians,* who had lain hid in the grafs, (that was as high as a Mans wafte) and gathered round them, till they had clos'd them in; being all arm'd with Guns, Spears, Hatchets, *&c.* with their hair trim'd and faces painted, in their Warlike ap-pearance. It was doubtlefs fome-what furprizing to our Gentleman at firft, but without any vifible difcovery of it, after a fmall filent paufe on each fide, He fpoke to *Awa-fhonks,* and told her, *That* George *had inform'd him that fhe had a defire to fee him, and difcourfe about making peace with the* Englifh. She anfwered, Yes. Then faid *Mr. Church, It is cuftomary when People meet to treat of Peace to lay afide their Arms, and not to appear in fuch Hoftile form as your People do:* defired of her that if they might talk about Peace, which he defired they might, *Her men might lay afide their Arms, and appear more treatable.*

---

[180] Doubtlefs to the rock itfelf. which, from 1200 to 1300 feet — from the as I have faid, is about 500 paces — or beach.

Upon which there began a confiderable noife and murmur among them in their own Language. Till *Awafhonks* ask'd him, What Arms they fhould lay down, and where? He (perceiving the *Indians* look'd very furly, and much difpleafed) Replied, *Only their Guns at fome fmall diftance, for 'formality fake.* Upon which with one confent they laid afide their Guns, and came and fat down.

Mr. *Church* pulled out his Callebafh[181] and asked *Awafhonks, Whether fhe had* [24] *lived fo long at* Wetu-fet,[182] *as to forget to drink* Occapechees;[183] and drinking to her, he perceived that fhe watch'd him very diligently, to fee (as he thought) whether he fwallowed any of the Rhum; he offered her the Shell, but fhe defired him to drink again firft, He then told her, *There was no poifon in it,* and pouring fome into the Palm of his hand, fup'd it up, and took the Shell and drank to her again, and drank a good Swig which indeed was no more than he needed. Then they all ftanding up, he faid to *Awafhonks, You wont drink for'f ar there fhould be poifon in it:* And then handed it to a little ill look'd fellow, who catched it readily enough, and as greedily would have fwallowed the Liquor when he had it at his mouth; But Mr. *Church* catch'd him by the throat and took it from him, asking him, *Whether he*

---

[181] A gourd veffel, or drinking cup, made of fome tough fhell; which, in thofe days, when pottery was coftlier than now, was in common ufe. They were, in the laft generation, often made of a cocoa-nut fhell.

[182] *Wachufett*, where Philip and his Indians had been gathered. (See note 149. *ante.*)

[183] *Occapeches* is a diminutive from *occapé,* or, as Eliot wrote it, *Onkuppe,* " ftrong drink." It means, therefore, " little ftrong drinks," " drams." (Ab-naki, " á'kSbi, *eau de vie*, Rafles.)

intended to fwallow Shell and all? And then handed it to *Awaſhonks*, ſhe ventured to take a good hearty dram, and paſs'd it among her Attendants.

The Shell being emptied, he pulled out his Tobacco, and having diſtributed it, they began to talk.

Awaſhonks demanded of him, the Reaſon why he had not (agreeable to his promiſe when ſhe ſaw him laſt) been down at *Sogkonate* before now; Saying that probably if he had come then according to his promiſe, they had never joyned with *Philip* againſt the *Engliſh*.

He told her he was prevented by the Wars breaking out ſo ſuddenly. And yet, he was afterwards coming down, & came as far as *Punkateeſe,* where a great many *Indians* ſet upon him, and fought him a whole afternoon, tho' he did not come prepared to fight, had but Nineteen Men with him, whoſe chief deſign was to gain an Opportunity to diſcourſe ſome *Sogkonate Indians.* Upon this there at once aroſe a mighty Murmur, confuſed noiſe, & talk among the fierce look'd Creatures, and all riſing up in an hubbub; and a great ſurly look'd fellow took up his *Tomhog,* or wooden *Cutlaſh,* to kill Mr. *Church,* but ſome others prevented him.

The Interpreter asked Mr. *Church,* if he underſtood what it was that the great fellow (they had hold of) ſaid ? He anſwered him, No. Why, ſaid the Interpreter, He ſays, you killed his Brother at *Punkateeſe,* and therefore he thirſts for your blood. Mr. *Church* bid the Interpreter tell him that his Brother began firſt : That if he had kept at

Sogkonate according to his defire and order, he fhould not have hurt him.

Then the chief Captain commanded *Silence*, and told them, That they fhould talk no more about old things, *&c.* and quell'd the tumult, fo that they fat down again, and began upon a difcourfe of making Peace with the *Englifh.* Mr. *Church* ask'd them, *What Propofals they would. make, and. on what terms they would break their League with* Philip? Defiring them to make fome Propofals that he might carry to his Mafter's, telling them that it was not in his Power to conclude a Peace with them, but that he knew that if their Propofals were reafonable, the Government would not be unreafonable, [25] and that he would ufe his Intereft in the Government for them. And to encourage them to proceed, put them in mind that the *Pequots* [184] once made War with the *Englifh,* and that

[184] The name *Pequot* was given by the neighboring tribes to what was properly an off-fhoot of the *Muhhekaneew* (*Mohican* and *Mohegan*) nation, and was poffibly affumed by themfelves, as " *the deftroyers*" of their enemies. The early Dutch voyagers called them *Pequattoos* and *Pequatoes ;* Roger Williams writes *Pequttóog,* &c.; Winthrop, *Pekoath,* elfewhere *Pequins,* &c. The Indian verb fignifying " to deftroy," " to make havoc," has, before an *inanimate* objeçt, *Paguatóog* (as Eliot writes it, e.g., Is. iii : 12) in the third perfon plural of the indicative, " they deftroy." This agrees almoft exaçtly with Roger Williams's form of the name. With an *animate* objeçt fpecified, the verb is *Paguanóog;* whence probably Winthrop's *Pequins.* It is fingular that fo obvious an etymology, or rather trauflation, has hitherto efcaped notice. The name, like that given to the " Mohawks," expreffes the terror with which this warlike race was regarded by other New-England tribes. [Winthrop, *Journal,* i: 52, 72, 122.]

Their territory extended from the *Niantic* on the weft to the *Paucatuck* on the caft; fome 30 miles in length by fome 20 in breadth, moftly in Connecticut. The " Pequot war " took place in 1636-8. [De Foreft's *Hift. Ind. of Conn.* 58; *R.-I. Hift. Coll.* iii : 161.]

after they fubjected themfelves to the *Englifh*, the *Englifh* became their Protectors, and defended them againft other Nations that would otherwife have deftroyed them, *&c.* After fome further difcourfe, and debate, he brought them at length to confent that if the Government of *Plymouth* would firmly ingage to them, *That they, and all of them, and their Wives and Children, fhould have their Lives fpared, and none of them tranfported out of the Country, they would fubject themfelves to them, and ferve them in what they were able.*

Then Mr. *Church* told them, That he was well fatisfyed the Government of *Plymouth* would readily concur with what they propofed, and would fign their Articles: And complementing them upon it, how pleafed he was with the thoughts of their return, and of the former friendfhip that had been between them, *&c.*

The chief Captain rofe up, and expreffed the great value and refpect he had for Mr. *Church;* and bowing to him faid, *Sir, If you'l pleafe to accept of me and my men, and will head us, we'l fight for you, and will help you to* Philips *head before Indian Corn be ripe* And when he had ended, they all exprefs'd their confent to what he faid, and told Mr. *Church* they loved him, and were willing to go with him and fight for him, as long as the *Englifh* had one Enemy left in the Country.

Mr. *Church* affured them, That if they proved as good as their word, they fhould find him their's and their Children's faſt friend. And (by the way) the friendſhip is maintain'd between them to this day.[185]

Then he propoſed unto them, that they ſhould chooſe five men to go ſtraight with him to *Plymouth* : They told him, No ; they would not chooſe, but he ſhould take which five he pleaſed: ſome complements paſſed about it, at length it was agreed, They ſhould chooſe Three, and he Two. Then he agreed, with that he would go back to the Iſland that Night, and would come to them the next Morning, and go thro' the Woods to *Plymouth*. But they afterwards objeƈted, That this travelling thro' the Woods would not be ſafe for him; the Enemy might meet with them, and kill him, and then they ſhould loſe their friend, and the whole deſign ruined beſide. And therefore pro-poſed, That he ſhould come in an Engliſh Veſſel, and they would meet him and come on board at *Sogkonate-point*,

---

[185] This was written in 1715 or 1716. In June, 1698, Rev. Grindal Rawſon, of Mendon, and Rev. Samuel Danforth, of Taunton, " Preachers to the Indians in their own tongue," viſited Little Compton, and reported that they found two plantations of Indians there, at *Saconet* and *Cokeſit* (on the borders of Dartmouth); that Samuel Church, alias *Sokchawahkam*, taught the firſt, and had ordinarily 40 hearers, of whom 20 were men; and that, at the ſecond, Daniel Hinckley taught eleven families twice every Sabbath. A ſchoolmaſter, named *Akam*, alſo labored at *Cokeſit*, and there were two Indian rulers at each place. [See original printed Re-port to *Comm. for Prop. Goſpel*, made July 12, 1698.] In 1700 there were ſaid to be 100 Indian men ſtill living in Little Compton. About 1750, a moſt deſtruƈtive fever cauſed great mortality among them; ſo that in 1774 the R.-I. cenſus reported there only 1 male and 13 females above 16 yrs., and 5 males and 6 females under that age, — 25 in all. In 1803 there were " not more than 10 " there. So far as I can learn in the town, there is not one perſon with any trace of Indian blood recogniz-able in his veins there now. [1 *Maſſ. Hiſt. Coll.* ix: 204; x: 114, 119.]

and Sail from thence to *Sandwich*: which in fine, was concluded upon.

So Mr. *Church* promiſing to come as ſoon as he could poſſibly obtain a Veſſel, and then they parted. He returned to the Iſland, and was at great pains and charge to get a Veſſel, but with unaccountable diſappointments; ſometimes by the falſeneſs, and ſometimes by the faint-heartedneſs of Men that he bargained with, and ſomething by Wind and Weather, *&c.* [26]

Until at length Mr. *Anthony Low*[186] put into the Harbour[187] with a loaden Veſſel bound to the Weſtward, and being made acquainted with Mr. *Churches* caſe, told him, *That he had ſo much kindneſs for him, and was ſo pleaſed with the buſineſs that he was ingaged in, that he would run the venture of his Veſſel & Cargo, to wait upon him.* Accordingly, next Morning they ſet Sail with a Wind that ſoon brought them to *Sogkonate-point*; but coming there they met with a contrary wind, and a great ſwelling Sea.

The *Indians* were there waiting upon the Rocks, but

---

[186] *Anthony Lowe (Loe)*, ſon of John, Boſton, removed after 1654 to Warwick, R.-I.; in 1658 was fined £3, by Plymouth Court for felling a piſtol to an Indian, at Eaſtham; in 1680 owned land adjoining Nathaniel Peck's in Swanſey, and in 1682–3 was living at Swanſey, and had an Indian ſlave named *James*, to whom the Plymouth Colony ordered his freedom and "a good ſuite of clothes." Whether he afterwards returned to Warwick, and was freeman there in May, 1704, and conſtable there in Oct., 1706; or whether that Anthony were his ſon, I cannot determine. [Savage's *Gen. Dict.* iii: 125; *Plym. Col. Rec.* iii: 137; vi; 56, 101; *R.-I. Col. Rec.* iii: 498, 571.]

[187] Newport Harbor, as I ſuppoſe. There is nothing that can be called a harbor on the eaſt ſhore of the iſland. Newport was not more than five or ſix miles from Capt. Almy's houſe in Portſmouth.

had nothing but a miferable broken Canoo to get aboard in. Yet *Peter Awafhonks* ventured off in it, and with a great deal of difficulty and danger got aboard. And by this time it began to Rain and Blow exceedingly, and forced them away up the Sound;[188] and then went away thro' *Briftol* Ferry, round the Ifland to *New-port*, carrying *Peter* with them.

Then Mr. *Church* difmifs'd Mr. *Low*, and told him, *That inafmuch as Providence oppos'd his going by Water, and he expected that the Army would be up in a few days, and probably if he fhould be gone at that juncture, it might ruine the whole defign; would therefore yield his Voyage.*

Then he writ the account of his tranfactions with the *Indians*, and drew up the Propofals, and Articles of Peace, and difpatch'd *Peter* with them to *Plymouth*; that his Honour the Governour if he faw caufe might fign them.

Peter was fet over to *Sogkonate* on the Lords day[189]

---

[188] That is the "Eaft Paffage," or Narraganfet River.

[189] This would feem to have been Sab., 25 June, 1676. The army, by the Court order (note 165, *ante*), were to be ready to march on Wednefday, 21 June; they ought to reach the neighborhood of Rhode-Ifland by the following Sabbath, and fo it would be natural that there fhould be "great looking for them," by this time. It is on record, alfo, that *Peter*, with *George* and *David*, alias *Chowahunna*, appeared before the Council at Plymouth on the following Wednefday, 28 June, 1676, in "the behalfe of themfelues and other Indians of Saconett, to the number of about 30 men, with theire wiues and children, and tendered to renew theire peace with the Englifh, and requefted libertie to fitt downe in quietnes on theire lands att Saconett." Their examination is detailed, at length. On being upbraided for the wrong done in joining Philip, &c., "*Chowohumma*, faid: Wee cannot make fatiffaction for the wronge don; but if our weemen and children can be cecured, wee will doe any feruice wee can by fighting againft the enimie." They further faid that *Succanowaffucke* was the firft man that ftirred up the Indians to join with

Morning, with orders to take thofe men that were chofen to go down, or fome of them at leaft with him. The time being expired that was appointed for the *Englifh* Army to come, there was great looking for them. Mr. *Church* on the Monday Morning (partly to divert himfelf after his fategue, and partly to liften for the Army) Rid out with his Wife and fome of his friends to *Portfmouth*,[190] under a pretence of Cherrying; but came home without any News from the Army: But by Midnight, or fooner, he was roufed with an Exprefs from Maj. *Bradford*, who was arrived with the Army at *Pocaffet*. To whom he forth with repaired,[191] and informed him of the whole of his pro ceedings, with the *Sogkonate Indians*. With the Majors

Philip, and that he was at Saconet, and promifed to try to furprife him as foon as they fhould return. The Council propofed that Peter fhould remain as a hoftage, to which he confented. It was finally decided that they fhould go back, and that fuch as Maj. Bradford defired for the army fhould join that, and the others give up their arms; that any "murdering" Indians of their number fhould be delivered up, and that they fhould not harbor the enemies of the Colony; on which conditions it was promifed that "they fhall haue a place affigned them for theire p'fent refidence in peace," with further promife for the future, "in cafe the warr doe feafe." [*Plym. Col. Rec.* v: 201-3.]

[190] If Church were ftill an inmate of Capt. Almy's houfe in Portfmouth, there feems a little ftrangenefs in his fpeaking thus of riding out *to* Portfmouth. He may have removed his family, before this, to Major Peleg Sanford's, in Newport (now in Middletown), where, it will be feen, they were at the time of Philip's capture. Or, as the firft fettlement of the northern part of the ifland was around a cove between Briftol ferry and the Stone bridge (the fettlement being firft called Pocaffet; changed to Portfmouth, 1639-40), the name of Portfmouth may, at the date of which Church is here fpeaking, have been more efpecially appropriated to the original fettlement in the extreme northern portion of the prefent town, fo that he naturally fpoke of riding over from Capt. Almy's toward the Stone bridge, as riding out to Portfmouth. [Arnold's *Hift. R.-I.* i: 71, 125, 136, 143.]

[191] Tuefday, 27 June, 1676.

confent and advice, he returned again next Morning[192] to the Ifland, in order to go over that way to *Awaſhonks*, to inform her that the Army was arrived, *&c.* Accordingly from *Sachueeſet-Neck*,[193] he went in a Canoo to *Sogkonate*; told her Maj. *Bradford.* was arrived at *Pocaſſet*, with a great Army, whom he had inform'd of all his proceedings with her. That if ſhe would be adviſed and obſerve order ſhe nor her People need not to fear being hurt by them. Told her, She ſhould call all her People down into the Neck, leaſt if they ſhould be found ſtraggling about, miſchief might light on them. That on the Morrow they would come down and receive her, and give her further orders. She promiſed to get as many of her People together as poſſibly ſhe could. Deſiring Mr. *Church* to conſider that it would be difficult for to get them together at ſuch ſhort [27] warning. Mr. *Church* returned to the Ifland, and to the Army the ſame Night: The next Morning[194] the whole Army Marched towards *Sogkonate* as far as *Punkateeſe;* and Mr. *Church* with a few Men went down to *Sogkonate* to call *Awaſhonks*, and her People to come up to the Engliſh Camp; as he was going down, they met with a *Pocaſſet Indian*, who had killed a Cow and got a Quarter of her on his back, and her Tongue in his Pocket; who gave them an account, That he came from *Pocaſſet* two days ſince in company with his Mother

---

192 Wedneſday, 28 June, 1676.
193 *Sachueeſet* [*Sachueſ*] neck is the fouth-eaſtern point of the iſland of Rhode-Ifland; the elongated heel of the foot of which the village of Newport forms the inſtep. It is diſtant about 3 miles, by water, due weſt, from Saconet.
194 Thurſday, 29 June, 1676.

and feveral other *Indians* now hid in a Swamp above *Nomquid*;[195] difarming of him, he fent him by two Men to Maj. *Bradford*, and proceeded to *Sogkonate*: they faw feveral *Indians* by the way skulking about, but let them pafs. Arriving at *Awafhonks* Camp, told her, *He was come to invite her and her People up to* Punkateefe, *where Maj.* Bradford *now was with the* Plymouth *Army, expeΩ-ing her and her SubjeΩs to receive orders, until 'further order could be had 'from the Government.* She complyed, and foon fent out orders for fuch of her SubjeΩs as were not with her, immediately to come in; and by Twelve a Clock of the next day,[196] fhe with moft of her Number appear'd before the Englifh Camp at *Punkateefe*. Mr. *Church* tender'd the Major to Serve under his Commiffion, provided the *Indians* might be accepted with him, to fight the Enemy. The Major told him, *his Orders were to im-* ιprove him, *if he pleafed, but as 'for the* Indians, *he would not be concerned with them.* And prefently gave forth orders for *Awafhonks*, and all her SubjeΩs both Men, Women and Children to repair to *Sandwich*, and to be there upon Peril, in Six days.[197] *Awafhonks* and her chiefs gather'd

---

[195] *Nomquid* [*Nonequit, Nonquit, Namquit, &c.,*], the cove or pond lying between *Punkateefe* neck and Tiverton.

[196] Friday, 30 June, 1676. Both Hubbard and Mather mention "about 90". as the number of thofe with Awafhonks in this fubmiffion. [*Narrative*, 97; *Brief Hift.* 39.]

[197] As this took place only two days after Peter and his two companions made their appearance at Plymouth to confer with the Council, — and we are told that it was " after fome time for confideration " that the Council reached its conclufion, — it is not probable that Maj. Bradford had been informed of their decifion. (Mather fays, Awafhonks with about 90 came and tendered themfelves " before the meffengers re-turned.") He was therefore aΩing on

round Mr. *Church*, (where he was walk'd off from the reft) expreffed themfelves concerned that they could not be confided in, nor improv'd. He told them, *'twas beft to obey Orders; and. that if he could not accompany them to* Sandwich, *it fhould not be above a Week before he would. meet them there; That be was confident the Governour would. Commiffion him to improve them.* The Major haftened to fend them away with *Jack Havens*,[198] (an *Indian* who had never been in the Wars) in the Front with a flag of Truce in his hand. They being gone, Mr. *Church*, by the help of his Man *Toby* (the *Indian* whom he had taken Prifoner, as he was going down to *Sogkonate*) took faid *Toby*'s Mother, & thofe that were with her, Prifoners. Next Morning[199] the whole Army moved back to *Pocaffet.* This *Toby* informed them that there were a great many *Indians* gone down to *Wepoifet*[200] to eat Clams, (other Provifions being very fcarce with them;) that *Philip* him. felf was expected within 3 or 4 dayes at the fame Place:

his own authority as commander-in-chief, and his objeĉt in ordering Awafhonks and her tribe to Sandwich was, clearly, to get them out of reach of temptation, at once, and opportunity, to join Philip in further hoftilities. His order was not a harfh one in the matter of time; for the diftance could not probably be more than 40 miles by the circuitous foreft-paths, for which he allowed them fix days. [*Plym. Col. Rec.* v: 202: Mather's *Brief Hiftory*, 39.]

[198] *Jack Havens* is on the lift of fourteen Indians, whofe names were entered on the Court Records under date of 6 March, 1676-7, "whoe haue approued themfelues faithfull to the Englifh during the late Rebellion," befides Mamanuett, their Sachem (and family), who is defcribed as "att or about Saconett." [*Plym. Col. Rec.* v: 225.]

[199] Saturday, 1 July, 1676.

[200] *Wepoifet* [*Weypoifet*, *Waypoyfet*, &c.,] was the Indian name for the narrow entrance of *Kikemuit* river feparating the northern part of Briftol, R.-I., from the fouth-eaftern part of Warren. [Feffenden's *Hift. Warren. R.-I.* 71.]

being asked, *What Indians they were?* He anfwered, Some *Weetemores Indians*, fome *Mount-hope Indians*, fome *Narraganfet Indians*, and fome other Upland *Indians*, in all about 300. The *Rhode-Ifland.* Boats by the Majors order meeting them at *Pocaffet*, they were foon imbark'd, it being juft in the dusk of the Evening, they could plainly difcover the Enemies fires at the Place the *Indian* directed to;[201] and the Army concluded no other but they were bound [28] directly thither, until they came to the North End of the Ifland, and heard the word of Command for the Boats to bare away.[202] Mr. *Church* was very fond of having this probable opportunity of furprizing that whole Company of *Indians* imbraced: But Orders, 'twas faid, muft be obeyed, which was to go to *Mount-hope* and there to fight *Philip.* This with fome other good opportunities of doing fpoil upon the Enemy, being unhappily mifs'd.[203]

[201] The exact fpot where the Indians were digging clams and eating them would feem to have been on the foutheaftern curve of what is now called Touiffett neck; from whence fires would be vifible acrofs the bay at Pocaffet; where Maj. Bradford's army could fcarcely be diftant from them five miles in a ftraight line.

[202] They probably embarked at what was then the Ferry, — now fpanned by the "Stone Bridge," — from whence, for two miles and a half, their natural courfe would lie directly towards the light of the fires. When well up with the north end of Rhode-Ifland, their courfe, if they were going to Mount-

Hope Cove, would haul ftraight to the weft, and, if they were to land at Briftol neck, fharp to the fouth-weft.

[203] The narrative does not certainly indicate whether the army kept Sabbath at Mount Hope, or, finding Philip was not there, pufhed on at once up Mount-Hope neck and acrofs Miles's bridge to Rehoboth; though the probabilities feem to be ftrong that they did not march to Rehoboth until they had, at leaft, fearched for the Indians whom they had feen the night before at Weypoifet. I imagine that the "other good opportunities" to which Church refers as being "miffed," had reference to feveral fruitlefs attempts, occupying feveral

Mr. *Church* obtain'd the Majors Confent to meet the *Sog-konate Indians,* according to his promife. He was offer'd a Guard to *Plymouth,* but chofe to go with one Man only, who was a good Pilot. About Sun-fet[204] he with *Sahin* his Pilot[205] mounted their Horfes at *Rehoboth,* where the Army now was, and by two Hours by Sun next Morning arrived fafe at *Plymouth*: And by that time they had refrefhed themfelves, the Governour and Treafurer[206] came to Town. Mr. *Church* giving them a fhort account of the affairs of the Army, *&c.* His Honour was pleafed to give him thanks for the good and great Service he had done at *Sogkonate,* told him, *He had confirmed. all, that he promifed* Awafhonks, *and. had 'fent the* Indian *back again*

days in Mount-Hope neck and its region, to damage the Indians, before the army went to the garrifon-houfe at Rehoboth, which (with one other) had efcaped deftruction on the 28th of March.

[204] This could not have been " funfet " of the next day after leaving Pocaffet (Sab., 2 July, 1676), becaufe then Church would have reached Plymouth two hours after funrife, on Monday, 3 July. But he told the Governor, on the day of his arrival, that " the *time had expired* that he had appointed to meet the Sogkonates at Sandwich "; and as he had promifed them, on the 30th of June, that " it fhould not be *above a week* before he would meet them," his promife could not expire until Friday, 7 July: therefore he could not have reached Plymouth until on or after the 7th July. Hence he could not have left

Rehoboth before Thurfday, 6 July, the fifth day after leaving Pocaffet, and landing at Mount Hope.

[205] *Sabin* [*Sabine*] was then a Rehoboth name. Savage mentions eight of the name, all (he thinks) of Rehoboth, and five of whom ferved in Philip's war either in perfon or by contributions. Blifs mentions *Jonathan,* as in the Narraganfett fight, and *Samuel,* as ferving under Maj. Bradford. He alfo gives the names of five (*Jofeph, William, Samuel, Benjamin,* and a *Widow Sabin*) as making advances of money to fuftain the war. Doubtlefs, Church's guide was one of this patriotic family. [*Gen. Dict.* iv: 1; *Hift. Rehoboth,* 117, 118.]

[206] Jofias Winflow and Conftant Southworth. The former refided in Marfhfield, and the latter in Duxbury. [See notes 20 and 68, *ante.*]

that brought his Letter. He asked his Honour, *Whether he had any thing later from* Awaſhonks? He told him he had not. Where-upon he gave his Honour account of the Majors orders relating to her and hers, and what diſcourſe had paſſed *pro & con* about them; and that he had prom-iſed to meet them, and that he had incouraged them, that he thought he might obtain of his Honour a Commiſſion to lead them forth to fight *Philip.* His Honour ſmilingly told him, *That he ſhould not want Commiſſion if he would accept it, nor yet good Engliſh men enough to mahe up a good Army.* But in ſhort, he told his Honour the time was expired that he had appointed to meet the *Sogkonates* at *Sandwich.* The Governour asked him, when he would go? He told him that afternoon, by his Honours leave. The Governour ask'd him, How many Men he would have with him? He anſwered, Not above half a dozen, with an order to take more at *Sandwich,* if he ſaw cauſe; and Horſes provided. He no ſooner moved it, but had his number of Men tendering to go with him, among which was Mr. *Jabez Howland,*[207] and *Nathanael South-*

---

[207] *Jabez Howland* was ſon of John, who came as attendant of Gov. Carver in the Mayflower; was fined at Plym-outh, March 5, 1666–7, 3s. 4d, for a breach of the peace, in ſtriking Joſeph Billing-ton; ſerved on a trial jury in 1671 and 1677, and on a coroner's jury in 1671 and 1673; was conſtable of Plymouth in 1675; petitioned for a grant of land in 1675, in virtue of the Court order preferring children born here to ſtran-gers; removed to Briſtol, R.-I., and was licenſed to keep an inn there in 1681, and was ſeleƈtman there in 1682, 1685, and 1690; was enſign of a mili-tary company there in 1684; deputy thence in 1689 and 1690. He married Bethia, dau. of Anthony Thacher, and had ten children. [Savage's *Gen. Diƈt.* ii: 479; *Plym. Col. Rec.* iv: 140; v: 82, 88, 122, 165, 170, 255; vi: 78, 84, 131, 169, 206, 241.]

worth ;[208] they went to *Sandwich* that Night; where Mr. *Church* (with need enough) took a Nap of Sleep. The next Morning with about 16 or 18 Men proceeded as far as *Agawom*,[209] where they had great expectation of meeting the *Indians,* but met them not; his Men being difcouraged about half of them returned; only half a dozen ftuck by him, & promifed fo to do until they fhould meet with the *Indians.* When they came to *Sippican River*,[210] Mr. *Howland.* began to tyre, upon which Mr. *Church* left him, and two more, for a Referve at the River, that if he fhould meet with Enemies and be forced back, they might be

[208] *Nathaniel Southworth*, fecond fon of Conftant, was born at Plymouth, 1648; furveyor of highways 1673; ferved on trial jury in 1677; was conftable of Plymouth, and ferved on coroner's jury in 1678; was fined 10s. in 1681, for refufing to aid the conftable of Plymouth; ferved on coroner's jury in 1684; was a felectman of Plymouth in 1689 and 1691, and grand juror in 1690. He was alfo a lieutenant. He died Jan. 14, 1711. Savage fays he lived at Middleborough; but I find no trace of it in the Colony Records. [Savage's *Gen. Dict.* iv: 143; *Plym. Col. Rec.* v: 115, 246, 257, 263; vi: 56, 148, 206, 237, 264.]

[209] *Agawam* was the Indian name of the fettlement near the Agawam River, in what is now Wareham. The name is ftill retained by a little village on the low lands through which the river winds into the "Narrows." The name is from *agwe*, "below"; hence fignifying fometimes *below*, as defcriptive of a

point down ftream from another on the fame river, and fometimes *a low place*, as defcriptive of flats, or low land without reference to higher elevations in the vicinity, as thefe flat meadows in Wareham, and the "low ilands of *Auguan*" of which Capt. Smith fpeaks. [*Advertifements for the Unexperienced, &c.*, p. 27.]

[210] *Sippican* River (confluent with the *Weweantitt*) runs into Buzzard's Bay about half way between the villages of Wareham and Marion; and its lower portion forms the boundary between thofe two towns. The word *Sippican* [*Sepaconnet, Seppekan*] is related to Sebago, from the Abnaki, s8bék8, "la mer, eau falée," Rafles, (but *brackifh* water, rather than *falt*, perhaps), the equivalent of Eliot's *feippag*, ufed in *James* iii: 12, for "falt water." The Indians of Maffachufetts had no word for *falt*. *See*, by itfelf, fignifies ufually, "four"; hence, doubtlefs, "difagreeable," "ill-tafted."

ready to aſſiſt them in getting over the River. Proceeding in their March, they croſſed another River,[211] and opened a great Bay,[212] where they might ſee many Miles along-ſhore, where were Sands and Flats; and hearing a great noiſe below them towards [29] the Sea. They diſmounted their Horſes, left them and crep'd among the buſhes, until they came near the bank, and ſaw a vaſt company of *Indians*, of all Ages and Sex*s*, ſome on Horſeback running races, ſome at Foot-ball,[213] ſome catching Eels & Flat-fiſh in the water, ſome Clamming, *&c.* but which way with ſafety to find out what *Indians* they were they were at a loſs. But at length, retiring into a thicket, Mr. *Church* hollow'd to them; they ſoon anſwered him, and a couple of ſmart young Fellows, well mounted, came upon a full Career to ſee who it might be that call'd, and came juſt upon Mr. *Church* before they diſcovered him;

[211] In the abſence of any tradition identifying this ſtream, and deciding merely by my knowledge of the localities, I conceive this to have been what is now called "Mill Creek," emptying into Aucoot Cove — which is the firſt inlet on the coaſt ſouth-weſt of Sippican Harbor.

[212] If I am right in the identification of Mill Creek as the ſtream laſt referred to, after Church paſſed over it, a progreſs of leſs than a mile would enable him to look out by the ſouth-eaſtern extremity of Charles Neck and the overlapping Butter's Point of Great Neck (a mile and a half further eaſt), and to "open" Buzzard's Bay, which

here has a breadth of ſix or ſeven miles; while it would give him ſight of a long coaſt diſtance down what is now the eaſtern and ſouthern ſhore of Mattapoiſett. I judge, therefore, that the ſands and flats on which Awaſhonks and her Indians were now encamped were thoſe between Aucoot Cove and Angelica Point, or between Angelica Point and Ned's Point, in Mattapoiſett aforeſaid.

[213] "A game of football in which he was expert, or of quoits, or a wreſtling-bout, or a dance in which women did not mingle, afforded ſome occaſional variety." [Palfrey's *Hiſt. N. E.* i: 32; Schoolcraft's *Hiſt. Ind. Tribes*, ii: 78.]

but when they perceived themfelves fo near *Englifh* Men, and Arm'd, were much furprized, and tack'd fhort about to run as faft back as they came forward, until one of the Men in the bufhes call'd to them, and told them his Name was *Church*, and need not fear his hurting of them. Upon which, after a fmall paufe, they turned about their Horfes, and came up to him; one of them that could fpeak *Englifh*, Mr. *Church* took afide and examin'd, who inform'd him, That the *Indians* below were *Awafhonks*, and her company, and that *Jack Havens* was among them; whom Mr. *Church* immediately fent for to come to him, and order'd the Meffenger to inform *Awafhonks* that he was come to meet her; *Jack Havens* foon came, and by that time Mr. *Church* had afk'd him a few Queftions, and had been fatisfyed by him, That it was *Awafhonks*, and her company that were below, and that *Jack* had been kindly treated by them; a company of *Indians* all Mounted on Horfe-back, and well Arm'd came riding up to Mr. *Church*, but treated him with all dew refpeéts. He then order'd *Jack* to go tell *Awafhonks*, that he defigned to Sup with her in the Evening, and to lodge in her Camp that Night. Then taking fome of the *Indians* with him, he went back to the River to take care of Mr. *Howland*:[214] Mr. *Church* being a Mind to try what Mettal he was made of, imparted his notion to the *Indians* that were with him, & gave them direétions how to aét their parts; when he came pretty

[214] It would be four and a half or five miles back to Sippican River, where Mr. Howland, with his referve of two men, had been left.

near the Place, he and his *Engliſh* Men pretendedly fled firing on their retreat towards the *Indians* that purſued them, and they firing as faſt after them. Mr. *Howland* being upon his guard, hearing the Guns, and by & by feeing the motion both of the *Engliſh* and *Indians*, concluded his friends were diſtreſſed, was ſoon on the full Career on Horſe-back to meet them, until he perceiving their laughing miſtruſted the Truth. As ſoon as Mr. *Church* had given him the News, they haſted away to *Awaſhonks*. Upon their arrival, they were immediately conducted to a ſhelter, open on one ſide, whither *Awaſhonks* and her chiefs ſoon came & paid their Reſpects: and the Multitudes gave ſhouts as made the heavens to ring. It being now about Sun-ſetting, or near the dusk of the Evening; The Netops[215] came running from all quarters loaden with the tops of dry Pines, & the like combuſtible matter making a hugh pile thereof, near Mr. *Churches* ſhelter, on the open ſide thereof: but by this time Supper was brought in, [30] in three diſhes, *viz.* a curious young Baſs, in one diſh, Eels & Flat-fiſh in a ſecond, and Shell-fiſh in a third, but neither Bread nor Salt to be ſeen at Table. But by that time Supper was over, the mighty pile of Pine

[215] See note 143, *ante.* The word intends friendly Indians. Mr. Drake ſuggeſts here that the term may be equivalent to *Sannop* (citing Winthrop [*Journal*, i: 49], and Hubbard [*Gen. Hist. N.E.*, 253]; though the latter has *Sannap*): but Mr. Trumbull ſays, " *Sannop* had, with the Indians, a more reſtricted and a definite application (though it was ſometimes uſed by the Engliſh, as equivalent to *Nétop*, or 'Indian'). It ſignified 'a brave,'—*vir*, as diſtinguiſhed from *homo;* and was never applied by an Indian to a *foreigner*, or except to the warriors of his own nation or tribe." [Drake's *Church* (2d ed.), 91.]

Knots and Tops, &c. was fired, and all the *Indians* great and ſmall gathered in a ring round it. *Awaſhonks* with the oldeſt of her People Men and Women mix'd, kneeling down made the firſt ring next the fire, and all the luſty, ſtout Men ſtanding up made the next; and then all the Rabble in a confuſed Crew ſurrounded on the out-ſide. Then the chief Captain ſtep'd in between the rings and the fire, with a Spear in one hand and an Hatchet in the other, danced round the fire, and began to fight with it, making mention of all the ſeveral Nations & Companies of *Indians* in the Country that were Enemies to the *Engliſh;* & at naming of every particular Tribe of *Indians*, he would draw out & fight a new fire brand, & at his finiſhing his fight with each particular fire-brand, would bow to him and thank him; and when he had named all the ſeveral Nations and Tribes, and fought them all he ſtuck down his Spear and Hatchet, and came out; and another ſtept in and acted over the ſame dance, with more fury, if poſſible, than the firſt; and when about half a dozen of their chiefs had thus acted their parts, The Captain of the Guard ſtept up to Mr. *Church* and told him, *They were mahing Souldiers ʾfor him, and what they had been doing was all one Swearing af them,*[216] *and having in that manner*

---

[216] "The principle of enliſtment is ſufficiently well preſerved. . . . Each warrior that riſes and joins the war-dance, thereby becomes a volunteer for the trip. He arms and equips himſelf; he provides his own ſuſtenance; and when he ſteps out into the ring, and dances, he chants his own ſong, and is greeted with redoubling yells. Theſe ceremonies are tantamount to 'enliſtment,' and no young man who thus comes forward can honorably withdraw." [*Schoolcraft's Information reſpecting the Indian Tribes of the U.S.* vol. ii : 59, 60.]

ingaged all the lufty ftout men. Awafhonks & her chiefs came to Mr. *Church*; and told him, *That now they were all ingaged to fight'for the* Englifh, *and he might call forth all, or any of them at any time as he'faw occafion to fight the Enemy*; and prefented him with a very fine Firelock. Mr. *Church* accepts their offer, drew out a number of them, and fet out next Morning before day for *Plymouth*, where they arrived fafe the fame day.

The Governour being informed of it, came early to Town next Morning: and by that time he had *Englifh* Men enough to make up a good Company, when joyned with Mr. *Churches* Indians, that offered their Voluntary Service to go under his Command in queft of the Enemy. The Governour then gave him a Commiffion, which is as follows,

CAptain Benjamin Church, *you are hereby Nominated, Ordered, Commiffion'd, and Impowred to raife a Com-'pany of Volunteers of about* 200 *Men,* Englifh *and. Indians; the Englifh not exceeding the number of* 60, *of which Com-'pany, or fo many of them as'you can obtain, or fhall fee caufe at prefent to improve, you are to tahe the command and con-duct, and. to lead. them forth now and hereafter, at fuch time, and unto fuch'places within this Colony, or elfe where, within the confederate Colonies, as you fhall think fit; to difcover, purfue, fight, furprize, deftroy, or fubdue our Indian Ene-mies, or any'part or'parties of them that by the Providence of God. you may meet with; or them or any of them by treaty and compofition to receive to mercy, if'you fee reafon (provided. they be not Murderous Rogues, or such as have been principal Actors in those Villanies:) And forasmuch as your Company may be uncertain, and* [31] *the Persons often changed, You are also hereby impowred with advice of your Company to chuse and Commissionate a Lieutenant, and to establish Serjeants, and Corporals as you see cause: And you herein improving your best judgment and discretion and utmost ability, faithfully to Serve the Interest of God, His Majesty's Interest, and the Interest of the Colony ; and carefully governing your said Company at home and abroad.: these shall be unto you full and ample Commission, Warrant and Discharge. Given under the Publick Seal, this 24th Day of July, 1676.*[217]

Per Jos. Winslow, GOV.

[217] There is a miftake in the infertion of this commiffion here, not unnatural when the lapfe of time before the record was made, is taken into the account. This is not the commiffion which Church firft received, and on which he firft went out (as Judge Davis thought, inferring a mifprint in the date, of the 24th for the 14th [Morton's *Memorial*, 449]); but that "enlarged" one which was afterwards given him. This is obvious, firft, from its date. If Church arrived at Plymouth on Friday, 7 July (fee note 204), he muft have found Awafhonks at Mattapoifett on Saturday, 8 July, and returned to Plymouth on Sunday, the 9th; in which cafe the Governor came to town and commiffioned him on Monday, the 10th July, and he fet off " the fame night into the woods," on his firft expedition as Captain. There are no data for abfolute certainty as to this. But the Colony Records make it clear that he muft have been out on at leaft one fuccefsful expedition before the *twenty-fecond* of July, becaufe they contain a Court order of that date, that all volunteers taking prifoners " fhall haue the one halfe of them for theire pains and venture, from the day of the date heerof, *includeing thofe prifoners alfoe laft brought in by Benjamine Church and his companie.*" [*Plym. Col. Rec.* v : 207.] The Rev. Mr. Walley, alfo, writing to the Rev. Mr. Cotton [Davis's Morton's *Memorial*, p. 449] under date of 18 July, 1676, fays, " I am glad of the fuccefs Ben. Church hath; it is the good fruit of the coming in of Indians

Receiving Commiſſion, he Marched the ſame Night into the Woods, got to *Middleberry* [218] before day, [219] and as ſoon as the light appeared, took into the Woods and Swampy thickets, towards a place where they had ſome reaſon to expeſt to meet with a parcel of *Narraganſet Indians,* with ſome others that belonged to *Mount-hope*: Coming near to where they expeſted them, Capt. *Church's* Indian Scout diſcovered the Enemy, and well obſerving their fires, and poſtures, Returned with the intelligence to their Captain, who gave ſuch direſtions for the ſurrounding of them, as had the direſt effeſt; ſurprizing them from every ſide ſo unexpeſtedly, that they were all taken, not ſo much as one eſcaped. And upon a ſtriſt examination, they gave intelligence of another parcel of the Enemy, at

to us; thoſe that come in are conquered and help to conquer others." But Church had done nothing in this campaign which could be ſo referred to, previous to his ſetting off into the woods, here ſpoken of. Therefore Mr. Walley muſt refer to the reſults of this expedition to Namasket and Monponſet, which muſt, by conſequence, have taken place between the 10th and 18th of July. It will be ſeen, alſo, further on, that Church twice ſtates that he kept up this guerrilla warfare "ſeveral weeks"; and then proceeds to narrate, as if taking place ſubſequently, his ſetting out for Bridgewater in purſuit of Philip; which, by his account, was on Sunday, 30th July. If his firſt expedition was, as I ſuggeſt above, on Monday, the 10th, only *three* weeks would

intervene to make good his "ſeveral." Then, in the ſecond place, the very terms of the commiſſion itſelf ſhow that it was that "enlarged" one to which he ſubſequently refers; becauſe it gives him authority to "commiſſionate officers under him," to "march as far as he ſhould ſee cauſe, within the limits of the three United Colonies," to "receive to mercy, give quarter or not, &c. &c." [See p. 104.]

[218] *Middleborough* is a very large town, whoſe eaſtern boundary is about 10 miles weſt of the village of Plymouth. *Namaſket* was its Indian name, — from *namas*, "fiſh"; *namas-ohbe-ut*, "at the fiſh-place": that portion of the town which ſtill bears the name, being a noted fiſhing-place among the Indians.

[219] Tueſday, 11 July, 1676?

a Place called *Munponfet-Pond*[220] Capt. *Church* haftning with his Prifoners, thro' the Woods to *Plymouth*, difpofed of them all, excepting only one *Jeffery*, who proving very ingenious & faithful to him, in informing where other parcels of the *Indians* harboured Capt. *Church* promifed him, that if he continued to be faithful to him, he fhould not be Sold out of the Country, but fhould be his waiting man, to take care of his Horfe, *&c.* and accordingly he Served him faithfully as long as he lived.

But Capt. *Church* was forth-with fent out again; and the Terms for his incouragement being concluded on: *viz. That the Country fhould find them Ammunition & Provifion; & have half the Prifoners, & Arms, they took: The Captain and his Englifh Souldiers to have the other half of the Prifoners, and. Arms; and. the Indian Souldiers the loofe Plunder.* Poor incouragement! But after fome time it was mended.

They foon Captivated the *Munponfets*,[221] and brought in, not one efcaping. This ftroke he held feveral Weeks,

---

[220] *Monponfet* (*Moonponfet, Maunipenfing*) pond is an irregularly oblong fheet of water — perhaps averaging a mile and a quarter in length by three-quarters of a mile in breadth, and almoft divided into two equal parts by a tongue of land running down from its northern fbore — lying in the northern portion of the town of Halifax, Mafs., near to its junction with Hanfon and Pembroke, and about 10 miles W.N. W. from Plymouth. In regard to the meaning of its name, Mr. Trumbull fays, " Monponfet I cannot refolve."

[221] I think Church ufes this term here to defignate that " parcel " of the " Narraganfetts " who were temporarily encamped at this notable fifhing-place, rather than to indicate that there was any hoftile tribe of that name having a permanent refidence fo near to Plymouth, and deriving their defignation from this pond. I find no trace of any such tribe in the records.

never returning empty handed. When he wanted intelligence of their Kennelling Places, he would March to fome place likely to meet with fome travellers or ramblers, and fcattering his Company, would lye clofe; and feldom lay above a day or two, at the moft, before fome of them would fall into their hands: Whom he would compel to inform, where their Company was; and fo by his method of fecret and fudden furprizes took great Numbers of them Prifoners.[222]

The Government obferving his extraordinary courage and conduct, and the fuccefs from Heaven added to it, faw caufe to inlarge his Commiffion; gave him power to raife, and difmifs his Forces, as he fhould fee occafion; [32] to Commiffionate Officers under him, and to March as far as he fhould fee caufe, within the limits of the three United Colonies: to receive to mercy, give quarter, or not; excepting fome particular & noted Murderers: *viz.* *Philip*, and all that were at the deftroying of Mr. *Clark*'s Garrifon, and fome few others [223]

Major *Bradford* being now at *Taunton* with his Army,[224]

---

[222] The arrangement mentioned above, by which thofe volunteers received one half of the value of the prifoners and arms which were taken, as their pay for fervice; fheds light upon their efpecial anxiety to capture the enemy alive.

[223] This is the commiffion dated 24th July, and inferted on p. 100. On the 21ft July, three days before, the names of eleven Indians were placed on the Colony Record as "coepartenors in the outrage comitted att William Clarke's houfe, att the Eelriuer, 12 March, 1676." [*Plym. Col. Rec.* v: 206.]

[224] By the kindnefs of Mr. Haven of the Antiquarian Society in Worcefter, and of Judge Collamore of Royalton, Vt., I am in poffeffion of copies of a letter written from Taunton, on the 16th of this month by Anthony Collamore, one of Bradford's army there, giving

and wanting Provifions; fome Carts were ordered from *Plymouth* for their fupply, and Capt. *Church* to guard

fome account of their procedure, and fhedding a little light upon what has been a very obfcure portion of the war. As the letter has never, to my knowledge, been printed, I infert it in full:—

"TANTON, this July y⁰ 16, 1676. [Sunday.]

"DEARE AND LOVEING WIFE,—After " my kind love to you prefented hopeing "thefe will find you in health, as bleffed "be God I am at writing hereof. So " likewife are all our Situate men & y⁰ "reft of our army. Yᵉ feventh [Mr. " Haven's copy makes this 'twelfth,' " and Judge Collamore queries whether " it be 'feventh' or 'twelfth;' but the "connection favors the former,] day of " this Inftant wee marched from tan-"ton towards Swanfy & from thence "to Matapoyfett [Gardner's neck, fee " note 48, *ante*]; & fo continued in yᵉ " perfuite of them untill yᵉ fourteenth " day of yᵉ above-faid Month; and wee " haue killed & taken upwards of a hun-"dred Indians; but never an Englifh " Man flain or wounded, only one or " two bewildered in yᵉ wood & fo taken " by yᵉ enemy [* * * MS. illegible "* * *], nor have we any of our " Indians flaine or wounded, but peter " Mahalen has a fmall wound in his " belly; wee intend to be in perfute of " Phillip tomorrow againe, we have per-" fued him fo clofe yᵗ do wee almoft " defpaire; wee have followed him very " clofe from fwamp to fwamp, fo yᵗ he " is enforced to fly with a very fmall "quantity of men with him becaufe

" wee fhall not find him out; but I " hope with yᵉ Bleffing of God wee fhall " accomplifh our defire yᵗ is to take " him; thofe captives yᵗ wee have taken "* * * * * they tell us yᵗ Robin " Bradifh & Cornelias yᵗ ftole Mr. " Cufhen's cow, are gon doune between "our town & hingum to do Mifchief " there; yᵉ 11ᵗʰ day of this Inftant there " was about a 100 Indians made an on-"fett on tanton; they had burnt only " two out houfes for there was 200 " Englifh & Indians there prefent, " which fruftrated them of their de-"figne; fo yᵗ they have killed never " a man there; but they have killed " one man fince; pray prefent my fer-" vice to my Uncle & Aunt with my duty " to my father and mother & my love " to my children & brother & fifters & " yᵉ reft of my friends; Sargᵗ [Bar-"ker?—Deane's *Scituate*, 129, 216] is " well fiting on a rock eating Biskett " & Cheefe & defires to be remembered " to his wife; this being all at prefent "from

"Yo. ever Lo. Husband, "ANTHONY COLLYMER.

" pray take an opportunity to gett two " bufhells of corn ground while yᵉ wa-" ter lafts.

"I hope there in no fear of yᵉ In-"dians making an onfett on our towne " at prefent."

[Anthony Collamore was nephew to Peter, one of the firft fettlers of Scituate, and received, by his will, a fhare of his eftate. He married, in 1666, Sarah,

them.[225]   But he obtaining other guards for the Carts, as
far as *Middleborough*, ran before with a fmall Company,
hoping to meet with fome of the Enemy, appointing the
Carts and their guards to meet them at *Nemafcut*[226]
about an hour after the Suns rifing next Morning: he
arrived there about the breaking of the day-light, difcovered a company of the Enemy; but his time was too
fhort to wait for gaining advantage; and therefore ran
right in upon them, Surprized and Captivated about 16 of
them: who upon examination, inform'd, That *Tifpaquin*,[227]

one of the twin daughters of Ifaac
Chittenden, and had five children
(Mary, Peter, Sarah, Martha, Elizabeth).   He was loft on a coafting
voyage from Scituate to Bofton, 16
Dec., 1693, on a ledge of rocks off Scituate beach, which, to this day, bears
the name of Collamore's Ledge.   He
was commander of the militia of the
town at the time, and was buried "under arms." — [Deane's *Scituate*, 239,
240.]

[225] This expedition feems to have
taken place 20–27 July.   Increafe Mather, writing under date of Saturday,
22 July, fays: "This week alfo, Capt.
Church, of *Plimouth*, with a fmall party
confifting of about 18 *Englifh* and 22
Indians [Hubbard (p. 100) gives the
fame as the number of the party] had
four feveral engagements with the enemy, &c."; going on to fpeak of the
capture of Tiafhq's fquaw, in a way to
identify this as the expedition to which
he refers. [*Brief Hiftory*, 42.]

[226] See note 218, *ante*.   The exact

place in Middleborough here intended,
I fuppofe to be, fay 30 rods above
the bridge where the road from the
Green to the Four Corners croffes the
Nemasket River; where were rapids,
and near which is now the Lower
Factory, or Star Mills.

[227] *Tifpaquin* (*Tufpaquin*, abbrev.
from *Watufpaquin*, alias the *Black
Sachem*) was Sachem of Affawompfett,
the territory furrounding the pond of
that name in Middleborough.   He received his land from "*Pamontaquafk*,
the Pond Sachem" (who was probably
his father), by will dated 29 Oct., 1668.
He deeded land, 9 Aug., 1667, to Henry Wood; 17 July, 1669, with his fon
William, to Experience Mitchel *et al.*;
10 June, 1670, to Edward Gray; 30
June, 1672, to Edward Gray and Jofias
Winflow; in 1673, to John Saufaman;
11 Mar., 1673, to Felix, Saufaman's
fon-in-law; 3 July, 1673, to Benjamin
Church and John Tompfon; 23 Dec.,
1673, to Saufaman's daughter, called
Affowetough; 1 March, 1674–5, he and

a very famous Captain among the Enemy was at *Aſſa-
wompſet*, with a numerous Company.

But the Carts muſt now be guarded, and the oppor
tunity of viſiting *Tiſpaquin* muſt now be laid aſide: The
Carts are to be faithfully guarded, left *Tiſpaquid* ſhould
attack them.

Coming towards *Taunton*, Capt. *Church* taking two
Men with him, made all ſpeed to the Town; and coming
to the River ſide,[228] he hollow'd, and inquiring of them that
came to the River, for Maj. *Bradford*, or his Captains; he
was inform'd, they were in the Town, at the Tavern. He
told them of the Carts that were coming, that he had the
cumber of guarding of them, which had already prevented
his improving opportunities of doing Service. Pray'd
therefore that a guard might be ſent over to receive the
Carts, that he might be at liberty; refuſing all invitations
and perſwaſions, to go over to the Tavern, to viſit the

his ſon William bail *Tobias* — accuſed
(and afterwards convicted) of Sauſaman's murder — in lands to the value
of £100; 14 May, 1675, they fell Aſſawompſett neck to John Tompſon *et al.*,
as a ſecurity againſt the claims of
others. In the ſpring of 1676 he was
at the head of ſome 300 men, and had
a hand in the attempt to burn Scituate,
20 April, and Bridgewater, 8 May.
[*Plym. Col. Rec.* xii: 229, 230, 235;
v: 159; Drake's *Boob of the Ind.* 193,
194, 241, 242.]

[228] The old road from Middleborough
to Taunton, on which Church may be

preſumed to have travelled, took ſomething of the general courſe now taken
by the Middleborough and Taunton
R.R., running ſouth of that *cul-de-ſac*
in which the Taunton River encloſes a
ſouth-eaſt portion of Raynham, ſtriking
the river for croſſing a few rods above
the place where it receives Little
River, and there connecting, as I am
informed, with what is now Summer
St. From the eaſt bank of the river,
where he now "hollow'd," to the town
and the "tavern," muſt have been
probably a third of a mile, or a little
more.

Major: he at length obtain'd a guard to receive the Carts; by whom alfo he fent his Prifoners to be convey'd with the Carts to *Plymouth*, directing them not to return by the way they came, but by *Bridgwater*.[229]

Haftening back he purpofed to Camp that Night at *Affawompfet* Neck.[230] But as foon as they came to the River that runs into the great Pond thro' the thick Swamp at the entering of the Neck;[231] the Enemy fired upon them, but hurt not a Man. Capt. *Churches* Indians ran right into the Swamp and fired upon them, but it being in the dusk of the Evening, the Enemy made their efcape in the thickets: The Captain then moving about a Mile into the Neck, took the advantage of a fmall Valley to feed his Horfes; fome held the Horfes by the Bridles, the reft on the guard look'd fharp out for the Enemy, within hearing on every fide, and fome very near; but in the dead of the Night, the Enemy being out of hearing, or ftill, Capt. *Church* moved out of the Neck (not the fame way he came in, leaft he fhould be Ambuf[33]cado'd)

[229] The road from Taunton to Plymouth by Bridgewater, to which Church here refers, appears to have taken a tolerably ftraight courfe in a north-north-eafterly direction to what is now Weft Bridgewater, and then bore away a little fouth of eaft toward Plymouth — through what are now Halifax, North Plympton, and Kingfton.

[230] The land, in what is now the town of Lakeville, inclofed between Affawompfett and Great Quitticas Ponds on the eaft and north, and Long Pond on the weft; fome four miles in length, and varying from two miles to 80 rods in width. This narroweft part is at the northern entrance to the neck, where Long Pond and Affawompfett come near together, and are connected by a little brook.

[231] The brook referred to in the laft note, which croffes the road to New Bedford a little fouth of what has long been known as Sampfon's Tavern; now dignified as the Lakeville Houfe.

toward *Cuſhnet*,[232] where all the Houſes were burnt; and
croſſing *Cuſhnet* River,[233] being extreamly fategued, with
two Nights and one Days ramble without Reſt or Sleep;
and obſerving good forage for their Horſes, the Captain
concluded upon baiting, and taking a Nap. Setting Six
Men to watch the paſſage of the River, two to watch at a
time, while the other ſlept, & ſo to take their turns; while
the reſt of the Company went into a thicket to Sleep under
the guard of two Sentinels more. But the whole Company being very drowſy, ſoon forgot their danger, and
were faſt a-ſleep, Sentinels, and all. The Captain firſt
awakes, looks up, and judges he had ſlept four Hours,
which being longer than he deſigned, immediately rouſes
his Company, and ſends away a file to ſee what were
become of the watch at the paſſage of the River, but they
no ſooner opened the River in fight, but they diſcovered a
company of the Enemy viewing of their tracts, where they
came into the Neck;[234] Capt. *Church* and thoſe with him
ſoon diſpers'd into the bruſh on each ſide of the way,

[232] *Cuſhnet* (*Acuſhnet, Accuſſhaneck, Acuſhenah, Cuſhenah, Cuſhenett*) was the name of the firſt ſettlement made at the head of Acuſhnet inlet, three miles north of New Bedford, where the river meets the tide. It is about 11½ miles almoſt due ſouth of that ſpot in the neck where Church pauſed to feed his horſes. With *Ponagaſett* and *Coak-ſett* it had been conſtituted a townſhip, named Dartmouth, 8 June, 1664; and burned by the Indians in the ſummer of 1675, — as, ſee note 109, *ante*. [*Plym. Col. Rec.* iv: 65.]

[233] They came down on the eaſt ſide of the river, and, where it runs into tide-water, croſſed to the weſtern ſide, on their way to Ruſſell's garriſon at Pona-ganſet.

[234] The neck between the great cedar ſwamp and the Paſcamanſet River, on the weſt, and the head of Acuſhnet inlet (now New-Bedford Harbor) on the eaſt.

while the file fent, got undifcovered to the paffage of the River, and found their watch all faft a fleep: but thefe Tidings thoroughly awakened the whole Company. But the Enemy giving them no prefent difturbance, they examined their Snapfacks, and taking a little refrefhment, the Captain orders one party to guard the Horfes, and the other to Scout,[235] who foon met with a Track, and following of it, they were bro't to a fmall company of *Indians*, who proved to be *Little Eyes*, and his Family, and near Relations, who were of *Sogkonate*, but had forfaken their Country men, upon their making Peace with the *Englifh*. Some of Capt. *Churches* Indians asked him, *If he did. not know that Fellow?* Told him, *This is the Rogue that would. have hilled you at* Awafhonks *Dance* ;[236] and fignified to him that now he had an opportunity to be revenged on him. But the Captain told them, *It was not Englifh-mans fafhion to feek revenge; and. that he fhould have the fame quarter the reft had.* Moving to the River fide, they found an old Canoo, with which the Captain ordered *Little Eyes* and his company to be carryed over to an Ifland ;[237] Telling him, *he would leave him on that Ifland until. he returned.* ;

---

[235] They muft have fcouted over the ground where the city of New Bedford now ftands.

[236] See note 19, *ante.*

[237] Probably what is now called Palmer's Ifland, on which the inner lighthoufe ftands, midway of the channel, juft as it narrows between Fair Haven and New Bedford, and in the range of the fouthernmoft wharves of the latter. Fifh, Pope's, and Crow Iflands, nearly a mile further up, would not have enabled Lightfoot to look over upon Sconticut neck, as he feems next day to have done; but the narrow entrance to that neck is in plain fight, two miles due eaft from the lower extremity of Palmer's.

and, left the English should, light on them, and hill, them, he would leave his coufin Light-foot[238] (*whom the English knew to be their Friend.*) *to be his guard.* Little Eyes expreffed himfelf very thankful to the Captain. He leaving his orders with *Light-foot,* returns to the Rivers fide towards *Poneganfet,* to *Ruffels* Orchard,[239] coming near the Orchard they clap'd into a thicket and there lodg'd the reft of the Night without any fire; and upon the Morning light appearing, moves towards the Orchard, difcovers fome of the Enemy, who had been there the day before, and had beat down all the Apples, and carryed them away; dif-covered alfo where they had lodg'd that Night, and faw the ground where they fet their baskets bloody, being as they fuppofed and as it was afterwards difcovered to be with the flefh of Swine, &c. which they had killed that day: They had lain under [34] the Fences without any fires; and feem'd by the marks they left behind them to be very numerous, perceived alfo by the dew on the grafs that they had not been long gone; and therefore mov'd a-pace in purfuit of them. Travelling three Miles, or more, they came into the Country Road, where the track parted, one parcel fteered towards the Weft end of the great Cedar Swamp, and the other to the Eaft end.[240]

[238] *Lightfoot* appears to have been one of Awafhonks' Indians who volun-teered at Mattapoifet (p. 99). Church afterwards gave him the title of cap-tain. He fought with Church in the firft expedition eaft, in 1689.

See note 110, *ante.*

[240] The three miles feem to have brought them near to what is now known as the village of North Dart-mouth. The eaftern path fkirting the fwamp ran over toward Acufhnet; the weftern would feem to have led up near where Turner's Mills now ftand, on

The Captain halted and told his *Indian Souldiers, That they had heard as well as he, what ʒome Men had ʒaid at* Plymouth *about them,* &c. *That now was a good opportunity for each party to prove themʒelves : The Track being divided they ʒhould ʒollow one, and the Engliʒh the other, being equal in number.* The *Indians* declined the Motion, and were not willing to move any where without him; faid, *they ʒhould not think themʒelves ʒafe without him.* But the Captain infifting upon it, they fubmitted; he gave the *Indians* their choice to follow which track they pleafed; they replyed, *They were light and able to Travel, therefore if he pleaʒed they would tahe the Weʒt Track.* And appointing the Ruins of *John Cooks* Houfe at *Cuʒhnet*[24] for

the weftern fide of the Pafcamanfet River, toward Saffaquin's Pond. The diftance round to the rendezvous at Acufhnet, by the latter, was much the greater, and on this account the Indians chofe it, becaufe "they were light and able to travel."

[241] *John Cooke* was fon of Francis, and came in the Mayflower with his father; married 28 March, 1634, Sarah, daughter of Richard Warren; was deacon of the Plymouth Church, but was caft out, in the latter part of Mr. Reyner's miniftry, for "having been the author of much diffenfion and divifion, and for afterwards running into fectarian and anabaptiftical principles"; had a grant of land in Dartmouth, in June, 1664; became one of the firft fettlers of Acufhnet; was deputy from there in 1666, 1667, 1668, 1673, 1674, 1675, 1678, 1679, 1680, 1681, 1683, and

1686; was authorized as a magiftrate there in 1667, 1684, and 1689; had a controverfy with fome of the inhabitants of Dartmouth in regard to "Ram Ifland," which was fettled by the Court, 1 July, 1672; died at Dartmouth, 23 Nov., 1695, probably the only one of the paffengers on board the Mayflower who lived through the entire exiftence of the Plymouth Colony! Backus fays he became a Baptift minifter and "preached the doctrine of election, with the other doctrines of fovereign grace in Dartmouth for a number of years"; and thinks he founded the Baptift Church, near the borders of Tiverton and Dartmouth, in 1685. His houfe — whofe ruins are here referred to — was fituated on the Fair-Haven fide of the Acufhnet, about a mile north of the New-Bedford and Fair-Haven Bridge, and about a third of a mile eaft of the river, in what is

the place to meet at; each Company fet out briskly to try their Fortunes. Capt. *Church* with his *Englifh* Soldiers followed their Track until they came near entring a miery Swamp, when the Capt. heard a Whiftle in the Rear, (which was a note for a halt) looking behind him, he faw *William Fobes* [242] ftart out of the Company and made towards him, who haften'd to meet him as faft as he could; *Fobes* told him they had difcovered abundance of *Indians*, and if he pleafed to go a few fteps back he might fee them himfelf: he did fo, and faw them a-crofs the Swamp, obferving them, he perceived they were gather-

now called " Brimblecome's Orchard." The fite is almoft directly oppofite the houfe of Mr. J. M. Howland now ftanding, and is a few rods fouth of the Woodfide Cemetery. A block-houfe alfo ftood upon his land, perhaps half way from his houfe to the river. His farm was bounded on the weft by the Acufhnet, and ran back toward the eaft a mile and a half or more, and north and fouth at leaft as far, his houfe being pretty nearly in the center of it north and fouth. [Savage's *Gen. Dict.* i: 447; *Plym. Col. Rec.* iv: 67, 122, 148, 153, 163, 180; v: 93, 97, 114, 144, 165, 256; vi: 10, 36, 61, 106, 147, 186, 217; Ricketfon's *Hift. New Bedford*, 35, 314; Backus's *Hift. N. E.* ii: 16, 18; *Abridgment of do.* 135; MS. letters from Mr. F. B. Dexter and Mr. Geo. H. Taber.]

[242] *William Fobes* (*Fobbes, Vobes, Forbes*) was the fourth fon of John Fobes (and Conftant, fifter of Experience Mitchel), who was one of the early fettlers at Duxbury, and fubfequently one of the original proprietors of Bridgewater, where he fettled and died about 1661. William married, about 1667, Elizabeth, youngeft daughter of Conftant Southworth of Duxbury, who feems to have been oppofed to the match, putting this item into his will: " I will and bequeath unto my daughter E. S. my next heft bed and furniture, with my wife's beft bed, provided fhee doe not marry William Fobbes; but if fhee doe, then to have five fhillings." William was, of courfe, at the time of this Indian campaign, a brother-in-law of Church. He afterwards fettled at Little Compton — I do not know whether on the land there allotted to his elder brother, Edward, who took it among the firft grantees in his father's right (fee note 7), — and went commiffary with Maj. Church, in the third expedition eaft, in 1692. [Savage's *Gen. Dict.* ii: 177; Winfor's *Duxbury*, 258, 314; Mitchell's *Bridgewater*, 159.]

15   113

ing of *Hurtle-Berries*, and that they had no apprehenfions of their being fo near them; The Captain fuppofed them to be chiefly Women, and therefore calling one Mr. *Dil-lano*,[243] who was acquainted with the ground, and the Indian Language, and another named Mr. *Barns*;[244] with thefe two Men he takes right thro' the Swamp as faft as he could, and orders the reft to haften after them. Capt.

[243] I think this was *Jonathan Delano* (*DeLauney, DeLa Noye, Delanoy, Dallanoy, Dellano, Delanoe*), fon of Philip, who came in the Fortune, in 1621, and was one of the firft fettlers of Duxbury. Jonathan was born in 1648, and was confequently near 28 years of age at this time. He married, 26 Feb., 1678, Mercy, daughter of Nathaniel Warren, of Plymouth, and had eleven children. He became one of the early fettlers of Dartmouth (probably in his father's right of one fhare among the 36 original proprietors, in 1652), which would account for his being "acquainted with the ground." He was "commiffion-ated" lieutenant (as I judge for his military experience in this war), 20 May, 1690; was conftable, town clerk, surveyor, felectman, and, in 1689, deputy from Dartmouth. He died 28 Dec., 1720; and his graveftone ftill remains in the old Acufhnet burying-ground. [Winfor's *Duxbury*, 251; Ricketfon's *New Bedford*, 208, 386; Savage's *Gen. Dict.* ii: 34.]

[244] The clew to identification here is flight; but Church's Englifh foldiers on this expedition, were likelieft to be of Plymouth and its vicinity; and the Barnes known to me as beft fulfilling this and other natural conditions, is Jonathan, fecond fon of John, of Plymouth, 1632 (probably of Yarmouth, 1639), who married Mary Plummer. Jonathan was born 3 June, 1643, and was, confequently, at this time, a little more than 33 years of age. In March, 1664-5, with his father, he had a controverfy with Mr. Maherfhalalhafhbaz (an extraordinary chriftening borrowed from *Isa.* viii: 1.) Dyer, of Newport, R.-I., in regard to a floop; in which he got the worft of it, to the amount of £13 and his own cofts. He married, 4 Jan., 1665, Elizabeth, daughter of William Hedge, of Yarmouth, and had eleven children. 29 Oct., 1671, he was appointed, with the widow, adminiftrator on his father's eftate; 3 June, 1673, the Court gave him, with another, liberty to act as guardian of the children of his fifter Mary, who had married Robert Marfhall; in 1677 he was conftable of Plymouth; in 1679 and 1684 he ferved on coroner's juries, and in 1667, 1672, 1681, 1684, and 1685, on trial juries. [Savage's *Gen. Dict.* i: 121; *Plym. Col. Rec.* v: 81, 216, 231; vi: 8, 148; vii: 121, 136, 172, 242, 243, 285, 298; viii: 31; Freeman's *Hist. Cape Cod*, ii: 16, 186.]

Church with *Dillano* & *Barns* having good Horfes, fpur'd on and where foon among the Thickeft of the *Indians*, and out of fight of their own Men: Among the Enemy was an *Indian* Woman (who with her Husband had been drove off from *Rhode-Ijland.*) notwithftanding they had an Houfe upon Mr. *Sanford*'s Land,[245] and had planted an Orchard before the War; yet the Inhabitants would not be fatif-fyed till they were fent off;[246] and Capt. *Church* with his Family, living then at the faid *Sanfords*, came acquainted with them, who thought it very hard to turn off fuch old,

[245] *Peleg Sanford* [*Sandford, Sam-ford*] was fon of John, who was one of the earlieft fettlers of Rhode-Ifland. He, before 1665, married Mary, daugh-ter of Gov. Brenton; was admitted freeman at Newport, 1666; was made affiftant in 1667, and again in later years; 1667 was chofen captain of a troop of horfe; was appointed a Com-miffioner to England in the fame year, but did not go; was General Treafurer in 1678, and afterward; was elected Major of all troops on the ifland in 1679; was chofen Governor, on Cran-fton's death in 1680, and again in 1681, 1682, and 1683, when he declined; came near being killed by pirates, in 1682; was chofen to go to England for the Colony in 1683, and had an Admi-ralty commiffion from the king in 1697-8, followed by a correfpondence with Lord Bellemont. It is not known when he died. His houfe was in New-port. [Savage's *Gen. Dict.* iv: 15; *R.-I. Col. Rec.* ii: 147, 186, 218, 241, 565; iii: 5, 8, 30, 80, 83, 97, 106, 120, 134, 394.]

[246] The following order of the Court, paffed 13 March, 1675-6, will fhow the ftate of feeling then exifting on the ifland in regard to the refidence of In-dians among them: "This Affembly doe order, that whatfoever perfon in Rhode Ifland, or elfewhere in this Col-lony, that hath either Indian or Indians in his cuftody, from 12 yeares old and upward, fhall be bound in the daytime (if he goeth abroad from his houfe), to have a fufficient keeper in company with him, and to be locked up in the night in a fufficient place of fecurity; and that if any fuch Indian be found without fuch keeper in the day or lockt up in the night as abovefaid, all fuch mafter foe offendinge fhall forfeitt £5; twenty-five fhillings fhall be to him that can take an Indian foe offendinge, and bring him before the Governor, or any magiftrate; or by two fufficient witneffes to teftify againft the offender, and the remainder to the Generall Treafury." This order was publifhed "by beate of drum." [*R.-I. Col. Rec.* ii: 534.]

quiet People: but in the end it prov'd a Providence & an advantage to him and his Family, as you may fee afterwards. This *Indian* Woman knew Capt. *Church*, and as foon as fhe faw him, held up both her hands and came running towards him, crying aloud, *Church, Church, Church.* Capt. *Church* bid her ftop the reft of the *Indians*, and tell them, *The way to fave their Lives was not to run, but yield themfelves Prifoners, and he would not hill them;* [35] fo with her help, and *Dillano*'s, who could call to them in their own Language, many of them ftop'd and furrendred themfelves; others fcampering and cafting away their baskets, *&c.* betook themfelves to the thickets, but Capt. *Church* being on Horfe-back foon came up with them, and laid hold on a Gun that was in the hand of one of the foremoft of the company, pull'd it from him, and told him he muft go back. And when he had turned them, he began to look about him to fee where he was, and what was become of his Company, hoping they might be all as well imploy'd as himfelf, but could find none but *Dillano*, who was very bufy gathering up Prifoners; the Captain drove his that he had ftop'd to the reft, inquiring of *Dillano* for their Company, but could have no news of them. But moving back picked up now and then a skulking Prifoner by the way. When they came near the place where they firft ftarted the *Indians*, they difcover'd their Company ftanding in a body together, and had taken fome few Prifoners; when they faw their Captain, they haftened to meet him: They told him they found it difficult getting thro' the Swamp, and neither feeing nor hearing any thing of him, they concluded the Enemy had kill'd him, and were at a great lofs what to do. Having brought their Prifoners together they found they had taken and kill'd 66 of the Enemy. Capt. *Church* then ask'd the old Squaw, *What company they belonged unto?* She faid, They belonged part to *Philip,* and part to *Qunnappin* [247] and the *Narraganfet-Sachem,* [248] difcovered alfo upon her declaration that both *Philip* and *Qunnappin* were about two Miles off in the great Cedar Swamp; [249] he enquired of her, *What company they had with them?* She anfwered, *Abundance of Indians: The Swamp,* fhe faid, *was full of Indians from one end unto the other, that were fettled there, that there were near an* 100 *men came from the Swamp with them, and left them upon that plain to gather Hurtle-berry's, and promifed to call them as they came back out of* Sconticut-Neck, [250] *whither they went to hill Cattel and Horfes for*

[247] *Quinnapin* (*Panoquin, Sowagonifh, &c.*) was a Narraganfett, and nephew of *Miantunnomoh.* He became an ally of Philip, — one of his three wives being a fifter of *Wootonekanufke,* Philip's wife, — was in the Narraganfett fwamp fight, and aided in the attack on Lancafter, 10 Feb., 1675; purchafing Mrs. Rowlandfon of the Narraganfett who captured her at that time. He was taken foon after the time of his prefent mention, and was fhot at Newport, on fentence of a Court-martial, 25 Auguft, 1676. [Drake's *Boob of Ind.* 239; *R.-I. Hift. Coll.* iii: 173.]

[248] Poffibly *Pumham,* who was killed at Dedham, 25-27 July, and who — doubtlefs with his followers — was likely to have been at this time with Philip. [Drake's *Boob of Ind.* 257.]

[249] That, as I fuppofe, which is ftill called by this name, two or three miles north-weft of the city of New Bedford, and through which the road to Turner's Mills now paffes.

[250] The fouthern portion of the town of Fair Haven, projecting like a finger pointing toward the Elizabeth Iflands, — fome 3 miles long by an average breadth of near ¾ of a mile, and forming the eaftern boundary of New-Bedford Harbor.

Provisions for the company. She perceiving Capt. *Church* move towards the Neck, told him, *If they went that way they would all be kill'd.* He ask'd her, *Where-about they crossed the River?* She pointed to the upper passing place.[251] Upon which Capt. *Church* passed over so low down as he thought it not probable they should meet with his Track in their return·[252] and hastened towards the Island, where he left *Little Eyes*, with *Light-foot.*[253] Finding a convenient place by the River side for the Securing their Prisoners,[254] Capt. *Church* and Mr. *Dillano* went down to see what was become of Capt. *Light-foot*, and the Prisoners left in his charge. *Light-foot* seeing and knowing them, soon came over with his broken Canoo;[255] and inform'd them, *That he had seen that day about* 100 *Men of the Enemy go down into* Sconticut Neck, *and that they were now returning again* : Upon which they three ran down immediately to a Meadow where *Light-foot* said the *Indians* had passed; where they not only saw their Tracks, but also them: Where-upon they lay close until the En-

[251] The "upper passing place" was where Church and his company had crossed, the night before, probably about where the bridge now is, at the Head of the River. [See note 233, *ante*.]

[252] Any lower crossing could hardly have been accomplished, even at ebb tide, without some swimming or the aid of a canoe. The likeliest place for this lower crossing seems to be from Belville to Island Marsh, where the river narrows so that they would have needed to swim not more than 100 yds. This is just north of the Wamsutta Mills in New Bedford.

[253] See note 238, *ante*.

[254] Probably just above Mill Creek, which flows into the Acushnet just below the present New-Bedford and Fair-Haven bridge.

[255] He doubtless landed near Fort Phœnix; then, with Church and Delano, ran along to the road up out of Sconticut neck and the meadow.

emy came into the faid [36] Meadow, and the fore-moft fat down his load and halted, until all the company came up, and then took up their loads & march'd again the fame way that they came down into the Neck, which was the neareft way unto their Camp; had they gone the other way along the River,[256] they could not have miffed Capt. *Churches* Track, which, would doubtlefs have expos'd them to the lofs of their Prifoners, if not of their lives. But as foon as the Coaft was clear of them, the Captain fends his *Light-foot* to fetch his Prifoners from the Ifland, while he and Mr. *Dillano* returns to the company, fent part of them to conduct *Light-foot* & his company to the aforefaid Meadow, where Capt. *Church* and his company met them; croffing the Enemies Track they made all haft, until they got over *Mattapoifet-river*,[257] near about four Miles beyond the ruines of *Cooks* Houfe, where he appointed to meet his *Indian* company, whither he fent *Dillano*, with two more to meet them; ordering them, that if the *Indians* were not arrived, to wait for them. Accordingly, finding no *Indians* there, they waited until late in the Night, when they arrived with their booty.[258] They

---

[256] The neareft path from Sconticut neck to the Acuſhnet croffing, probably was then very nearly where the road now is; which averages a diftance of about a mile from the eaftern ſhore of the Acuſhnet. Church's path hugged that ſhore, and, as he croffed lower down, his track nowhere touched theirs.

[257] *Mattapoºfet* River empties into Mattapoifet Harbor, and its courfe for its laft 5 miles averages about 4 miles eaft of the Acuſhnet, on whofe ſhore ftood Cook's houfe.

[258] The weftern path around the great cedar fwamp required much longer time than the eaftern, over which Church had come; and the Indians had that in mind in choofing it. (See note 240, *ante*.)

difpatch'd a Poft to their Captain to give him an account
of their Succefs; but the day broke before they came to
him: And when they had compared Succeffes, they very
remarkably found that the number that each Company
had taken and flain, was equal. The *Indians* had kill'd 3
of the Enemy, and taken 63 Prifoners, as the *Englifh* had
done before them, both *Englifh* and *Indians* were fur-
priz'd at this remarkable Providence, and were both
parties rejoycing at it; being both before afraid of what
might have been the event of the unequal Succefs of the
parties.[259] But the *Indians* had the fortune to take more
Arms than the *Englifh*. They told the Captain, *That they*
bad. miffed a brave Opportunity by parting; They came
upon a great Town of the Enemy, viz *Capt.* Tyasks[260] *com-*
pany, (*Tyasks* was the next man to *Philip*) *They fired.*
upon the Enemy before they were difcovered, and ran upon
them with a fhout; the Men ran and left their Wives and.
Children, and many of them their Guns:[261] *They took*

---

[259] The reference is to the prejudice
— which Church referred to when he
made to the Indians of his party the
propofition to go by themfelves — ftill
exiftent in the Colony againft the Indians as foldiers in that war; a prejudice paralleled in obftinate perfiftence
by that fo long entertained by many
againft the colored troops in our recent
ftruggle.

[260] *Tyafks* (*Tiafhq*) I find nothing of
more than is here narrated, except that
Mather fays of this fight, " *Tiafhq*
Philip's Chief Captain ran away leav-

ing his Gun behind him, and his *Squaw*,
who was taken"; and *Hubbard* fays,
" In June laft," — his chronology, of
courfe, is in fault, — " one *Tiafhq*, a
great captain of his [Philip's], his wife
and child, or children, being taken;
though he efcaped himfelf, at firft, yet
came fince and furrendred himfelf."
[*Brief Hift.* 42; *Narrative*, 106.]

[261] Mr. Drake fays, in his late edition
of Mather's *Brief Hiftory* (p. 181, note),
that " the place where these prifoners
were taken was probably in fome part
of what is fince Rochefter." It is haz-

Tyasks *Wife and Son, and tho't that if their Captain &
the English company had been with them they might have
taken some hundreds of them: And now they determined not
to part any more.*

That Night *Philip* fent (as afterwards they found out) a
great Army to way-lay Capt. *Church* at the entring on of
Affawompfet Neck, expecting he would have returned the
fame way he went in; but that was never his method to
return the fame way that he came; & at this time going
another way he efcaped falling into the hands of his Enemies. The next day they went home by *Scipican*,[262] and
got well with their Prifoners to *Plymouth*.

He foon went out again; and this ftroke he drove many
Weeks;[263] and when he took any number of Prifoners, he
would pick out fome that he took a fancy to, and would
tell them, *He took a particular fancy to them, and bad.
chofe them for himfelf to make Souldiers of; and if any
would. behave themfelves well, he would. do well by them, and
they fhould be his men and not Sold out of the Country.* [37]
If he perceived they look'd furly, and his *Indian* Souldiers

ardous for a neophyte to venture to
differ from one fo long and largely
familiar with Indian affairs; but I think
if Mr. Drake would take with him
Church's account over the country
traverfed, he would agree with me in
fixing the place of Tiafhq's capture as
fomewhere on the northern and weftern
fkirts of the " great cedar fwamp," in
what is now New Bedford.

[262] It would be a fhort four miles from
their prefent pofition, on the eaft bank
of the Mattapoifett River, to that point
in the road to Plymouth, by Sippican,
where Church difcovered Awafhonks
and her party. [See note 212, *ante*.]

[263] This is to be taken as a general
remark, covering Church's relation to
this fummer of the war, and not as
intimating that many weeks paffed
before the period of the next incident
which he fpecifically fets down.

call'd them treacherous Dogs, as fome of them would fometimes do, all the notice he would take of it, would only be to clap them on the back, and tell them, *Come, come, you look wild and furly, and mutter, but that fignifies nothing, thefe my beft Souldiers were a little while a go as wild and furly as you are now; by that time you have been but one day along with me, you'l love me too, and be as brisk as any of them.* And it prov'd fo. For there was none of them but (after they had been a little while with him, and fee his behaviour, and how chearful and fuccefsful his Men were) would be as ready to Pilot him to any place where the *Indians* dwelt or haunted (tho' their own Fathers or neareft Relations fhould be among them) or to fight for him, as any of his own Men.

Capt. *Church* was in two particulars much advantaged by the great *Englifh* Army[264] that was now abroad. One was, that they drove the Enemy down to that part of the Country, *viz.* to the Eaftward of *Taunton* River by which means his bufinefs was nearer home. The other was that when ever he fell on with a pufh upon any body of the Enemy (were they never fo many) they fled expecting the great Army. And his manner of Marching thro' the Woods was fuch, as if he were difcovered, they appeared

---

[264] Befides the Plymouth troops under Major Bradford, to whom Church has herein referred; Major Talcot was in the field with fome 250 Englifh and 200 Mohegans from Connecticut, and two companies from Maffachufetts, under Capts. Brattle and Mofely, were affociated with Bradford's men; befides Henchman's forces, which were fcouring the interior woods. [Palfrey's *Hift. N. E.* iii: 197; Barry's *Hift. Mafs.* i: 444, 445.]

to be more than they were. For he always Marched at a wide diftance one from another, partly for their fafety: and this was an *Indian* cuftom, to March thin and fcatter. Capt. *Church* inquired of fome of the *Indians* that were become his Souldiers, *How they got fuch advantage often of the Englifh in their Marches ibro' the Woods?* They told him, That the *Indians* gain'd great advantage of the *Englifh* by two things; The *Indians* always took care in their Marches and Fights, not to come too thick together. But the *Englifh* always kept in a heap together, that it was as eafy to hit them as to hit an Houfe. The other was, that if at any time they difcovered a company of *Englifh* Souldiers in the Woods, they knew that there was all, for the *Englifh* never fcattered; but the *Indians* always divided and fcattered.

Capt. *Church* now at *Plymouth,* fomething or other happen'd that kept him at home a few days, until a Poft came to *Marfhfield* on the Lords day Morning,[265] informing the Governour that a great army of *Indians* were difcovered, who it was fuppofed were defigning to get over the River towards *Taunton* or *Bridgwater,* to Attack thofe Towns that lay on that fide the River.[266] The Governour haftned to *Plymouth,* raifed what Men he could by the way, came to *Plymouth* in the beginning of the forenoon Exercife;

[265] Sunday, 30 July, 1676.
[266] Philip had been in the neighborhood of Affawompfet Pond, in Middleborough, on the fouthern and eaftern fide of Taunton (*Titicut,* i.e. *Keh-teih-tuk-qut* [*Eliot,* Gen. xv: 18], "on-the-great-river") River. In order to get at Taunton and Bridgewater, which were on the northern and weftern fide, it was needful for him to crofs; and, both for eafier croffing and to avoid the "great army," he would move north to do it.

fent for Capt. *Church* out of the Meeting-houfe, gave him the News, and defired him immediately to Rally what of his Company he could; and what Men he had raifed fhould joyn them. The Captain beftirs himfelf, but found no Bread in the Store-houfe, and fo was forc'd to run from Houfe to Houfe to get Houfe-hold Bread for their March; but this nor any thing elfe prevented his Marching by the beginning of the afternoon Exercife; March-[38]ing with what Men were ready, he took with him the Poft that came from *Bridgwater* to Pilot him to the Place, where he tho't he might meet with the Enemy.[267]

[267] Mitchell [in 2 *Mafs. Hift. Coll.* vii: 157, and in his *Hift. Bridgewater*, 39] gives an extract from an old manu-fcript which he fuppofes to have been written by Comfort Willis, who was "Town Trooper" at this time, which gives fome details flightly at variance with Church's account of the matter, but which, if genuine, muft take pre-cedence in authenticity. He fays, "On Saturday [29 July], Capt. Hay-ward, Sergt. Packard, John Willis, and Ifaac Harris, went out to fee if the In-dians were coming down upon them, and they faw an Indian, which made them think the enemy was at hand; and they immediately preffed Comfort Willis and Jofeph Edfon to go poft to the Governor the fame day at night to tell him of it. And he [the Gover-nor] went to Plymouth with them the next day, [Sunday, 30 July] to fend Capt. Church with his company. And Capt. Church came with them to Mon-ponfet [Halifax] on the Sabbath, and came no further that day; and he told them he would meet them the next day. And Comfort Willis and Jofeph Edfou came home at night, and told their friends of it, and Enfign Haward, Sam-uel Edfou, Jofiah Edfou, Jofeph Edfou, John Wafhburn, Samuel Wafhburn, Thomas Wafhburn, John Field, Nicholas Byram, Samuel Allen, Samuel Allen, jr., John Gordon, John Hayward, John Packard, John Ames, Comfort Willis, Guido Bailey, Nathaniel Hayward, John Whitman, John Packard, and Samuel Leach went out on Monday, fuppofing to meet with Captain Church; but they came upon the enemy, and fought with them, and took feventeen of them alive, and alfo much plunder, and they all returned, and not one of them fell by the enemy, and received no help from Church."

I incline to accept the verfion of this MS., and I reconcile its ftatements with thofe of Church by fuppofing him, in his reminifcence of the events, forty

In the Evening they heard a fmart firing at a diftance from them, but it being near Night, and the firing but of fhort continuance, they mifs'd the place and went into *Bridg-water* Town.[268]   It feems, the occafion of the firing, was, That *Philip* finding that Capt. *Church* made that fide of the Country too hot for him, defign'd to return to the other fide of the Country that he came laft from.[269]   And coming to *Taunton* River with his company,[270] they fell'd

years after, to have dropped out one day from his reckoning, — if his language was meant to be taken, as it would naturally be, as implying that "in the evening" was the evening of the fame day on which he left Plymouth. I think that he went no further than Monponfet on the Sabbath; that on Monday he fcouted fouth-weftward toward Bridgewater, along the upper fkirt of thofe great cedar fwamps which ftill occupy fo many miles of the northern part of Middleborough, and where he would be likelieft to find Philip, but failed to fall in with him; that the "fmart firing at a diftance" which he heard, was that of Comfort Willis's party (*Increafe Mather* fays it was "about 3 *h. p. m.*"); and that "miffing the place" of that, he went into Bridgewater Town on *Monday* evening, 31 July. Hubbard and both the Mathers fix the date of the expedition of the Bridgewater men — as the old MS. does — on Monday, 31 July; while, if the apparent ftatement of Church were taken, it would fix it on Sunday, the 30th. Four to one, and that one dictating fo long afterward, muft carry

the day. [Hubbard's *Narrative*, 101; *Brief Hiftory*, 44; *Magnalia* (ed. 1853) ii : 575.]

[268] *Bridgewater Town* then was what is now known as Weft Bridgewater; the firft fettlement having been made on Town River, lefs than three miles eaft of the prefent eaftern boundary line of Eafton.

[269] That is, on the weftern fide of Titicut River, toward the Nipmuck country, north-wefterly, or toward the Narraganfett country on the fouth-weft.

[270] After long inquiry, I have failed to get any evidence, of much value, fixing the pofition of this croff-ing-place where the tree was felled. The only tradition of any fort which has come to my knowledge, with regard to it, was furnifhed me by Williams Latham, Efq., of Bridgewater, who informs me that Mr. Stillman B. Pratt, late editor of the *Middleborough Gazette*, once told him that the tree was felled near the junction of the Nemafket, with the Taunton River. This fpot is about three quarters of a mile a little eaft of fouth of the prefent Titicut Station on the Old-Colony and Fall-

a great Tree a-crofs the River for a Bridge to pafs over
on; and juft as *Philips* old Uncle *Akkompoin*,[271] and fome
other of his chiefs were paffing over the Tree, fome brisk
Bridgwater Lads, had Ambufh'd them, fired upon them,
and killed the old man, and feveral others, which put a
ftop to their coming over the River that Night.

Next Morning[272] Capt. *Church* moved very early with
his Company which was increafed by many of *Bridgwater*
that lifted under him for that Expedition, and by their
Piloting, he foon came very ftill, to the top of the great
Tree which the Enemy had fallen a-crofs the River; and
the Captain fpy'd an *Indian* fitting upon the ftump of it on
the other fide of the river; and he clap'd his Gun up, and
had doubtlefs difpatch'd him, but that one of his own
Indians called haftily to him, Not to fire, for he believed it
was one of his own men; upon which the *Indian* upon

River Railroad. I diftruft this tradition, however, and am of opinion that
Philip kept up feveral miles further on
the eaft bank of Town River, before
croffing, for thefe reafons: (1) it feems
to me, intrinfically, quite as probable
that he would do fo; (2) the ftream
would be much lefs in width, and could
be much eafier croffed upon a tree, in
the manner fuggefted; (3) the requifites
of the fubfequent narrative feem to me
to require them to be further north on
the ftream next day than they would
have been if the tree had been as low
down as Titicut; and (4) that my fuppofition would bring their "firing" up
more nearly within Church's hearing,
in his natural route from Monponfet.
I fhould be inclined, then, to place the
probable pofition of the tree much nearer to Sprague's Hill than to Titicut.

[271] *Unkompoin* [*Uncompowett*] figned
a treaty of friendfhip with the Englifh
at Plymouth, 6 Aug, 1662, with Philip,
and is there ftyled "Vnkell to the aboue-
faid fachem." With Philip, he claimed
land in Swanfey, in 1668. Mather fays
he was "one of his [Philip's] chief
Councellors." Mr. Drake fays he was
alfo called *Woonkaponehunt* and *Woh-
kowpahenitt*. [*Plym. Col. Rec.* iv:
26; v: 79; *Brief Hift.* 44; *Boob of
Ind.* 199, 203, 204.]

[272] Tuefday, 1 Aug.

the ſtump look'd about, and Capt. *Churches Indian* feeing his face perceived his miſtake, for he knew him to be *Philip;* clap'd up his Gun and fired, but it was too late, for *Philip* immediately threw himſelf off the ſtump, leap'd down a bank on the ſide of the River, and made his eſcape. Capt *Church* as foon as poſſible got over the River, and ſcattered in queſt of *Philip,* and his company; but the Enemy ſcattered and fled every way; but he pick'd up a conſiderable many of their Women and Children, among which was *Philip*'s Wife, and Son of about Nine Years Old.[273] Diſcovering a conſiderable new Track

[273] Philip's wife's name, Mr. Drake fays, was *Wootonekanuſke;* and he adds that ſhe was a fifter of one of the three wives of Quinnapin. Judge Davis gives an intereſting account of the diſcuſſion that took place in the Colony in regard to the diſpofition to be made of Philip's fon. The Court ſeem — as they often did, on queſtions concerning which they had doubt, and the more eſpecially when thoſe queſtions were of a moral nature — to have confulted the principal Reverend Elders. Samuel Arnold (paſtor of the church in Marſhfield) and John Cotton (Plymouth) write, 7 Sept., 1676, thus: "Upon ferious confideration, we humbly conceive that the children of notorious traitors, rebells and murtherers, eſpecially of fuch as have bin principal leaders and actors in fuch horrid villanies, and that againſt a whole nation, yea the whole Ifrael of God, may be involved in the guilt of their parents, and may, *falva republica,* be adjudged to death, as to us

ſeems evident by the fcripture inftances of *Saul, Achan, Haman,* the children of whom were cut off by the fword of Juſtice for the tranfgreffions of their parents, although, concerning fome of thoſe children, it be manifeft that they were not capable of being coacters therein." Increafe Mather, of Boſton, wrote to Mr. Cotton, 30 Oct., 1676: "It is neceſſary that fome effectual courfe fhould be taken about him [Philip's fon]. He makes me think of Hadad, who was a little child when his father (the chief fachem of the Edomites) was killed by Joab; and, had not others fled away with him, I am apt to think, that David would have taken a courfe, that Hadad fhould never have proved a fcourge to the next generation." Rev. James Keith, of Bridgewater, alfo wrote to Mr. Cotton, 30 Oct., 1676, but as follows: "I long to hear what becomes of Philip's wife and fon. I know there is fome difficulty in that *Pfalm,* cxxxvii: 8, 9, though I think it

along the River, and examining the Prifoners, found that it was *Qunnappin* and the *Narraganfets,* that were drawing off from thofe parts towards the *Narraganfet* Country, he inquired of the Prifoners, *Whether* Philip *were gone in the fame Track* ? they told him, *They did not know, for he fled in a great fright when the firft* Englifh *Gun was fired, and they had none of them feen or heard any thing of him fince.* Capt. *Church* left part of his Company there to fecure the Prifoners they got, and to pick up what more they could find; and with the reft of his company hafted in the Track of the Enemy to over-take them, if it might be, before they got over the River, and ran fome Miles along the River until he came unto a place where the *Indians* had waded over·[274] and he with his Company waded over after them up to the Arm-pits; being almoft as wet before with Sweat as the River could make them: Following about a Mile further, and not overtaking them, and the

---

may be confidered, whether there be not fome fpecialty and fomewhat extraordinary in it. That law, *Deut.* xxiv: 16, compared with the commended example of *Amaziah,* 2 *Chron.* xxv: 4, doth fway much with me in the cafe under confideration. I hope God will direct thofe whom it doth concern to a good iffue, &c. &c." By a letter from Mr. Cotton to Dr. Mather, 20 March, 1677, which contains this paffing remark, "Philip's boy goes now to be fold," it is made almoft certain that, with his mother, he fhared the fate of fo many of his nation, and went to fpend his fpared life in Cadiz, or the

Bermudas. [Davis's *Morton's Mem.* 454.]

[274] While bathing, when a boy, in this river, I have often waded acrofs on a bar which a local tradition affigns as the place where the Indians croffed on this occafion. It is, if I remember correctly, perhaps a mile and a quarter up ftream from the junction of the Nemafket with the Taunton, and nearly due weft of the refidence of the late Cephas Thompfon, Efq., in Middleborough. If the pofition of the tree was where I fuppofe it to have been (fee note 270, *ante*), this fuits very well the demands of the narrative.

Captain being under a neceffity [39] to return that Night to the Army, came to an halt, told his Company, *he muft return to his other men.* His *Indians* Souldiers moved for leave to purfue the Enemy (tho' he return'd;) faid, *The* Narraganfets *were great Rogues, and, ibey wanted, to be revenged on them for hilling fome of their Relations*; named, *Tokkamona*[275] (*Awafhonks* Brother) and fome others. Capt. *Church* bad them go & profper, and made *Light-foot* their chief,[276] and gave him the title of Captain, *Bid them go and quit themfelves like men.* And away they fcampered like fo many Horfes. Next Morning[277] early they returned to their Captain, and informed him, *That they had come up with the Enemy, and bill'd feveral of them, and brought him Thirteen of them Prifoners;* were mighty proud of their Exploit, and rejoyced much at the opportunity of avenging themfelves. Capt. *Church* fent the Prifoners to *Bridgwater,* and fent out his Scouts to fee what Enemies or Tracks they could, difcovering fome fmall Tracks, he follows them, found where the Enemy had kindled fome fires, and roafted fome flefh, *&c.* but had put out their fires and were gone. The Captain followed them by the Track, putting his *Indians* in the Front; fome of which were fuch as he had newly taken from the

---

[275] *Takanumma,* "a Sachem at Saconett," appeared at Plymouth Court, 3 Nov., 1671, "with Philip, cheife Sachem," and engaged fubjeftion "to the Kinges ma^{tie} of England, this gou'ment, and the lawes thereof," &c., agreeing to pay yearly one wolf's head to the Treafurer, and Philip engaged for his "performance of the faid engagement in all points thereof." [*Plym. Col. Rec.* v: 80.

[276] See note 238, *ante.*

[277] Wednefday, 2 Auguft, 1676.

Enemy, and added to his Company. Gave them order to March foftly, and upon hearing a whiftle in the Rear to fit down, till further order. Or upon difcovery of any of the Enemy to ftop, for his defign was, if he could, difcover where the Enemy were, not to fall upon them (unlefs neceffitated to do it) until next Morning. The *Indians* in the Front came up with many Women and Children, and others that were faint and tired, and fo not able to keep up with the Company; thefe gave them an account that *Philip* with a great number of the Enemy were a little before. Capt. *Churches Indians* told the others, *They were their Prifoners, but if they would. fubmit to order and be ftill no one fhould hurt them* : They being their old acquaintance, they were eafily perfwaded to conform. A little before Sun-fet there was a halt in the Front until the Captain came up, and they told him, *They difcovered the Enemy* : He order'd them, to dog them, and watch their motion till it was dark. But *Philip* foon came to a ftop, and fell to breaking and chopping Wood, to make fires : and a great noife they made. Capt. *Church* draws his company up into a ring, and fat down in the Swamp[278]

[278] I find no data in any of the accounts of this purfuit for an accurate determination of the locality of this fwamp; our only guide being general conjecture founded upon the lay of the land, the time taken, and the probabilities of the cafe. We muft affume as the point of departure fome place on *Titicut* River where it divides the prefent towns of Bridgewater and Middle-borough, probably not far from the pofition of the State Alms Houfe in the former. From this point, where the Indians waded acrofs to the Bridgewater fide, they unqueftionably fhaped their general courfe for the Narragan-fett country. But in doing fo they muft make a detour to the weft to avoid the " army " in Taunton; as following the neareft route along the weftern bank of

without any noiſe or fire: The *Indian* Priſoners were much ſurprized to fee the *Engliſh* Souldiers; but the Captain told them, *If they would be quiet and not mabe any diſturbance or noiſe, they ſhould meet with civil treatment, but if they made any diſturbance, or offered to run, or make their eſcape, he would immediately bill them all;* ſo they were very ſubmiſſive & obſequious. When the day broke,[279] Capt. *Church* told his Priſoners, *That his Expedition was ſuch at this time that he could not afford them any guard.:* Told them, *They would find it to be their intereſt to attend the orders he was now about to give them; which was, That when the fight was over, which they now expeſted; or as*

the river would bring them directly upon that town. A glance at the configuration of the country will make it moſt probable, then, that they paſſed between *Nunkateſt* (*Nippenicket*) and *Guſhee* ponds, over into the north part of what is now Raynham, and thence into the north part of what is now Taunton, between *Winniconnet* and Watſon's ponds, and ſo fouth-weſt, about as the diviſion line between Taunton and Norton runs, toward Rehoboth. I aſſume that from 15 to 18 miles through thoſe rough wood-paths and ſwamps would be as much as ſuch a mixed company, many of whom were "faint and tired," could accompliſh in a day. This, by the route which I have indicated, would bring them near to three cedar ſwamps; one now called Crooked-Meadow Swamp, through which the town line between Taunton and Norton runs; one called Seekonk Swamp,

in the ſouthern angle of Norton; and a ſmaller one, three-quarters of a mile into Rehoboth, and ſome two miles north of *Squannakonk* Swamp, where *Annawon* was afterwards taken. It is my impreſſion that the latter beſt meets all the conditions of the cafe. Philip feems to have camped on an upland on the edge of or within the ſwamp, as was their cuſtom. Mr. Drake, in his edition of Church, places the ſwamp which ſheltered them in Mattapoiſett neck in Swanſey. But that muſt have involved a return march on the part of Church and his priſoners of 25 to 30 miles back to Bridgewater, which waſ more than they could well accompliſh before "that night"; beſides that from Swanſey Church's natural route would have led through Taunton, where he would moſt likely have delivered his priſoners, as on a ſubſequent occaſion.

[279] Thurſday, 3 Auguſt, 1676.

*ſoon as the firing ceaſed, ihey muſt ʔfollow the Tracks of his
Company and come to them.* (An [40] *Indian* is next to
a blood-hound to follow a Track.) He ſaid to them, *It
would be in vain for them to think of diſobedience, or to
gain any thing hy it, for he had tahen and. hilled. a ʒreat
many of the* Indian *Rebels, and. ſhould in a little time hill.
and tahe all the reſt,* &c. By this time it began to be ſo
light, as the time that he uſually choſe to make his on-
ſet. He moved ſending two Souldiers before to try if
they could privately diſcover the Enemies poſtures. But
very unhappily it fell out, that the very ſame time
Philip had ſent two of his as a Scout upon his own
Track, to ſee if none dog'd them; who ſpy'd the two
Indian men, and turn'd ſhort about, and fled with all
ſpeed to their Camp: and Capt. *Church* purſued as faſt
as he could; the two *Indians* ſet a yelling and howling,
and made the moſt hideous noiſe they could invent, ſoon
gave the Alarm to *Philip* & his Camp; who all fled at the
firſt tydings, left their Kittles boiling & Meat roaſting
upon their wooden Spits, & run into a Swamp with no
other Break-faſt, than what Capt. *Church* afterwards treated
them with. Capt. *Church* purſuing, ſent Mr. *Iſaac Howland*[280] with a party on one ſide of the Swamp, while him-

[280] *Iſaac Howland* was youngeſt ſon
of John, and brother of Jabez (ſee note
207, *ante*); was one of the firſt ſettlers of
Middleborough; married Eliza, daughter of George Vaughan; was ſurveyor
of highways at M., in 1672; ſelectman
-at M., in 1674, 1684, 1685, 1686; admitted freeman in 1681; was a member
of the " grand enqueſt," in 1682; ſerved
on a trial jury, in 1683; was licenſed to
keep an ordinary at M., in 1684; was
deputy for M., in 1689, 1690, 1691; re-

felf with the reft ran on the other-fide, agreeing to run on
each fide, until they met on the further end: placing fome
men in fecure Stands at that end of the Swamp where
Philip entered, concluding that if they headed him and
beat him back, that he would take back in his own Track.
Capt. *Church* and Mr. *Howland.* foon met at the further
end of the Swamp (it not being a great one) where they
met with a great number of the Enemy, well armed, coming out of the Swamp. But on fight of the *Englifh* they
feemed very much furprized, & tack'd fhort. Capt.
Church called haftily to them, and faid, *If they fired. one
Gun they were all dead. men; for he would have them
know that he had them hem'd in, with a force fufficient to
command. them; but if they peaceably furrender'd they
fhould have good. quarter,*[281] &c. They feeing both *Indians*
and *Englifh* come fo thick upon them, were fo furprized
that many of them ftood ftill and let the *Englifh* come and

ceived £7 of Thomas Joflen, of Little
Compton, for "a yoak of oxen, unjuftly
detained." [Savage's *Gen. Dict.* ii:
479; *Plym. Col. Rec.* v: 93, 145; vi:
62, 86, 129, 131, 168, 186, 198, 206, 212,
222, 240, 246, 263, 268.]

281 Hubbard fays, "In this engagement God did appear in a more then
ordinary manner to fight for the Englifh, for the Indians by their number,
and other advantages of the place, were
fo conveniently provided, that they
might have made the firft fhot at the
Englifh, and done them much damage;
but one of their own Country-men in

Capt. *Churches Company,* efpying them,
called aloud unto them in their own Language, telling them, *that if they fhot a
Gun, they were all dead men;* with
which they were fo amazed, that they
durft not once offer to fire at the Englifh, which made the victory the more
remarkable." [*Narrative,* 102.] Mather [*Brief Hiftory,* 44] adds that the
Indian's name was *Matthias.* As Church
could not himfelf fpeak Indian, this is
probably the correct verfion of what
took place; or perhaps he fpoke in Englifh, and his Indian foldiers repeated
his words in their tongue.

take the Guns out of their hands, when they were both charged and cock'd. Many both Men, Women and Children of the Enemy were imprifoned at this time; while *Philip, Tifpaquin, Totofon,*[282] &c. concluded that the *English* would purfue them upon their Tracks, fo were way-laying their Tracks at the firft end of the Swamp, hoping thereby to gain a fhot upon Capt. *Church* who was now better imploy'd in taking his Prifoners & running them into a Valley, in form fomething fhap'd like a Punch-bole, and appointing a guard of two files trible armed with Guns taken from the Enemy. But *Philip* having waited all this while in vain, now moves on after the reft of his company to fee what was become of them. And by this time Capt. *Church* was got into the Swamp ready to meet him; and as it happen'd made the firft difcovery, clapt behind a Tree until *Philips* company came pretty near, and then fired upon them, kill'd many of them, and a clofe skirmifh followed. Upon this *Philip* having grounds fufficient to fufpe&t the event of his com[41]pany that

[282] *Tatofon* (*Totofon, Tautozen*) is faid to have been the fon of *Sam Barrow*, whofe death is mentioned further on. There is a tradition that his camp was upon what — it is thought by corruption from his name — is now called *Towfer's* neck, an upland penin-fula proje&ting into Great-Bear Swamp, about a mile and a half fouth-weft of the village of Rochefter, Mafs., and a fhort diftance eaft of the road to Matta-poifett. *Tatofon* was witnefs to a deed of lands upon *Weequancett* neck in 1666; with others "engaged his Fidelitie" to the Colony at Plymouth, 6 July, 1671; led the party that murdered Clark's Garrifon, 12 March, 1676 (fee note 156, *ante*), whereupon "four coates" were offered to *Capt. Amos* as a reward if he would "bring him in"; and feems to have died miferably, foon after Philip's death, as will appear further on. [Drake's *Boob of the Ind.* 244; *Plym. Col. Rec.* v : 72, 205, 206, 209.]

went before them, fled back upon his own Track; and coming to the place where the Ambufh lay, they fired on each other, and one *Lucus* of *Plymouth*,[283] not being fo

[283] *Thomas Lucas* (*Lucafe*) has a fingularly and perfiftently bad record. He firft appears before the Court, 3 Feb., 1656, when he had a controverfy with the widow Dotey, and was caft in 3s.; 2 Oct., 1658, he was fined 10s. for a fecond conviction of drunkennefs, and 5s. for retailing ftrong liquors; 6 Oct., 1659, he was fined 10s. for being drunk; 7 Mar., 1659–60, he was fined 30s. for abufive conduct toward James Cole, sen.'s wife and James Cole, jr.'s child; 2 Oct., 1660, he was fined 10s. for being drunk twice; 5 Mar., 1660–1, he was bound in £20 to find fureties for good behavior, but prefenting himfelf in Court, "diftempered with drinke," and with "vnbefeeming behauiour" he was committed to prifon and fined 40s.; 7 May, following, he was found drunk, and broke his bonds, and his cafe was referred to the next Court, which "upon fome confiderations" remitted £10 of his forfeiture; 3 Mar., 1662–3 he was fentenced to be "whipt" for drunkennefs, but the fentence was fufpended if he did not offend again; 1 Mar., 1663–4, he got his whipping, and was alfo bound over in £20, for abufing his wife and reviling others; 8 June, 1664, he was put in the ftocks for fwearing; 9 June, 1665, was imprifoned 24 hours for the fame offence; 3 Oct., 1665, he was fined 10s. for being drunk; 2 Mar., 1668–9, his wife teftified that he had not abufed her fince he was bound over;

and he, promifing amendment, was releafed of that prefentment; 7 June, 1670, he was fined 3s. 4d. for breaking the king's peace; 3 June, 1673, he was arrefted for being drunk, but "releafed with admonition"; 1 June, 1675, "for being diftempered with drinke, it being foe often, and that hee hath borne feuerall p'ticular punifhments gradually, and can not be reclaimed, it was ordered concerning him that all that fell drinke be ftrictly ordered and prohibited to let him haue none"; 30 Oct., 1675, for being drunk, and for reviling fome deceafed magiftrates, he was "whipt att the poft." The only countervailing records concerning him — fo far as they are fuch — which I have found, are that, 5 Mar., 1651-2, he gained £3 12s. in a jury trial from Richard Hawes; 15 July, 1660, he affixed his mark to the verdict of a coroner's inqueft on the death of James Peirfe; and that, 29 Oct., 1669, a jury gave him cofts when fued by Jofeph Bartlett, for 258 lbs. of "beife delivered att his houfe." He was clearly a miferable, drunken, profane, quarrelfome fellow, and his life — as Church intimates by careleffnefs (he could hardly have been drunk fo early in the morning) — found fit ending. He had five children, viz: John, born 15 July, 1656; Mary, born 15 Mar., 1658; Benoni, born 30 Oct., 1659; Samuel, born 15 Sept., 1661; and William, born 13 Jan., 1662.

careful as he might have been about his Stand, was kill'd by the *Indians*. In this Swamp skirmifh Capt. *Church* with his two men which always ran by his fide as his guard, met with three of the Enemy, two of which furrendred themfelves, and the Captains guard feized them, but the other being a great ftout furly fellow, with his two locks ty'd up with red and a great Rattle-fnake skin hanging to the back part of his head, (whom Capt. *Church* concluded to be *Totafon*) ran from them into the Swamp Capt. *Church* in perfon purfued him clofe, till coming pretty near up with him, prefented his Gun between his Shoulders, but it miffing fire, the *Indian* perceiving it, turn'd and prefented at Capt. *Church*, and miffing fire alfo; their Guns taking wet with the Fog and Dew of the Morning; but the *Indian* turning fhort for another run, his foot trip'd in a fmall grape-vine, and he fell flat on his face; Capt. *Church* was by this time up with him, and ftruck the Muzzle of his Gun an inch and half into the back part of his head, which difpatch'd him without another blow. But Capt. *Church* looking behind him faw *Totofon* the *Indian* whom he tho't he had kill'd, come flying at him like a dragon: But this happened to be fair in fight of the guard that were fet to keep the Prifoners, who fpying *Totafon*, and others that were following of him, in the very feafonable junâ‹ture made a fhot upon them, and refcued their Captain; tho' he was in no fmall

[*Plym. Col. Rec.* iii: 110, 150, 173, 181,   51, 55, 66, 101, 106; v: 16, 39, 118, 169, 196, 200, 206, 207, 212, 220, 223; iv: 33,   182; vii: 57, 157; viii: 23.]

danger from his friends bullets, for fome of them came fo near him that he tho't he felt the wind of them. The skirmifh being over, they gathered their Prifoners to_gether, and found the number that they had killed and taken was 173 [284] (the Prifoners which they took over Night included) who after the skirmifh came to them, as they were ordered.

Now having no Provifions, but what they took from the Enemy, they haftened to *Bridgwater,* fending an exprefs before to provide for them, their Company being now very numerous. The Gentlemen of *Bridgwater* met Capt. *Church* with great expreffion of honour and thanks, and received him and his Army with all due refpect and kind treatment.

Capt. *Church* drove his Prifoners that Night into *Bridgwater* Pound,[285] and fet his *Indian* Souldiers to guard them. They being well treated with Victuals and drink, they had a merry Night; and the Prifoners laugh'd as loud as the Souldiers, not being fo treated a long time before.

Some of the *Indians* now faid to Capt. *Church, Sir, You have now made* Philip *ready to dye, for you have made him*

[284] Hubbard fays Church had in his own force but "30 Englifhmen and 20 reconciled Indians," and that he took and killed "about" 153 of the enemy. [*Narrative,* 102.] Increafe Mather fays the fame [*Brief Hiftory,* 44], and fo does his fon, Cotton. [*Magnalia,* ed. 1853, ii: 575.] But, in this, Church's memory, and notes, are the beft authority; the more efpecially as the fact that his pay, and that of his company, depended on the number, would fix it in his mind.

[285] The pound was fituated on the north bank of the Town River, in what is now Weft Bridgewater, within five rods of the river, and ten rods below the old town bridge; oppofite to the fite formerly occupied by the office of William Baylies, Efq.

as ipoor, and miferable as he us'd to mahe the Englifh; *for you have now killed. or taben all his Relations. That they believed. he would now foon have his head, and. that this bout bad. almoft broke his heart.*

The next day Capt. *Church* moved and arrived with all his Prifoners fafe at *Plymouth.*[286] The great *Englifh* army were now at *Taunton*, and Maj. *Talcot*[287] [42] with the *Connecticut* Forces being in thefe parts of the Country, did confiderable fpoil upon the Enemy.[288]

Now Capt. *Church* being arrived at *Plymouth,* received thanks from the Government for his good Service, &c. many of his Souldiers were difbanded; and he tho't to reft himfelf awhile, being much fategued and his health impared, by exceffive heats and colds, and wading thro' Rivers, &c. But it was not long[289] before he was call'd

---

[286] Friday, 4 Auguft, 1676.

[287] *John Talcott (Tailecoat, Taylcoat)* was fon of John (who came in the " Lion," to Cambridge, in 1632, and removed with Hooker to Hartford); was born in England; after ferving in various offices was made chief military officer of Hartford Co., 26 June, 1672; was made Major, 7 Aug., 1673, and, 26 Nov., 1673, Commander-in-chief of all forces then raifing againft New York; 15 May, 1676, he was fimilarly appointed over the troops raifed for Philip's war, and was very active and fuccefsful in his command. He died, 23 July, 1688. He had 14 children, by Helena Wakeman and Mary Cook. [Savage's *Gen. Dict.* iv : 250; *Colonial Records of*

Connecticut, ii : 183, 206, 218, 279, 443, 444, 447-55, 458-65.]

[288] Maj. Talcott, with the Connecticut forces, after having killed and taken many of the Indians in the Narraganfett country, returned to Connecticut about 5 July. Having recruited his men a fhort time, he took his ftation at Weftfield, where he fell with great fuccefs upon Indians fleeing weftward. [Trumbull's *Hift. Conn.* i : 348.]

[289] Church's language here, and a little further on, is mifleading; as it would feem to imply a much greater lapfe of time than really took place. He returned to Plymouth from his laft Bridgewater expedition, as we have feen, on Friday, 4 Aug., 1676. As

upon to Rally, upon advice that fome of the Enemy were difcovered in *Dartmouth* woods. He took his *Indians,* and as many *Englifh* Volunteers as prefented, to go with him, and fcattering into fmall parcels. Mr. *Jabez Howland.* (who was now, and often his Lieutenant and a worthy good Souldiers)²⁹⁰ had the fortune to difcover and imprifon a parcel of the Enemy. In the Evening they met together at an appointed place, and by examining the Prifoners, they gain'd intelligence of *Totofons* haunt; ²⁹¹ and being brisk in the Morning, they foon gain'd an advantage of *Totofons* company, tho' he himfelf with his Son of about Eight Years old made their efcape, and one old Squaw with them, to *Agawom* ²⁹² his own Country. But *Sam Barrow,*²⁹³ as noted a Rogue as any among the Enemy, fell into the hands of the *Englifh,* at this time. Capt. *Church* told him, *That becaufe of his inhumane Murders and Barharities, the Court had allow'd him no quarter, but was to be forthwith put to Death, and therefore he was to prepare for it.* *Barrow* reply'd, *That the Sentence of*

Philip was killed one week from the next day, and as Church muft have been at leaft one day on the route to Pocaffet and Rhode-Ifland, only four week-days are left after the Sabbath following his return from Bridgewater, for the expedition toward Dartmouth woods. It would feem, then, that Church only laid ftill over Saturday and Sunday, — which, literally, was " not long, " — and " rallied " for Dartmouth on Monday, 7 Aug.

²⁹⁰ See note 207, *ante.*

²⁹¹ See note 282, *ante.* If this refers to *Towfer's* neck in Rochefter, the party probably did not crofs the Acufhnet River at this time.

²⁹² See note 209, *ante.*

²⁹³ *Sam. Barrow* is ftated to have been *Tatofon's* father (fee note 282, *ante*). I find nothing elfe concerning him, except that he appears to figure upon the Colony Records in the lift of the party deftroying Clark's Garrifon, under the name of *Sanballett.* [*Plym. Col. Rec.* v: 206.]

Death againſt him was juſt, and. that indeed. he was aſhamed to live any longer, and deſired no more favour. than to Smoke a Whiff of Tobacco before his Execution. When he had taken a few Whiffs, he ſaid, *He was ready;* upon which one of Capt. *Churches Indians* funk his Hatchet into his Brains. The famous *Totoſon* arriving at *Agawom,* his Son which was the laſt which was left of his Family (Capt. *Church* having deſtroyed all the reſt) fell ſick: The wretch reflecting upon the miſerable condition he had bro't himſelf into, his heart became as a ſtone within him, and he dy'd.[294] The old Squaw flung a few leaves and bruſh over him, and came into *Sandwich,* and gave this account of his death, and offered to ſhew them where ſhe left his body; but never had the opportunity, for ſhe immediately fell ſick and dy'd alſo.

Capt. *Church* being now at *Pl1 mouth* again weary and worn, would have gone home to his Wife and Family, but the Government being Solicitous to ingage him in the Service until *Philip* was ſlain, and promiſing him ſatisfaction and redreſs for ſome miſtreatment that he had met with: He fixes for another Expedition; he had ſoon Volunteers enough to make up the Company he deſired and Marched thro' the Woods, until he came to *Pocaſſet.*[295]

[294] It is preſumable that this ſon of eight years, who thus fell ſick, died before his father; as the ſquaw apparently made no further mention of him.

[295] He muſt have left Plymouth by Thurſday night, 10 Aug., or very early on Friday morning, at the lateſt, thus to have ·reached Pocaſſet in time to croſs the ferry, and ride 8 miles down the iſland, while it was yet light enough on the afternoon of Friday, the 11th, to "ſpy" horſemen coming "at a great pace," at a diſtance.

And not feeing nor hearing of any of the Enemy, they went over the Ferry to *Rhode-Ifland*, to refrefh them- felves. The Captain with about half a dozen in his com- pany took Horfe & rid about eight Miles down the *Ifland*, to Mr. *Sanfords* [296] where he had left his Wife; who no

---

[296] See note 245, *ante*. Since that was in type, I have gained fome ad- ditional facts, which may be fet down here.

Maj. Sanford lived about half a mile fouth of (the prefent) Portfmouth line, in what is now Middletown (then New- port); which made his farm about "eight miles down the Ifland" from Tripp's Ferry. [*MS. letter* of Mr. Richard Sherman.]

In 1682, he rendered an account, amounting to £103 9s. 9d., to Plym- outh-Colony Court, for fervices ren- dered the wounded men of the army, after the great Narraganfett Swamp fight. (See p. 60, &c., *ante*.) Some items of that account are of intereft enough to warrant its infertion here, as cafting light upon that portion of the war. [I copy from *Plym. Col. Rec.* vi· 118-120, fupplying conjecturally fome miffing words, and condenfing fome items.]

"Peleg Sanford, Efq. his Account, appointed to be recorded, at June Court, 1682.

"Rhode-Ifland, anno 1675. Gen. Jo- fiah Winflow's Debitʳ.

	£	s.	d.
"To treatment of 28 wound- ed men fr. — Dec. vntell yᵉ 25ᵗʰ day	4	04	0

	£		
"To Almy for 244 lbs. of mutton	3	01	c
"To Almy, 10 yds. duffles for wounded	3	00	c
"To Almy, 2½ cord of wood for do	1	00	0
"To firkin of butter — 66 lbs. at 6d pr. lb. (firkin 18d)	1	14	6
"To 451½ lbs. mutton deliv- ered at the houfe of Mr. Brinton & Robᵗ. Carr for tenders of wounded men	5	12	9
"To 12 lb. candles & 10 lb. butter, to do houfes,	0	12	10
"To 6 bufhels Ind. Corn, to do,	1	04	0
"To 2 gall. mallaffas to do,	0	05	0
"To 102 lb. falt beefe & 7 lb. porke to do	1	07	6
"To 16½ cords wood, at 8s, & 4 load of wood	7	16	0
"To 3 qts rum to Lowell	0	03	9
"To 15 lbs. flax, with 6 lb. fent to the garifon	0	15	0
"To Capt. Green, for bear for the wounded	0	02	6
"To cafh for buriall of Link- horn, Harrifs, Sumerf- bury, and one more	1	10	0
"To 74 lb. fugar among wounded	1	17	c

fooner faw him but [43] fainted with the furprize; and by that time fhe was a little revived, they fpy'd two Horfe-men coming a great pace. Capt. *Church* told his company that thofe men (by their riding) came with Tydings. When they came up they prov'd to be Maj. *Sanford.* and Capt. *Golding;*[297] who immediately ask'd Capt. *Church, What he would. give to hear fome News of* Philip? He reply'd, *That was what he wanted.* They told him, *They*

	£	s.	d.
" To 28⅔ gall. rum to Doctor for wounded	7	03	1½
" To 2 fat fheep to Doct. Hawkins for wounded that went in y⁰ veffell with him	0	18	0
" To 8 yds duffles to Serg⁴. Witherly, Jams Bell & other Tanton men, y⁴ came wounded to my houfe Dec. 24	2	08	0
" To cafh to J. Bell to bear his charges home	0	04	0
" To Serg⁴. Witherell, Jams Bell & White for diatt, lodg'g & attendance, 2 one month & 1 three weeks, at 8s. per week .	4	08	0
" To Left. Sauage, Doct. Cuttler, & their men &c. &c.	15	03	0
" To Doct. Hawkins diet &c about a month. . .	1	12	0
" To Lieut. Vpham, fr. 24 Dec. to 14 March, & his kinfman for diet &c. at 8s each, his fifter alfo a confiderable p⁴ of y⁰ time . .	9	02	0

	£		d.
" To do. Vpham 1½ gall. rum, & 15 lb. mutton when he went away . .	0	11	3
" To eftate Wᵐ Brenton for hire of room fr. 24 Dec. to 17 Oct. 1676, y⁰ day that Serjañ Witherell went out of it, at £5 pr year.	4	01	7½
" To do. Witherly for fundryes, as p. his acct . .	3	12	11
" To damage fuftained in my beding and other houfehold ftuffe, with things péloined by incomers, which here charge £20, att prefent, for thought the damage be far more	20	00	0
	£103	9	9

" Dated in New Port, on Rhode Ifland, y⁰ 26ᵗʰ day Jan. 167⅚."

[There were credits given, amounting to £22 9s. 0d. The balance of the fhare of Plymouth in the account was then paid.]

[297] See note 93, *ante.*

*had. rid hard. with 'fome hopes of overtaking of him, and
were now come on purpofe to inform him, That there was
juft now Tydings'from* Mount-hope; *An* Indian *came down
'from thence (where* Philips *Camp now was) on to* Sand-
point[298] *over. againft* Trips,[299] *and hollow'd, and. made figns
to be fetch'd over; and being fetch'd over, he reported, That
he was fled'from* Philip, *who* (faid he) *has hill'd my Brother
juft before I came away, for ;giving 'fome advice that difpleafed him.*[300] And faid, *he was fled for 'fear. of meeting
with the fame his Brother had. met with.* Told them alfo,
That Philip *was now in* Mount-hope *Neck.* Capt. *Church*
thank'd them for their good News, and faid, he hop'd by
to Morrow Morning to have the Rogues head. The
Horfes that he and his company came on ftanding at the
door, (for they had not been unfaddled) his Wife muft
content her felf with a fhort vifit, when fuch game was
a-head; they immediately Mounted, fet Spurs to their
Horfes, and away. The two Gentlemen that bro't him
the Tydings, told him, *They would;gladly wait upon him to*

---

[298] *Sandy Point* is on the Briftol fide of Briftol Ferry, near where the light-houfe now ftands. [*MS. letter* of Mr. Richard Sherman.]

[299] *Tripp's* was the name then, or foon after (long before Church dictated, at leaft), current for Briftol Ferry, which was run by Abial Tripp, who lived on the Portfmouth fide, and who, with John Burden, received the formal right to the "ferry privilege" for feven years, 2 Aug., 1698, which was renewed, 19 June, 1705, "as formerly," for feven

years. [*R.-I. Col. Rec.* iii: 535; *MS. letter* of Mr. Richard Sherman.]

[300] "He caufed one of his Confederates to be killed for propounding an expedient of peace." [Hubbard's *Narrative*, 103.] Increafe Mather fays, "One of *Philip's* men (being difgufted with him for killing an *Indian* who had propounded an expedient for peace with the *Englifh*) ran away from him, and coming to Road-Ifland, informed that Philip was now returned again to *Mount-Hope*, &c." [*Brief Hiftory*, 46.]

fee the event of this Expedition. He thank'd them, and told them, he fhould be as fond of their company as any Mens; and (in fhort) they went with him. And they were foon as *Trips* Ferry (with Capt *Churches* company) where the deferter was; who was a fellow of good fenfe, and told his ftory handfomely: he offered Capt. *Church* to Pilot him to *Philip*, and to help to kill him, that he might revenge his Brothers death. Told him, That *Philip* was now upon a little fpot of Upland that was in the South end of the miery Swamp juft at the foot of the Mount,[301] which was a fpot of ground that Capt. *Church* was well acquainted with. By that time[302] they were got over the Ferry, and came near the ground half the Night was fpent, the Capt. commands a halt, and bringing the company together, he asked Maj *Sanford.* & Capt. *Goldings* advice, what method was beft to take in making the onfet, but they declining giving any advice, telling him, *That his great Experience & Succefs forbid. their taking upon them to give advice.* Then Capt. *Church* offered Capt. *Golding*, that he fhould have the honour (if he would pleafe accept of it) to beat up *Philips* headquarters. He accepted the offer and had his alotted number drawn out to him, and the Pilot. Capt. *Churches* inftructions to him were to be very careful in his approach to the Enemy, and be fure not to fhew himfelf until by day light they

---

[301] "Philip was furprifed and killed by Col. Church at a little knoll on the fouth-weft fide, at the foot of Mount Hope." [Feffenden's *Warren, R.-I.,* 40.]

[302] The diftance of the fwamp in which Philip was concealed was not much more than two miles from the landing of the ferry on the Briftol fide.

might fee and difcern their own men from the Enemy.
Told him alfo, That his cuftom in the like cafes was to
creep with his company on their bellies, until they came
as near as they could; and that as foon as the Enemy difcovered them they would cry out; and that was the word
[44] for his Men to fire and fall on. Directed him when
the Enemy fhould ftart and take into the Swamp,[303] they
fhould purfue with fpeed, every man fhouting and making
what noife they could; for he would give orders to his
Ambufcade to fire on any that fhould come filently. Capt.
Church knowing it was *Philips* cuftom to be fore-moft in
the flight, went down to the Swamp and gave Capt. *Williams* of *Situate*[304] the command of the right wing of the
Ambufh, and placed an *Englifh-man* and an *Indian* together behind fuch fhelters of Trees, *&c.* that he could
find, and took care to place them at fuch diftance as none
might pafs undifcovered between them, charg'd 'em to be
careful of themfelves, and of hurting their friends: And to
fire at any that fhould come filently thro' the Swamp:
But it being fome-what further thro' the Swamp than he

---

[303] Philip was on an upland ifland in
the midft of the fwamp; of courfe when
alarmed he would run into the fwamp
in the endeavor to efcape through it, —
their habitual courfe on fuch occafions.

[304] *John Williams* (oldeft child of
John, of Scituate) bore arms in 1643,
and was a houfeholder in 1647; was
Captain in Philip's war; was Deputy
from Scituate, in 1676, 1681, and 1691;
was fined 40s. 1 July, 1672, for "doing

feruill worke" on the Sabbath; had
various controverfies and lawfuits, and
died 22 June, 1694, aged 70, leaving
one of the largeft eftates at that time
exifting in the country; his farm having
been faid to be the beft in the Old Colony. He appears never to have married. [Deane's *Scituate*, 385; Savage's *Gen. Dict.* iv: 562; *Plym. Col.
Rec.* v: 99, 214; vi: 24, 61, 173, 174,
198, 202, 259.]

was aware of, he wanted men to make up his Ambuſcade; having placed what men he had, he took Maj. *Sanford.* by the hand, ſaid, *Sir, I have ſo placed them that 'tis ſcarce poſſible* Philip *ſhould eſcape them.* The ſame moment a Shot whiſtled over their heads, and then the noiſe of a Gun towards *Philips* camp. Capt. *Church* at firſt tho't it might be ſome Gun fired by accident: but before he could ſpeak, a whole Volley followed, which was earlier than he expected. One of *Philips* gang going forth to eaſe himſelf, when he had done, look'd round him, & Capt. *Golding* thought the *Indian* looked right at him (tho' probably 'twas but his conceit) ſo fired at him, and upon his firing, the whole company that were with him fired upon the Enemies ſhelter, before the *Indians* had time to riſe from their ſleep, and ſo over-ſhot them. But their ſhelter was open on that ſide next the Swamp, built ſo on purpoſe for the convenience of flight on occaſion.[305] They were ſoon in the Swamp and *Philip* the foremoſt, who ſtarting at the firſt Gun threw his Petunk[306] and Powder-horn over his

[305] A kind of *ſhed* wigwam, in the New-England ſenſe of that adjective, with the open ſide toward the ſwamp.

[306] *Petunk,* literally, "that into which ſomething is put," i. e., the pouch, or haverſack, which the Indian always carried by way of pocket. Eliot uſes the word (in 1 *Sam.* xvii: 40,) for David's "ſcrip"; and for "purſe" (in *Lube* xxii: 35), and uniformly tranſlates "quiver" by *petan,* a word of nearly the ſame ſignification. Roger Williams [Key *R.-I. Hiſt. Coll.* i: 33]

ſays (under the head of *Nôkehick,* i. e., "parched meal"), "I have travelled with neere 200 of them at once, neere 100 miles through the woods, every man carrying a *little Baſket* of this at his *back,* and ſometimes in a hollow *Leather Girdle* about his middle, ſufficient for a man for three or four daies. With this readie proviſion, and their *Bow* and *Arrowes* [this was printed in 1643, before the Indians had acquired the uſe of fire-arms], are they ready for *War,* and *travell* at an *houres* warning.

head, catch'd up his Gun, and ran as faft as he could fcamper, without any more clothes than his fmall breeches and ftockings, and ran directly upon two of Capt. *Churches* Ambufh; they let him come fair within fhot, and the *Englifh* mans[307] Gun miffing fire,[308] he bid the *Indian*[309] fire away, and he did fo to purpofe, fent one Musket

With a *fpoonfull* of this *meale* and a *fpoonfull* of water from the *Brooke*, have I made many a good dinner and fupper." [Compare Schoolcraft's *Information refpect. Ind. Tribes*, i : 80.]

[307] Baylies [*Hift. Mem. New Plym.* iii : 168] fays that this Englifhman's name was Francis Cook. But the Mafs. Hiftorical Collections [2d *Series* iv : 63] for 1816, (14 years before Efq. Baylies publifhed), contain a note from John Lothrop, affirming that the name of this foldier of Church was *Caleb* Cook. The latter Chriftian name is fupported by the fact, that the Colony Records fhow the exiftence, in 1676, of a Caleb Cook, then aged 25; while Francis, who came in the Mayflower, had been dead 13 years; his grandfon Francis, born 5 Jan., 1663, died at lefs than two years of age; and no other Francis appears.

Caleb Cook was oldeft fon of Jacob (youngeft fon of *Mayflower* Francis) and Damaris, daughter of Stephen Hopkins, and was born 29 Mar., 1651; he ferved on a coroner's jury at Plymouth, 20 Oct., 1675, in the cafe of John Fallowell; is down for a fine of £1 10s., 12 June, 1685; and ferved on a trial jury in the July Court of 1686. He had a great grandfon, Silvanus, of Kingfton, Mafs., who held in his pof-

feffion the gun with which the Indian fhot King Philip (which, according to family tradition, Cook exchanged with him for his own), and who gave the lock to one of the Lothrops, from whom John Lothrop gave it to the Cabinet of the Mafs. Hiftorical Society, where it ftill is. Many years after, the barrel was prefented by John Cook, of Kingfton, to the Cabinet of the Pilgrim Society in Plymouth, in which cuftody it remains. [Savage's *Gen. Dict.* i : 446; *Plym. Col. Rec.* v : 182; vi : 196; viii : 165; Ruffell's *Pilgrim Mem.* 105.]

[308] Hubbard adds that " the morning being wet and rainy," — which Church's fubfequent ftatement about the fun and the dew does not confirm, — " the Englifh man's gun would not fire, the Indian having an old Musket with a large touch-hole, it took fire the more readily." [*Narrative*, 105.]

[309] Church's teftimony is conclufive as to the identity of this Indian with that one known as *Alderman* among the colonifts; and both Hubbard and Mather affert the fame. I doubt, however, the truth of the common averment that *Alderman* was the Indian whofe brother Philip had killed, and who guided Church's party to the fwamp. Neither Church, Hubbard, nor Mather fay that, — however, on a cafual reading,

Bullet thro' his heart, and another not above two inches from it; he fell upon his face in the Mud & Water with his Gun under him. By this time the Enemy perceived they were way laid on the eaſt ſide of the *Swamp,* tack'd ſhort about. One of the Enemy who ſeem'd to be a great ſurly old fellow, hollow'd with a loud voice, & often called out, *iootaſh, iootaſh,*[310] Capt. *Church* called to his *Indian*

the latter two might appear to ſay it. A careful examination of their words ſhows that they only aſſert that Philip was ſlain by one of his own race, who had kept himſelf neutral until now; and ſpeak of his killer as *an* Indian, rather than *the* Indian, to whom they had before referred. It ſeems to me more natural if *Alderman* had been his informant and guide, that Church ſhould have mentioned the remarkable faɛt diſtinɛtly, when deſcribing his agency in the death of the chieftain. Hutchinſon appears to be reſponſible for the firſt ſtatement abſolutely identifying the pilot with the ſlayer; ſaying [*Hiſt. Maſs.* i: 277], "One of his own men, whom he had offended, and who had deſerted to the Engliſh, ſhot him through the heart," which he might eaſily baſe, by a miſapprehenſion, upon Hubbard and Mather. Trumbull [*Hiſt. Conn.* i: 349] repeats (probably from Hutchinſon) the ſtatement: "The Indian who had been guide to the party, ſhot him through the heart." Drake, Thatcher, Fowler, Arnold, and others have followed Trumbull. Jones's letter to Gov. Leet, publiſhed by Mr. Trumbull [*Col. Rec. Conn.* ii: 470], is probably the freſheſt document bearing on the

queſtion; and his language naturally implies a diſtinɛtion in his mind between the guide and the killer.

Hubbard [*Narrative,* 106] ſays *Alderman* was "of Sakonet." But Mather [*Brief Hiſt.* 47] with more particularity adds, "the *Indian* who thus killed *Philip,* did formerly belong to the Squaw-Sachim of *Pocaſſet* (*Weetamoe*), being known by the name of *Alderman.* In the beginning of the war, he came to the Governor of *Plymouth,* manifeſting his deſire to be at peace with the *Engliſh,* and immediately withdrew to an Iſland, not having engaged againſt the *Engliſh* nor for them, before this time." I find no confirmation of this ſtatement on the Court Records.

[310] *Iootaſh* is a verb in the imperative, 2d perſon, ſingular, and means "Fight!" Eliot would have written *Ayeuteaſh.* He has *Ayeuteak,* for the plural "fight ye," (in 1 *Sam.* iv: 9.) Roger Williams ſpells this laſt [*Key,* chap. xxix] "*Júhetteke,* Fight, which is their word of incouragement which they uſe when they animate each other in warre; for they uſe their tongues in ſtead of drummes and trumpets." [*R.-I. Hiſt. Coll.* i: 148.]

Peter [311] and ask'd him, *Who that was ihat called. fo?* He
anfwered, It was old *Annowon Philips* great Captain,[312] calling on his Souldiers to ftand to it and fight ftoutly. Now
the Enemy finding that place of the *Swamp* which was not
Ambufh'd, many of them made their efcape in the *Englifh*
Tracks.[313] The Man that had fhot down *Philip*, ran with all
fpeed to Capt *Church*, and informed him of his exploit, who
commanded him to be Silent about it, & let no man more
know it, until they had drove the *Swamp* [45] clean; but
when they had drove the *Swamp* thro' & found the Enemy
had efcaped, or at leaft the moft of them; and the Sun

[311] Probably *Peter*, fon of *Awafhonks.*
[See note 12, *ante*, and p. 87.]

[312] *Annawon* (*Annowan, Anowon*)
was one of Maffafoit's chiefs, and fo
one of Philip's oldeft braves. The only
record which I find of him, previous to
his connection with this war, is his appearance as a witnefs, in 1672, to two
fales of land by Philip to William
Brenton and others. His capture and
fate will foon be referred to. [Drake's
Boob of Ind. 200.]

His name fuggefts a probable derivation from *Nanawunnum*, " he rules " or
" has authority " (Eliot), or the verbal
Nananuwaen, " a ruler," " an overfeer."
Roger Williams has *Naunôuwheant*,
" a nurfe " or " keeper." [*R.-I. Hift.
Coll.* i: 52.] The primary fignification
of the verb is " to keep with care," " to
take care of."

[313] Hubbard fays Philip had " a few
of his beft friends " with him; and that
" 5 of his truftieft followers — of whom
one was faid to be the Son of his chief

Captain, that had fhot the firft gun at the
Englifh the year before " — were killed.
Mather fays that " he, with 7 of his
men," were in this fwamp and that "5
of his men were killed with him, — one
of which was his chief Captain's Son,
being (as the *Indians* teftifie) that very
Indian who fhot the firft gun at the *Englifh* when the War began." Wm. Jones
fays, — writing a fortnight after, from
New Haven, and repeating the teftimony to him of " one James Shore,
come in this week to Fairfield, in a vef-
fell from Rhod Ifeland," — " Philip in
labouring to efcape was fhot at ıft by
ye Englifh, but miffed, and then fhot
downe by an Indian. All ye reft, but
one more killd and one or two wounded, efcaping." Church's own language
would feem to imply that there were
more than feven men with Philip; that
more than one befides Philip was
ftopped; and that many of them got
away. [*Narrative*, 103; *Brief Hift.*
47; *Col. Rec. Conn.* ii: 471.]

149

now up, and fo the dew gone, that they could not fo eafily Track them, the whole Company met together at the place where the Enemies Night fhelter was; and then Capt. *Church* gave them the news of *Philips* death; upon which the whole Army gave Three loud *Huzza*'s. Capt *Church* ordered his body to be pull'd out of the mire on to the Upland, fo fome of Capt. *Churches Indians* took hold of him by his Stockings, and fome by his fmall Breeches, (being otherwife naked) and drew him thro' the Mud unto the Upland, and a doleful, great, naked, dirty beaft, he look'd like.[314] Capt. *Church* then faid, *That forafmuch as he had caufed many an* Englifh-mans *body to lye unburied, and rot above ground, that not one of his bones fhould be buried.* And calling his old *Indian* Executioner, bid him behead and quarter him [315] Accordingly, he came with

[314] This is the plain profe comment of an obferver upon the facts as they appeared to him. Dr. Palfrey has well referred to it, in his very juft remarks on the poetic exaggeration with which moft of our later literature has dealt with Philip. [*Hift. N. E.* iii: 223.]

[315] The idea in New England at that time feems to have been that Philip was a rebel againft King Charles 2d, and, as fuch, deferved the State punifhment of treafon, which, in England, until the 30th year of George 3d, was 1. To be drawn (latterly, on a hurdle, fo as to avoid the extreme torment of being dragged over the ground) to the gallows; 2. To be hanged by the neck, and cut down alive; 3. To have the entrails cut out and burned, while the

fufferer ftill lived; 4. To be beheaded; 5. That the body be cut into four quarters; 6. That the head and quarters be at the king's difpofal. [4, *Blackftone's Comm.* 92.] . Church's action, in the light of the public fentiment of that day, was far from indicating an inhuman revenge, or a cruel difpofition. It could fcarcely be expected that thefe remote and backwoods colonies were to go beyond the mother country in refinement. And it was not yet 17 years fince Parliament had voted the *difinterment* of Cromwell, Ireton, and Bradfhaw, and their decaying remains had been hanged at Tyburn, and their heads ftuck on poles on the top of Weftminfter Hall fronting Palace Yard; while nearly 20 years later than Philip's

his Hatchet and ſtood over him, but before he ſtruck he
made a ſmall Speech directing it to *Philip*; and ſaid, *He
had been a very great Man, and had made many a man
afraid of him, but ſo big as he was he would now chop his
Aſs for him*; and ſo went to work, and did as he was
ordered. *Philip* having one very remarkable hand being
much ſcarr'd, occaſioned by the ſplitting of a Piſtol in it
formerly. Capt. *Church* gave the head and that hand[316] to

death, Evelyn entered in his Diary (10
April, 1696), "The quarters of Sir William Perkins and Sir John Friend,
lately executed on the plot, with Perkins's head, were ſet up at Temple-Bar;
a diſmal ſight." Indeed, Walpole wrote
to Montague, 16 Aug., 1746, "paſſed
under the new heads at Temple Bar,
where people make a trade of letting
ſpying-glaſſes at a halfpenny a look";
and it is on record that Goldſmith
joked Johnſon in regard to ſimilar
adornments of that ſtructure; and, as
late as 1 April, 1772, a news-writer ſet
down: "yeſterday one of the rebels'
heads on Temple Bar fell down. There
is only one head now remaining."
Theſe facts ſhould have protected our
fathers from Peter Oliver's malignant
ſneer about "orthodox vengeance."
[See *Diary of Sam. Pepys*, ed. 1856,
i: 129, 152; *Diary of John Evelyn*, ed.
1857, ii: 340; Cunningham's *Hand
Book of London*, 437, 542; *Puritan
Commonwealth*, 145.]

[316] Increaſe Mather [*Brief Hiſt.* 47]
ſays, "his head being cut off and carried away to *Plymouth*, his Hands were
brought to *Boſton*." Cotton Mather
[*Magnalia*, ed. 1853, ii: 576] ſays,
"this Agag was now cut into quarters,
which were then hanged up, while his
head was carried in triumph to Plymouth." Niles [*Hiſt. Ind. and Fr.
Wars*, 3 *Maſs. Hiſt. Coll.* vi: 190] ſays
Philip "was cut into quarters, and
hanged up in the woods, and his head
carried to Plymouth." The ſtory, carried from this country to London by
the maſter of a veſſel ſoon ſailing from
Rhode-Iſland [Abbott's *Wars of the
Colonies*, 131], adds, "they quartered
his body, and hung it upon four trees."
By collating theſe we probably get all
the facts.

The head was placed upon a pole at
Plymouth, where it is ſaid to have
remained expoſed for more than 24
years [Felt's *Eccles. Hiſt. N. E.* ii:
638; Thacher's *Plymouth*, 389]; at any
rate Cotton Mather ſaid, in his *Magnalia* (firſt publiſhed in 1702, 26 years
after), "it was not long before the hand
which now writes, upon a certain occaſion took off the jaw from the expoſed
ſkull of that blaſphemous leviathan."
[ed. 1853, i: 566.] It is hardly probable that there is any truth in the tradi-

Alderman, the *Indian* who fhot him, to fhow to fuch Gentlemen as would beftow gratuities upon him; and accordingly he got many a Peny by it. This being on the laft day of the Week,[317] the Captain with his Company returned to the Ifland, tarryed there until Tuefday; and then went off and ranged thro' all the Woods to *Plymouth,*[318] and received their *Præmium,* which was *Thirty Shillings per* head, for the Enemies which they had killed or taken, inftead of all Wages; and *Philips* head went at the fame price.[319] Methinks it's fcanty reward, and poor incourage-

tion mentioned by Dr. Fobes in his defcription of Raynham [1 *Mafs. Hift. Coll.* iii: 171], that Philip's head was "depofited for a confiderable time" in the cellar under the "Leonard houfe" in that town.

[317] Saturday, 12 Auguft, 1676.

[318] Leaving Rhode-Ifland on Tuefday, the 15th, Church and his company muft have "ranged thro' all the woods" two days before reaching Plymouth; for the Mathers and Niles agree that the head reached Plymouth on Thurfday, the 17th, which had been fet apart as a day of Thankfgiving for fucceffes againft the Indians, perhaps before they had heard of Philip's death. [*Brief Hift.* 47; *Magnalia,* ed. 1853, ii: 576; 3 *Mafs. Hift. Coll.* vi: 190.]

[319] Affuming Hubbard and Mather's ftatement to be true, that 5 befides Philip were killed, and that there were no prifoners taken, — no mention being made of any, — the fum total of receipts for divifion would be £9. This, at 4s. 6d. a piece, — which Church fays was

each one's fhare, — would make the number of the party exactly 40. At 4s. 6d. each, their week's work would average a little lefs than 7d. 3qrs. per day, befides the honor! Hoyt, ftrangely confufing this with one day of the Bridgewater expedition, fays, "130 were killed and captured." [*Antiquarian Refearches,* 140.] This would have fwelled their compenfation to an aggregate of £195!

It may here be added, that there is, in the Cabinet of the Maffachufetts Hiftorical Society, a wooden difh, which is traditionally reprefented to have been a trophy of this expedition, and which was authenticated to the Society by the following receipt [*Proceedings Mafs. Hift. Soc.* 1863-4, 267.]: "Plymouth Sep. 14, 1803, Rec^d. of Ifaac Lothrop Eight Dollars, in full for a wooden bowle, formerly belonging to that illuftrious Soldier known by the name of King Philip, fon of the celebrated indian Sachem, Maffafoiet, and was a portion of the trophy affigned to Eleazer Rich-ment; tho' it was better than what had been fome time before. For this March they received *Four Shillings* and *Six Pence* a Man, which was all the Reward they had, except the honour of killing *Philip*. This was in the latter end of *Auguſt*, 1676 [320]

Capt. *Church* had been but a little while at *Plymouth*, before a Poſt from *Rehoboth* came to inform the Government, that old *Annawon*, *Philips* chief Captain was with his company ranging about their Woods, & was very offenſive & pernicious to *Rehoboth* & *Swanſey* [321] Capt. *Church* was immediately fent for again, & treated with to ingage one Expedition more; he told them, *Their incouragement was ſo poor he feared his Souldiers would be dull about going again*: But being a hearty friend to the cauſe, he Rally's again, goes to Mr. *Jabeſh Howland* his old Lieutenant,[322] and fome of his Souldiers, that us'd to go out with him; told them how the cafe was circumſtanced, and that he had intelligence of old *Annawon*'s walk, & haunt, and wanted hands to hunt him; they did not want

---

ard, Great Grandfather of the Subſcriber, who made one of the party, that terminated the exiſtence of the once princely proprietor.

" ELEAZER + RICHARD."
his mark.

Church's narrative furniſhes no evidence, either way, in regard to the genuineneſs of this relic. I find, however, no trace, either in Savage's fertile pages, or the Colony Records of Plymouth, Maſſachuſetts, or Rhode-Iſland, of any

Eleazer Richard (or Richards or Richardſon) as then living in New England; nor any evidence that any perſon of that furname ferved under Church in this campaign.

[320] Church ſpeaks here even more vaguely than he was apt to do, of the time of events.

[321] " By their ſhooting at the Engliſh Horſes, and other cattle." [Hubbard's *Narrative*, 107.]

[322] See note 207, *ante*.

much intreating; but told him, *They would. go with him,* *as long as there was an* Indian *left in the Woods.* He moved [323] & ranged thro' the Woods [46] to *Pocaſſet.* It being the latter end of the Week, he propoſed to go on to *Rhode-Iſland* and reſt until Monday. But early on the Lords day Morning,[324] there came a Poſt to inform the Cap

[323] He muſt have left Plymouth about Wedneſday or Thurſday (6th or 7th September), 1676 ? Hubbard ſays he had with him "but 5 Engliſhmen and 20 Indians." [*Narrative*, 107.]

[324] The queſtion of the date of this expedition is one of the moſt perplexing ones in the hiſtory of the time; ſtrangely enough, ſo far as I can learn, no record of it, or of any circumſtance which would exactly identify it, having a place in any of the early hiſtories or cotemporaneous records. Mr. Drake, in his ſecond edition of this narrative (1827, p. 142), is the firſt to attempt to ſettle it. He does ſo on the ſtrength of the fact that Annawon was taken on a Monday night, when the moon was ſhining, "not long after dark." He ſtates that the moon was at the full in 1676, on Saturday, the 26 Auguſt, whence he infers that Monday, 28 Auguſt, was the date of the capture (ſee alſo note to Mr. Drake's ed., Mather's *Brief Hiſtory*, 1862, p. 180), which would throw back the date of the ſtarting of the expedition from Plymouth to Wedneſday or Thurſday, the 23d or 24th. Dr. Palfrey [*Hiſt. N. E.* iii: 206] adopts this as the true date, and Arnold [*Hiſt. R.-I.* i: 417] ſpeaks vaguely of Annawon's capture as " a

few nights after the death of Philip." But John Foſter's Almanac for 1676 gives the full moon of Auguſt of that year as being on " the 13th day, at 26m. paſt 6 in the morn "; while Sherman's Almanac for the ſame year, ſtates it as on the " 13th day, at 25m. paſt 6 in the morn." This was the Sabbath, the next day after the day of the death of Philip. Church (ſee p. 152, *ante*) ſays he ſtaid at Rhode - Iſland until Tueſday, the 15th, and then " ranged thro' all the woods to Plymouth," which he could ſcarcely have reached before Friday or Saturday, the 18th or 19th. Then he was " a little while at Plymouth," a phraſe which might cover two or three weeks, while it would ſcarcely have been uſed for a leſs time than *one* week (which leſſer time he would more likely have ſtyled " a few days "), before the " poſt from Rehoboth " came with news of Annawon, and he was " ſent for " and " treated with " for " one expedition more "; and began to gather ſoldiers to go out again. From all this, it ſeems very clear that the Auguſt moon muſt have diſappeared long before he could have been ready to ſtart on this expedition. If this were ſo, we are thrown over into September for the true date of this expedition; and

tain, That early the fame Morning a Canoo with feveral *Indians* in it paffed from *Prudence Ifland* [325] to *Pappafquafh.*

the probabilities of the cafe would feem to fix the capture of Annawon as being on the firft Monday evening of September, on which the moon was fhining a few hours after dark. Fofter gives the full moon for September, 1676, as on "the 11 day, 54 m. paft 6, P.M.," and Sherman gives it as on "the 11 day, 55 m. paft 6 at night." This was on Monday evening, four weeks and two days after the death of Philip. On the previous Monday evening (4 Sept.), the moon (then juft in her firft quarter) muft have fet from one to two hours before midnight, and, in the denfe forefts furrounding Squannaconk Swamp, her (then) feeble light muft have ceafed to be available for much help to vifion at leaft an hour before her fetting; fo that (there) it would be hardly fafe to prefume on feeing by moonlight on the evening of 4 Sept., much later than 9 P.M. But it was "pretty dark" before Church arrived; then followed the capture, the parley with all the companies, the preparation for the fupper, the fupper, and the meffage to the outlying Indians, and the return of the meffengers; then Church laid down with the intention of fleeping two hours, laid a little while and grew wakeful, and roufed to look after his guard, then lay looking at the equally wakeful Annawon, "perhaps an hour"; then Annawon got up and retired into the thick woods "out of fight and hearing," and was gone a long time; "at length" Church heard him coming back, and *then*, "the moon

now fhining bright," he faw him coming with fomething in his hands, &c. All this detail of delays makes it almoft certain that the hour of Annawon's converfe with Church muft have been well on toward midnight, at leaft; fo that it is impoffible that the date could have been that of 4 Sept. Befides, Church's expreffion, "the moon fhining *bright*," is moft confonant with the *full* moon; fo that I am led to conclude that the true date of this capture is that of the Monday of the September full moon, viz., 11 Sept., 1676.

It is worthy of notice in this connection, that Hubbard [*Narrative*, 106] expreffly fays that Church took *Tifpaquin* "in September," yet places his capture *before* that of *Annawon*, faying, "the next that was feized after the former (ie., *Tifpaquin*) was one called *Annawon*, &c." Church himfelf, in this narrative (fee p. 175), inverts this order; but I am ftrongly inclined to believe that Hubbard was right, and that, if Church had fat down to the work of his annals at an earlier date, and before the frefhnefs of his memory had faded, he would fo have arranged them.

[325] *Prudence* is the ifland in Narraganfett Bay, fome 7 or 8 miles in length, of irregular fhape, lying weft of the northern part of Rhode-Ifland, and, in its fouthern half, feparated from it by a channel averaging perhaps a mile and a half in width. Its Indian name was *Chibacuwefet* (*Chippacurfett*).

Neck.[326] Capt. *Church* tho't if he could poffibly furprize them, he might probably gain fome intelligence of more game; therefore he made all poffible fpeed after them: the Ferry-boat[327] being out of the way, he made ufe of

Canonicus, in 1634, gave it to John Oldham, if he would fettle on it; which he did not. In 1637, Roger Williams and John Winthrop purchafed it, and Williams gave it its prefent name. [Winthrop's *Journal* i: 147; Letter of Williams, 3 *Mafs. Hift. Coll.* i: 165; Arnold's *Hift. R.-I.* i: 105.]

[326] *Poppafquafh* (*Papoofquafh, Papafquafh, Pappafqua*) Neck is a thumb-like promontory, perhaps 2½ miles in length by an average of ¾ in breadth, projecting from the weftern fide of the town of Briftol into the bay. Plymouth Court, 1 June 1669, granted 100 acres of it "to Mr. John Gorum, if it can be purchafed of the Indians"; and 5 July, 1669, granted the remainder to the "towne of Swanfey, for the promoting of a way of trade in this collonie." 1 July, 1672, "Mr. Conftant Southworth, Mr. James Browne, and Mr. John Gorum are appointed by the Court, to purchafe a certaine p'fell of land of the Indians, granted by the Court to the faid John Gorum, lying att Papafquafh neck." 13 July, 1677, the Court "rattified, eftablifhed, fettled, and confirmed the aforefaid 100 acres of land" to John Gorum's heirs and fucceffors for ever. It feems foon after to have paffed to Nathaniel Byfield, who is faid to have occupied nearly the whole of it as his farm for over 40 years, until his removal to Bofton in

1724. [*Plym. Col. Rec.* v: 20, 24, 95, 241; Shepard's *Hift. Dis. Briftol, R.-I.,* 49.]

As to the name, Mr. Trumbull fays, "This name was alfo given to a tract of land now in Voluntown, Conn., in a grant of 1681, as *Paupafquachuke;* the *uke* reprefenting *ohke* i.e., " place." Two derivations are equally probable, and plaufible, from *papafku,* 'double'— which is applicable to the fouthern end of Briftol, divided by the bay, or, as it may be tranflated, 'oppofite to,' 'over againft.' Otherwife, from *pohpohquffu* or *pahpahkfhas,* of Eliot; *paupockfu* of Roger Williams, i.e., ' the partridge.' With the addition of *ohke* it would be ' the partridge country,' or 'Partridge Point,' or rather 'Quail Point,' as we fhould tranflate it in Connecticut. I think the latter the more probable. derivation; though I do not *know* that a quail ever flew within a dozen miles of Poppafquafh."

The diftance for a canoe, acrofs from Prudence, would not be much more than 1½ miles, and the croffing would be in full view from Rhode-Ifland and probably not more than 3 miles diftant from it.

[327] The ferry to Briftol at Tripps; the fame which he croffed on his laft expedition after Philip. His object was to go up fome 4 miles through what is now the town of Briftol, and

Canoo's: But by that time they had made two fraights, and had got over the Captain, and about 15 or 16 of his *Indians*, the Wind fprung up with fuch violence that Canoo's could no more pafs.[328] The Capt. feeing it was impoffible for any more of his Souldiers to come to him, he told his *Indians*, *If they were willing to go with him, he would go to* Poppafquafh, *and fee if they could catch fome of thofe Enemy* Indians. They were willing to go, but were forry they had no *Englifh* Souldiers;[329] fo they March'd thro' the thickets that they might not be difcovered, until they came unto the Salt Meadow, to the Northward of *Briftol* Town,[330] that now is. Then they heard a Gun, the Capt. look'd about, not knowing but it might be fome of his own Company in the rear; fo halting till they all came up, he found 'twas none of his own Company that fired. Now tho' he had but a few Men, was minded to fend fome of them out on a Scout. He moved it to Capt. *Lightfoot*[331] to go with three more on a Scout; he faid he was willing provided the Captains man *Nathanael* (which was an *Indian* that they had lately taken) might be one of them, becaufe he was well acquainted with the Neck,[332]

---

endeavor to furprife the Indians as they fhould pafs out of Poppafquafh neck toward the main land.

[328] See note 175, *ante.*

[329] It will appear, further on, that his Lieutenant and Englifh foldiers fubfequently croffed and joined him next day.

[330] Probably thofe juft north-weft of Silver Creek.

[331] See note 238, *ante.*

[332] He means here, evidently, Mount-Hope neck, and not Poppafquafh neck. Church himfelf with his party proceeded to fearch the latter for the enemy; and Lightfoot with his three compauions muft have fcouted off toward what are now Warren and Swanfey, in the direction of Kikemuit.

and coming lately from among them, knew how to call them.[333] The Capt. bid him choofe his three companions, and go; and if they came a-crofs any of the Enemy not to kill them if they could poffibly take them alive; that they might gain intelligence concerning *Annawon*. The Capt. with the reft of his company moved but a little way further toward *Poppafquafh*, before they heard another Gun, which feemed to be the fame way with the other, but further off. But they made no halt until they came unto the narrow of *Poppafquafh* Neck;[334] where Capt. *Church* left three men more, to watch if any fhould come out of the Neck, and to inform the Scout when they returned which way he was gone. He parted the remainder of his company, half on one fide of the Neck, and the other with himfelf went on the other fide of the Neck, until they met; and meeting neither with *Indians* nor Canoo's returned big with expectations of Tydings by their Scout: But when they came back to the three men at the narrow of the Neck, they told their Captain the Scout was not returned, had heard nor feen any thing of them, this fill'd them with tho'ts what fhould become of them; by that time they had fat down & waited an hour longer, it was very dark, and they defpaired of their returning to them. Some of the *Indians* told their Captain, *They 'feared his new man* Nathanael

---

[333] The Indians were accuftomed to have fome call — like a wolf's howl, a loon's cry, or fomething of that fort — by which they could fignal each other in the woods. This was changed as often as there was danger of its becoming known to their enemies. *Nathanael*, being recently captured, would know what that fignal of his tribe now was.

[334] Perhaps 120 rods in width.

had met with his old. Mount-hope *friends, and was turned Rogue.* They concluded to make [47] no fires that Night, (and indeed they had no great need of any) for they had no Victuals to cook, had not fo much as a morfel of Bread with them. They took up their lodging fcattering, that if poffibly their Scout fhould come in the Night, and whiftle (which was their fign) fome or other of them might hear them. They had a very folitary, hungry Night; and as foon as the day broke[335] they drew off thro' the brufh to a hill without the Neck, and looking about them they efpy'd one *Indian* man come running fomewhat towards them, the Captain ordered one man to ftep out of the brufh and fhow himfelf. Upon which the *Indian* ran right to him, and who fhould it be but Capt. *Lightfoot,* to their great joy. Capt. *Church* ask'd him, *What News?* He anfwered, *Good. News, they were all well and had catch'd Ten* Indians, *and that they guarded them all Night in one of the Flankers of the old.* Englifh *Garrifon;*[336] *that their prifoners were part of* Annawons *company, and that they had left their Families in a Swamp above* Mattapoifet Neck.[337] And as they were Marching towards the old Garrifon *Lightfoot* gave Capt. *Church* a particular account of their Exploit, *viz. That prefently after they left him, they heard another Gun, which feem'd to be towards the* Indian

---

[335] Monday, 11 September, 1676.
[336] That on the fhores of the *Kikemuit,* about which Church had been fo exercifed the year before. (See note 65, *ante.*) He muft have thought its ufe had been found at laft.
[337] The neck of this name (Gardner's neck) in Swanfey.

burying place,[338] *& moving that way, they discovered two of the Enemy fleeing of an Horse.* The Scout *claping into the brush,* Nathanael *bid them fit down, and he would presently call all the* Indians *thereabout unto him.* They hid, *and he went a little distance back from them and fat up his note & howled like a Wolf : One of the two immediately left his Horse & came running to see who was there ; but* Nathanael *howling lower and lower drew him in between those that lay in wait for him, who feized him ;* Nathanael *continuing the fame note, the other left the Horse also following his mate, & met with the fame. When they caught these two they examined them apart, and found them to agree in their Story, that there were Eight more of them come down into the Neck to get Provifions, and had agreed to meet at the burying place that evening. These two being fome of* Nathanaels *old acquaintance, he had great influence upon them, and with his inticing Story, (telling what a brave Captain he had, how bravely he lived fince he had been with him, & how much they might better their condition by turning to him, &c.) per-*

---

[338] Concerning this, Gen. Feffenden fays, "In regard to the location of the 'Old Indian burying-ground,' I have long fince endeavored to find the fite of it. A farmer informed me that when he was a boy, about the year 1800, the people ftraightened the direct road from this place (Warren, R.-I) to Briftol; and, on the top of a hill, about half way between the two places (2 miles from each), they dug through a burying-ground, and carried off for interment more than one cart-load of human bones. There are now no appearances of a cemetery there. This was doubtlefs *a* burying-ground; but whether it was *the* burying-ground cannot be determined." [*MS. letter.*] The probability feems urgent that this was an *Indian* burying-place, as all which have been ufed by the white fettlers are doubtlefs well known. If fo, it is reafonable to infer that it was that to which reference is here made.

swaded and ingaged them to be on his side, which indeed, now began to be the better side of the hedge. They waited, but a little while before they espy'd the rest of theirs coming up to the burying place, and Nathanael *soon howl'd them in as he had done their mates before.* When Capt. *Church* came to the Garrison, he met his Lieutenant and the rest of his company;[339] and then making up good fires they fell to roasting their Horse-beaf,[340] enough to last them the whole day, but had not a morsal of Bread; tho' Salt they had which they always carryed in their Pockets, which at this time was very acceptable to them. Their next motion was towards the place where the Prisoners told them they had left their Women and Children,[341] and surprized them all, and some others that were newly come to them. And upon examination they held to one Story, that it was hard to tell where to find *Annawon*, for he never roosted twice in [48] a place. Now a certain *Indian* Souldier that Capt. *Church* had gain'd over to be on his side, pray'd that he might have liberty to go and fetch in his Father, who he said was about four Miles from that place, in a *Swamp*[342] with no other than one Young *Squaw;* Capt. *Church* in-

---

[339] Lieut. Howland and his squad, on getting acrofs the ferry and following Church, may have fallen in with one of Lightfoot's scouts, or may have gone to the old garrison, at a venture, as a likely place of meeting him, or news from him.

[340] Which the Indians had just killed.

[341] A swamp in Swanfey, probably not far from what is now Swanfey village.

[342] *Manwhague* swamp in the southeastern corner of Rehoboth, anfwers this requifition of diftance; befides lying near the rout to *Squannakonk* fwamp, where Annawon was, and whence thefe Indians whom Church had captured had come.

clined to go with him, thinking it might be in his way to gain fome intelligence of *Annawon ;* and fo taking one *Englifh* Man and a few *Indians* with him leaving the reft there, he went with his new Souldier to look his Father; when he came to the *Swamp,* he bid the *Indian* go fee if he could find his Father: he was no fooner gone but Capt. *Church* difcover'd a Track coming down out of the Woods, upon which he and his little company lay clofe fome on one fide of the Track & fome on the other. They heard the *Indian* Souldier make a howling for his Father; and at length fome body anfwered him, but while they were liftening, they thought they heard fome body coming towards them, prefently faw an old man coming up with a Gun on his Shoulder, and a young Woman following of him in the Track which they lay by: They let them come up between them, and then ftarted up and laid hold on them both. Capt. *Church* immediately examined them a part,[343] telling them, *What they muſt truſt too if they told falſe Stories*: He ask'd the young Woman, *What company they came laſt from?* She faid, *from Capt.* Annawons. He asked her, *How many were in company with him when ſhe left him?* She faid, 50 *or* 60. He ask'd her *How many Miles it was to the place where ſhe left him?* She faid, *She did not underſtand Miles, but he was up in* Squannaconk *Swamp?*[344] The old man who had been one of *Philips*

[343] Through one of his Indian foldiers as an interpreter.

[344] *Squannakonk* fwamp is on the eaftern fide of the town of Rehoboth, Mafs., about midway between its northern and fouthern boundaries, and

Council, upon examination, gave exactly the fame account. Capt. *Church* ask'd him, *If they could get there that Night?* He faid, *If they went prefently and travelled ftoutly, they might get there by Sun fet.*[345] He ask'd *Whither he was going?* He anfwered, *That* Annawon *had fent him down to look for fome* Indians, *that were gone down into* Mount_hope *Neck to kill Provifions:* Capt. *Church* let him know that thofe *Indians* were all his Prifoners. By this time came the *Indian* Souldier & brought his Father and one *Indian* more. The Captain was now in great ftraight of mind what to do next he had a mind to give *Annawon* a vifit, now knew where to find him, but his company was very fmall, but half a dozen men befide himfelf, and was under a neceffity to fend fome body back to acquaint his Lieutenant & company[346] with his proceedings. However he asked his fmall company that were with him, *Whither they would willingly go with him and give* Annawon *a vifit?* They told him, *They were always ready to obey his com-mands,* &c. But withal told him, *That they knew this Capt.*

nearly touches, at fome points, the weft line of Dighton; *Little Squanna-konk* and *Bad-Luck* fwamps lie be-tween it and Refervoir pond on the fouth, out of which flows the main feed-er of Palmer's (Warren) River. Mr. Drake fays [edition of Mather's *Brief Hiftory*, 180], that *Squannakonk* prob-ably fignifies the " Swamp of Night," or " Night-fwamp." But Mr. Trumbull fays, " I can make nothing of this name. It is certainly corrupted, and has loft at leaft one (initial) fyllable."

[345] It could fcarcely have been more than 9 or 10 miles to Annawon's camp; but the way was, unqueftionably, — through that miry country, — tedious and difficult, and the day was evi-dently waning; as Church had already marched, with many delays, from the narrow of Poppafquafh neck, a diftance which, by their finuous route, could hardly have been lefs than fifteen miles.
[346] Whom he had left at the fwamp above *Mattapoifett* neck.

163

Annawon *was a great Souldier; that he had been a valiant
Captain under* Afuhmequn, Philips *Father,*[347] *and that he
had been* Philips *Chieftain all this War; a very fubtle man,
and of great refolution, and had often faid, that he would
never be taking alive by the* Englifh; *and moreover they knew
that the men that were with him were refolute fellows, fome
of* Philip's *chief Souldiers; and therefore feared whether it
was practicable to make an attempt upon him with fo* [49]
fmall a handful of affiftants as now were with him. Told
him further, *That it would be a pitty that after all the Great
Things he had done, he fhould throw away his Life at laft,*
&c. Upon which he replyed, That he doubted not *Annawon* was a fubtle & valiant Man: that he had a long time
but in vain fought for him, and never till now could find
his quarters; and he was very loth to mifs of the opportunity; and doubt not but that if they would chearfully go
with him, the fame Almighty Providence that had hitherto
protected and befriended them would do fo ftill, *&c.* Upon this with one confent they faid, *They would go.* Capt.
Church then turned to one *Cook* of *Plymouth,*[348] (the only

---

[347] *Maffafoit* had two names, each of
which, in accordance with the humor
of the times, had a various fpelling.
Bradford wrote one *Maffafoyt* and
Maffafoyet; Winflow wrote it *Mafa-
foyt* and *Maffaffowat;* Prince fays,
"I find the ancient People from their
Fathers in *Plimouth Colony* pronounce
his name *Ma-faf-fo-it*"; to which
Thatcher adds (as if from Belknap,
what Belknap does not fay), "with the
accent on the fecond fyllable." The
other was written *Woofamequin, Wafa-
megin, Uffamequen, Afuhmequin, Oofa-
mequen, Ofamekin, Owfamequin, Owf-
amequine,* &c. &c. [Bradford's *Hift.
Plym.* 94, 102; Young's *Chronicles
Plym.* 191, 313; Prince's *Annals,* 101;
Belknap's *Amer. Biog.* ii: 212; Thatcher's *Ind. Biog.* i: 117; Drake's *Book of
Ind.* 81.]

[348] Beyond queftion this was Caleb

English Man then with him) and ask'd him, *What he thought of it?* Who replyed, *Sir, I, am never afraid of going any where when you are with me.* Then Capt. *Church* asked the old *Indian*, if he could carry his Horfe with him? (for he conveyed a Horfe thus far with him:) He reply'd that it was impoffible for an Horfe to pafs the Swamps. Therefore he fent away his new *Indian* Souldier with his Father and the Captains Horfe to his Lieutenant, and orders for him to move to *Taunton* with the Prifoners, to fecure them there, and to come out in the Morning in the *Rehoboth* Road, in which he might expect to meet him, if he were alive and had fuccefs.³⁴⁹ The Captain then asked the old fellow, If he would Pilot him unto *Annawon?* He anfwered, that he having given him his life he was obliged to ferve him. He bid him move on then; and they followed: The old man would out-travel them, fo far fometimes that they were almoft out of fight; looking over his Shoulder and feeing them behind, he would halt. Juft as the Sun was fetting, the old man made a full ftop and fat down, the company coming up alfo fat down, being all weary. Capt. *Church* asked, *What news?* He anfwered, That about that time in the Evening Capt. *Annawon*, fent out his Scouts to fee if the Coaft were clear, and as foon as it began to grow dark the Scouts return. And then (faid he) we may move

Cook, who fo narrowly miffed being the flayer of Philip. (See note 307, *ante.*)

³⁴⁹ It was probably twelve or thirteen miles from the fwamp where Lieut. Howland and his company were, northeafterly up the weft bank of the *Titicut* (Taunton) River to Taunton.

again fecurely. When it began to grow dark the old man ftood up again, Capt. *Church* asked him if he would take a Gun and fight for him? He bowed very low and pray'd him not to impofe fuch a thing upon him, as to fight againft Capt. *Annawon* his old friend. But fayes he, I will go along with you, and be helpful to you, and will lay hands on any man that fhall offer to hurt you. It being now pretty dark they moved clofe together; anon they heard a noife, the Captain ftay'd the old man with his hand, and asked his own men what noife they thought it might be? they concluded it to be the pounding of a Mortar. The old man had given Capt. *Church* a defcription of the Place where *Annowon* now lay, and of the Difficulty of getting at him: being fenfible that they were pretty near them, with two of his *Indians* he creeps to the edge of the Rocks,[350] from whence he could fee their Camps; he saw

---

[350] A continuous tradition has pre-ferved the identity of this fpot. It is an out-cropping ledge of rocks in a bit of upland in the northern part of *Squannakonk* fwamp in Rehoboth. It may now be reached by the old turn-pike from Taunton to Providence, and is between the houfes on that road now occupied by Seneca Blifs and Noah Fuller; on the left fide as you go to-ward Providence, and about 6½ miles from Taunton. This portion of the fwamp is owned by Nathan Pratt of Taunton, who married a daughter of Dea. Blifs, its former proprietor. The building of this road through the north-ern end of the fwamp, with the natural change of years, has made the pofition more acceffible than of old, although wet ground ftill furrounds the rock. The traveller will find, perhaps 80 rods beyond Mr. Blifs's houfe (which ftands in the angle where another road croffes the pike), a tree on the left, larger than any near it, which bears the marks of being often ufed as a hitching-poft; with a path leading thence fouth-eafterly into the woods. Following that path, fay 80 paces, he will begin to afcend the ledge which flopes up before him at an angle of perhaps 40 degrees, and the length of which lies acrofs his way up, and apparently not far from north-eaft and fouth-weft. From pacing it,

three companies of *Indians* at a little diftance from each other, being eafy to be difcovered by the light of their fires. He faw alfo the great *An*[50]*nawon* and his company, who had formed his Camp or Kennelling-place, by falling a Tree under the fide of the great clefts of Rocks, and fitting a row of birch bufhes up againft it, where he himfelf, and his Son, and fome of his chiefs had taken up their lodging, and made great fires without them, and had their Pots and Kittles boiling, and Spits roafting. Their Arms alfo he difcovered, all fet together in a place fitted for the purpofe ftanding up an end againft a ftick lodged in two crotches, and a Mat placed over them, to keep them from the wet or dew. The old *Annawons* feet and his Sons head were fo near the Arms as almoft to touch them: But

I judge that this ledge may average 125 feet in length by 75 feet in width, terminating on its fouthern and weftern fide in rugged cliffs from 30 to 40 feet in hight. The rock is a pudding-ftone, thick fet with pebbles, and has evidently felt the effect of convulfion, or other rough treatment, along its fouthern and fouth-weftern edge, which is jagged, and from which huge bowlders, now lying at its bafe, have been torn. About two-thirds of the way weft, along this fouthern face, is a deep recefs, acceffible from above with difficulty by the aid of the bufhes growing in the clefts, which anfwers well to Church's defcription of the fpot in which Annawon was now encamped. The growth of trees around the rock has recently been felled; and the firft feeling of the vifitor is one of furprife that a retreat fo expofed on the fouthern fide as this now feems to be, fhould have anfwered the conditions of Annawon's camp. But, on reflection, one will fee, that, with the fwamp as it then was, the rock could be reached only from the upland ifthmus which connected it with the main land, which lay probably in the direction from which the path now approaches the fpot; while the fide which now feems expofed was not only protected by the furrounding water and mire, but fhut in and concealed by the old foreft growth. From the edge of the cliff, Church could look down upon Annawon, his fon, and chiefs, almoft directly under him, and upon the three companies around their fires, fcattered along its fouthern face.

the Rocks were fo fteep that it was impoffible to get down but as they lowered themfelves by the bows, and the bufhes that grew in the cracks of the Rock. Capt. *Church* creeping back again to the old man, asked him, If there was no poffibility of getting at them fome other way? He anfwered, no, That he and all that belonged to *Annawon* were ordered to come that way, and none could come any other way without difficulty or danger of being fhot. Capt. *Church* then ordered the old man and his daughter to go down fore-moft with their baskets at their backs, that when *Annawon* faw them with their baskets he fhould not miftruft the intregue; Capt. *Church* and his handful of Souldiers crept down alfo under the fhadow of thefe two and their baskets, and the Captain himfelf crept clofe behind the old man, with his Hatchet in his hand, and ftep'd over the young mans head to the Arms, the young *Annawon* difcovering of him, whip'd his blanket over his head and fhrunk up in a heap: The old Capt. *Annawon* ftarted up on his breech, and cryed out *Howoh*,[351] and defpairing of efcape[352] throw himfelf back again, and lay filent until Capt. *Church* had fecured all the Arms, *&c.* And having fecured that company, he fent his *Indian* Souldiers to the

---

[351] *Howoh!* i.e. *Awàun ewò?* "Who is that?" [Roger Williams's *Key. R.-I. Hift. Coll.* i: 29.] or *Howan?* "who?" e.g., *Howan yeuoh wag Edom &c.*, "Who is this that cometh from Edom, &c.?" [*Eliot, Ifaiah* lxiii: 1.] This feems to have been the ufual challenge: "Who's there?"

[352] Annawon probably had no idea that Church would have the boldnefs thus to beard him in his den, without an abundant force furrounding and irrefiftibly enclofing him on every fide; as was reprefented to be the fact to the other companies, by his Indian folldiers.

other fires & companies, giving them inſtructions, what to do and ſay. Accordingly, they went into the midſt of them: When they diſcovered themſelves who they were, told them that their Capt. *Annawon* was taken, and it would be beſt for them quietly and peaceably to ſurrender themſelves, which would procure good quarter for them: Otherwiſe if they ſhould pretend to reſiſt or make their eſcape, it would be in vain, and they could expect no other but that Capt. *Church* with his great Army, who had now entrap'd them, would cut them to pieces: told them alſo if they would ſubmit themſelves, and deliver up all their Arms unto them, and keep every man his place until it was day; they would aſſure them that their Capt. *Church* who had been ſo kind to themſelves when they ſurrendred to him, ſhould be as kind unto them. Now they being old acquaintance, and many of them Relations did much the readier give heed to what they ſaid, and complyed & ſurrendred up their Arms unto them, both their Guns and Hatchets, *&c.* and were forthwith carryed to Capt. *Church.* Things being ſo far ſettled, Capt. *Church* asked *Annawon,* What he had for Supper, for (ſaid he) I am come to Sup [51] with you. *Taubut*[353] (ſaid *Annowon*) with a big voice; and looking about upon his Women, bid them haſten and get Capt. *Church* and his company ſome Supper; then turned to Capt. *Church* and asked him, Whether he would

---

353 *Taubut:* Literally, "It is ſatiſfactory," "très bien," e.g., *Taubut paump maúntaman,* "I am glad you are well;" *Taubot ne paump maúntaëttit,* "I am glad they are well." [Roger Williams *R.-I. Hiſt. Coll.* i: 27.]

eat Cow-beaf or Horfe-beaf, The Captain told him Cow-beaf would be moft acceptable: It was foon got ready, and pulling his little bag of Salt out of his Pocket, which was all the Provifion he brought with him; this feafon'd his Cow-beaf fo that with it and the dry'd green-corn, which the old Squaw was pounding in the Mortar,[354] while they were fliding down the Rocks, he made a very hearty Supper. And this pounding in the Mortar proved lucky for Capt. *Churches* getting down the Rocks, for when the old Squaw pounded they moved, and when fhe ceafed to turn the corn, they ceafed creeping, the noife of the Mortar prevented the Enemies hearing their creeping: and the corn being now dreffed fupplyed the want of Bread, and gave a fine relifh with the Cow-beaf. Supper being over, Capt. *Church* fent two of his men to inform the other companies, that he had killed *Philip,* and had taken their friends in *Mount-hope* Neck,[355] but had fpared their lives, and that he had fub dued now all the Enemy (he fuppofed) excepting this company of *Annawons,* and now if they would be orderly and keep their places until Morning, they fhould have good quarter, and that he would carry them to *Taunton,* where they might fee their friends again, *&c.* The Meffengers

[354] "The mode of pounding dry maize, by the grain-raifing tribes, varied confiderably. It was a fpecies of work left wholly to the women, who generally exercifed their ingenuity in its reduction. When circumftances favored it, mortars and peftles of ftone were employed. The mortar was fome- times a depreffion in the face of a rock." [Schoolcraft's *Inf. refpecting the Ind. Tribes* iii: 466.]

[355] That is, thofe whom Annawon had fent down to Poppafquafh, and the regions beyond it, after provifions; whom Church had captured the day before.

return'd, that the *Indians* yielded to his propofals. Capt. *Church* tho't it was now time for him to take a Nap, hav_ing had no fleep in two days and one night before; told his men that if they would let him fleep two hours, they fhould fleep all the reft of the night. He lay'd himfelf down and endeavoured to fleep, but all difpofition to fleep departed from him. After he had lain a little while he looked up to fee how his Watch managed, but found them all faft a-fleep. Now Capt. *Church* had told Capt. *Anna-wons* company, as he had ordered his *Indians* to tell the others, that their lives fhould all be fpared, excepting Capt. *Annawons*, and it was not in his power to promife him his life, but he muft carry him to his Mafters at *Plymouth*,[356] and he would intreat them for his life. Now when Capt. *Church* found not only his own men, but all the *Indians* faft a-fleep *Annawon* only excepted, whom he perceived was as broad awake as himfelf; and fo they lay looking one upon the other perhaps an hour; Captain Church faid nothing to him, for he could not fpeak *Indian*, and tho't *Annawon* could not fpeak *Englifh;* at length *Annawon* raifed himfelf up, caft off his blanket, and with no more clothes than his fmall breeches, walked a little way back from the company: Capt. *Church* tho't no other but that he had occafion to eafe himfelf, and fo walked to fome dif-

---

356 It will be remembered, that Church's commiffion (fee p. 101, *ante*) expreffly excepted from· his power of " receiving to mercy" fuch as were " Murderous Rogues, or fuch as have been *;principal Actors* in thofe Villa‐nies." Compare the action of Ply‐mouth Court, 7 July, 1676; and alfo 4 November following. [*Blym. Col. Rec.* v: 205; xi: 242.]

tance rather than offend him with the ſtink: but by and by he was gone out of ſight and hearing; and then Capt. *Church* began to ſuſpect ſome ill deſign in him, and got all the Guns cloſe to him, and crouded himſelf cloſe under young *Annawon,* that if he ſhould any where [52] get a Gun he ſhould not make a ſhot at him without indangering his Son; lying very ſtill a while waiting for the event: at length, he heard ſome body coming the ſame way that *Annawon* went. The Moon now ſhining bright, he ſaw him at a diſtance coming with ſomething in his hands, and coming up to Capt. *Church,* he fell upon his knees before him, and offer'd him what he had bro't, and ſpeaking in plain *Engliſh,* ſaid, *Great Captain, you have killed. Philip, and conquered. his Country for I believe, that I & my company are the laſt that War againſt the* Engliſh, *ſo ſuppoſe the War is ended. by your means ; and therefore theſe things belong unto ·you.* Then opening his pack, he pull'd out *Philips* belt curiouſly wrought with *Wompom,*[357] being Nine

---

[357] *Wompom* (plural *Wompompeag*) was the Indian name for the *white* beads uſed as currency, or for the payment of tribute from tribe to tribe; from *wompi,* "white." The *black,* or, more properly, the ·*purple* beads, made from the margin of the ſhell of the round clam (*Venus mercenaria*), were called *ſuckauhock,* "dark-colored-ſhell." Theſe beads when ſtrung, in bands or girdles, were called, generally, ·*peag;* when looſe, *ſéawhóog* (*ſawhoog,* Roger Williams's *Key. R.-I. Hiſt. Coll.* i: 131); by the Dutch and other traders, *ſeawan,* *ſewan,* i.e., "ſcattered," "looſe." The Engliſh, not underſtanding, or diſregarding, the diſtinction of colors, aſfumed the name of the cheaper and more common *womp*ompeag as generic, and called *all* ſhell-money *wompom.*

Dr. Palfrey ſays theſe beads were a quarter of an inch long, and in diameter leſs than a pipe-ſtem, drilled lengthwiſe. Gookin and Roger Williams teſtify, that the white beads (or *wompom* proper) were rated at half the value of the black. Palfrey adds that the former paſſed for a farthing each in tranſac-

inches broad,³⁵⁸ wrought with black and white *Wompom*,
in various figures and flowers, and pictures of many birds
and beasts. This when hung upon Capt. *Churches* shoulders it reach'd his ancles. And another belt of *Wompom*
he presented him with, wrought after the former manner,
which *Philip* was wont to put upon his head; it had two
flags on the back part which hung down on his back: and
another small belt with a Star upon the end of it, which
he used to hang on his breast; and they were all edg'd
with red hair, which *Annawon* said they got in the Muh-
hogs³⁵⁹ Country. Then he pulled out two horns of glazed
Powder, and a red cloth Blanket: He told Capt. *Church*,
these were *Philips* Royalties³⁶⁰ which he was wont to

tions between the natives and the col-
onists; that is, 960 to the pound sterling.
A law was passed, however, in the Mass.
Colony, 2 June, 1641, to this effect:
"It is ordered that *wampampege* shall
passe currant at 6 a penny for any
summe under £10, for debts hereafter
to bee made." In Sept., 1648, the com-
missioners of the United Colonies, from
the fact that the Indians and traders
cheated in dealing with wampum,
"smaule & great uncomly & disorderly
mingled," recommended an order that
none should "bee payed or Rescaiued"
but what is "in som measure strunge
sutably;" but the General Courts did
not agree to it. In 1660 it was rated
at 5s. a fathom. [Palfrey's *Hist. N. E.*
i: 31; *Mass. Col. Rec.* i: 329; *Blym.
Col. Rec.* ix: 136, 149; x: 251; 1 *Mass.
Hist. Coll.* i: 152; *R.-I. Hist. Coll.* i:
130.]

³⁵⁸ "They [*peag*] were used for orna-
ment as well as for coin, and 10,000
have been known to be wrought into a
single war-belt four inches wide."
[Palfrey's *Hist. N. E.* i: 32.] "They
make girdles curiously, of one, two,
three, foure and five inches thicknesse
and more, of this money, which (sometimes to the value of £10 and more)
they weare about their middle and as a
scarfe about their shoulders and breasts.
"Yea, the Princes make rich Caps and
Aprons (or small breeches) of these
Beads thus curiously strung into many
formes and figures: their blacke and
white finely mixt together." [Roger
Williams's *Key. R.-I. Hist. Coll.* i:
131.]

³⁵⁹ Mohawk's country.

³⁶⁰ It is an interesting question what
became of these "royalties" after they
were thus passed into the hands of

adorn himfelf with when he fat in State. That he tho't him-
felf happy that he had an opportunity to prefent them to
Capt. *Church,* who had won them, *&c.* fpent the remainder
of the night in difcourfe; and gave an account of what
mighty fuccefs he had formerly in Wars againft many
Nations of *Indians,* when ferved *Afuhmequin,*[361] *Philips*
Father, *&c.* In the Morning[362] as foon as it was light, the
Captain March'd with his Prifoners out of that *Swampy*
Country towards *Taunton,* met his Lieutenant and Compa

Church. I find no note of their prefervation in Church's houfehold, nor any evidence that the tradition to which Mr. Drake refers, tracing them to the cuftody of a family in Swanfey, [*Book of Ind.* 239] has any foundation in fact. It is moft reafonable to fuppofe that Church turned them over to the Government, and evidence has juft been brought to light which indicates that moft, if not all, of the articles here referred to, were fent as prefents by the Plymouth Governor to King Charles the Second. Dr. Palfrey has depofited with the Mafs. Hiftorical Society the copy of a letter obtained by him from the State-Paper Office [*Colonial Papers* No. xlvi, Art. 149], from Jofias Winflow to the king, of date " New Plymouth, 26 June, 1677," in which the Governor craves His Majefty's acceptance " of thefe few Indian rarities, beeing the beft of our fpoyles, and the beft of the ornaments and treafure of fachem Philip the grande Rebell, the moft of them taken from him by Capt. Benja-min Church (a perfon of great loyalty and the moft fuccefsful of our com-

manders) when hee was flayne by him; being his Crowne, his gorge, and two belts of theire owne makeing of theire golde and filver." [*Mafs. Hift. Soc. Proceedings,* 1863-4, p. 481.] This defcription accords very well with that given by Church. The "crowne" was, doubtlefs, the belt "which *Philip* was wont to put upon his head"; the "gorge" [*gorget,* "a crefcent-fhaped plate worn round the neck by officers on duty," — *Worcefter*] may have been the "fmall belt with a Star upon the end of it, which he ufed to hang upon his breaft."

[361] It has been ufual to regard *Maffafoit* as a man of peace. Mr. Thatcher fays he " did not diftinguifh himfelf as a warrior; nor is he known to have been once engaged in any open hoftilities, even with the inimical and powerful tribes who environed his territory." [*Ind. Biog.* i: 140]. But this teftimony of Annawon, as well as other evidence which might eafily be cited, intimates that he was much like other Indians in that refpect.

[362] Tuefday, 12 September?

ny, about four Miles out of Town,[363] who expreffed a great deal of joy to fee him again, and faid, 'twas more than ever he expected. They went into *Taunton*, were civily and kindly treated by the Inhabitants, refrefhed and refted themfelves that night. Early next Morning,[364] the Captain took old *Annawon*, and half a dozen of his *Indian* Souldiers, and his own man, and went to *Rhode-Ifland*, fending the reft of his Company and his Prifoners by his Lieutenant to *Plymouth*. Tarrying two or three days upon the Ifland, he then went to *Plymouth*, and carried his Wife and his two Children with him.

Capt. *Church* had been but a little while at *Plymouth*, before he was informed of a parcel of *Indians*, that haunted the Woods between *Plymouth* and *Sippican*, that did great damage to the *Englifh* in killing their Cattel, Horfes and Swine; and the Captain was foon in purfuit of them: Went out from *Plymouth* the next Monday[365] in the afternoon; next Morning early[366] they difcovered a Track; the

---

[363] Church would moft likely ftrike the old Taunton and Providence road, then a trail, near the eaft flank of "Great-Meadow Hill," a half-mile north of the rock where he had encamped; from whence it would be nearly eight miles to Taunton. As he met his Lieutenant about half way, they muft have come together a little eaft of the *Segreganfet* River, probably not far from the prefent refidence of G. Dean.

[364] [Wednefday, 13 September?] As his occafions led him to Rhode-Ifland, Church doubtlefs took Annawon with

him from motives of kindnefs to that chief, left the Plymouth authorities might make fhort work with him before his return.

[365] See note 314, *ante*. It is my impreffion that this expedition is here mifplaced, really belonging in the laft week of Auguft or the firft week of September, before Annawon's capture. This Monday may, then, have been Monday, 28 Aug., or poffibly the 4th September.

[366] Church himfelf gives fmall clew to the geography of this expedition. It is obvious, however, that the marau-

Captain fent two *Indians* on the Track to fee what they could difcover, while he and his Company followed gently after, but [53] the two *Indians* foon returned with Tydings that they had difcovered the Enemy fitting round their fires, in a thick place of brufh. When they came pretty near the place, the Captain ordered every man to creep as he did; and furround them by creeping as near as they could, till they fhould be difcovered, and then to run on upon them and take them alive, if poffible, (for their Prifoners were their pay:) They did fo, took every one that was at the fires, not one efcaping. Upon examination they agreed in their Story, that they belonged to *Tifpaquin*,[367] who was gone with *John Bump*,[368] and one more,

ders of whom he was in fearch were "between Plymouth and Sippican"; and as he did not leave Plymouth until afternoon, he could not have been many miles on his way (unlefs he marched all night, which is not probable) when he difcovered their track. Hubbard fays [*Narrative* 107] that "the place was near *Lakenham* upon *Pocaffet* Neck." He was probably right in the place, and wrong in its relative pofition. *Lakenham* was the name very early given to the meadows lying eaft of Six-mile Brook and near Wenham Pond, on the road to Nemafket, in what is now Carver; at leaft 28 miles, air-line diftance, from *Pocaffet*, yet exactly where Church would be likelieft to be, on a fcout for Indians lurking between Plymouth and Sippican. It is about 6 miles from Plymouth.

[867] See note 227, *ante*.

[868] Few family names have had a more curious transformation, in the procefs of popular ufe, than that which is here attached to this Indian. Originally the Huguenot *Bompaffe* (from *Bon-pas*), it became corrupted firft to *Bumpafs*, then to *Bumpus*, and finally to *Bump*! Edward, who came over in the Fortune, in 1621, founded a very worthy family, which ftill holds its own in the Old Colony. Mr. Drake, in his edition of Church, fuppofes that the Indian here referred to may have derived his name from fome affociation with members of this family. It feems to me more probable, that his genuine Indian name fo refembled theirs in found as to have become confufed with it. There was a John *Wampees*, who appears on the lift of "diuers Indians inhabiting att *Agawaam, Sepecan, and Weweante*, with other Places adjoyn-

to *Agawom* [369] and *Sippican* [370] to kill Horfes, and were not expected back in two or three days. This fame *Tifpaquin* had been a great Captain, and the *Indians* reported that he was fuch a great *Pouwau*,[371] that no bullet could enter him, *&c.* Capt. *Church* faid, He would not have him killed, for there was a War broke out in the Eaftern Part of the Country, and he would have him faved to go with them to fight the *Eaftern Indians.*[372] Agreeably he left two old Squaws of the Prifoners, and bid them tarry there until their Capt. *Tifpaquin* returned, and to tell him, that *Church* had been there, and had taken his Wife, Children, and company, and carried them down to *Plymouth;* and would fpare all their lives, and his too, if he would come down

---

ing," who "engaged theire Fidelitie to the Gou'rment of New Plymouth, 6 July, 1671." *Bompaffe* and *Wampees,* as then popularly pronounced, could not, I think, have feemed very unlike; and it is my impreffion that this was the fame John; who, like *Tautozen* in the fame lift, proved faithlefs to the fidelity which he engaged. [*Plym. Col. Rec.* v: 72.]

[369] See note 209, *ante.*

[370] See note 210, *ante.*

[371] *Pauwau (Powow).* Eliot ufes this word in the form in which Church writes it, for a "witch," or "wizard," or "magician." [e.g., *Exod.* xxii: 18; *Dan.* iv: 7.] Roger Williams gives *Powwáw,* and defines: "thefe doe begin and order their fervice, and Invocation of their Gods, and all the people follow, and joyne interchangeably in a laborious bodily fervice, unto

fweating, efpecially of the Prieft, who fpends himfelfe in ftrange Antick Geftures, and Actions even unto fainting." [*Key. R.-I. Hift. Coll.* i: 111.] De Vries fays of the Indians at *Cayenne,* "Their priefts they call *peoayos;* we call them forcerers." So the word muft have had a wide range, territorially, and a very refpectable antiquity. Though not exactly a fimple or primitive word, its etymology is too obfcure to be given without a preliminary treatife on Indian roots.

[372] Wakely (Hubbard calls him *Waterly*) and his family, were murdered by the Indians at Falmouth, Me., in the fecond week of September; and other outbreaks at Saco, Scarborough, Wells, Kittery, &c., foon followed. [Hubbard's *Narrative of Troubles, &c., from Pafcataqua to Pemmaquid,* 16; Palfrey's *Hift N. E.* iii: 207.]

to them and bring the other two that were with him, and they fhould be his Souldiers, &c. Capt. *Church* then returned to *Plymouth,* leaving the old Squaws well provided for, and Bisket for *Tifpaquin* when he returned: Telling his Souldiers, that he doubted not but he had laid a Trap that would take him.[373] Capt. *Church* two days after went to *Bofton*; (the Commiffioners then fitting)[374] and waited upon the Honourable Governour *Leverett* who then lay Sick;[375] who requefted of Capt. *Church* to give him fome account of the War: who readily obliged his Honour therein, to his great Satisfaction, as he was pleafed to exprefs himfelf; taking him by the hand, and telling him, if it pleafed God he lived, he would make it a brace of a hundred pounds advantage to him out of the *Maffachufetts* Colony, and would endeavour the reft of the Colonies fhould do Proportionably;[376] but he dyed within a Fort-

[373] This language is to be interpreted honorably. Church does not mean that he had laid a trap to take the Black Sachem by a falfe promife, as might feem, in the light of fubfequent events; but that, in offering him a Captaincy under him to fight the Eaftern Indians, he had held out an inducement fufficient to fecure his capitulation, as the refult proved.

[374] The Commiffioners of the three Confederate Colonies.

[375] *John Leverett* was the only fon of Elder Thomas Leverett, and was born in England in 1616, and came to New England with his parents in Sept., 1633; joined Bofton Church 14 July, 1639; joined the Ancient and Honorable

Artillery Company, 1639, holding fucceffively all its offices; was freeman 13 May, 1640; 27 May, 1663, he was chofen Major-General, and every year afterwards, until he was chofen Governor, in 1673, which office he held until his death; befides being felectman, deputy, affiftant, &c. &c. No fact can be better eftablifhed than that he died 16 March, 1678-9, or about 2 years and 5 months later than the date to which Church would here affign his deceafe; another proof that the old warrior dictated from a memory not always accurate in minutiæ. [See *N. E. Hift. and Gen. Reg.* iv: 125-32.]

[376] Gov. Leverett, on behalf of the General Court of Mafs., wrote to the

night after, and fo nothing was done of that nature. The fame day[377] *Tifpaquin* came in and thofe that were with him, but when Capt. *Church* return'd from *Bofton*, he found. to his grief that the heads of *Annawon*, *Tifpaquin*, &c. cut off, which were the laft of *Philips* friends.[378] The General Court of *Plymouth* then fitting[379] fent for Capt. *Church* who waited upon them accordingly, and received their Thanks for his good Service, which they Unanimoufly Voted, which was all that Capt. *Church* had for his aforefaid Service.

Afterwards in the Year 1676. in the Month of *January*[380] Capt. *Church* received a Commiffion[381] from Gover

Governor of Plymouth, 17 Oct., 1676, in regard to fending an expedition caft againft the hoftile Indians there. " Wherein," he fays, " wee defire & expect yoᵗ concurrance wᵗʰ us, & affiftance of us wᵗʰ fome Englifh, & alfo fome of your Indians, & *Capt. Church, whom we haue fpoken with here, & finde him ready to ferve God & the country;* requeft therefore your fpeedy fending of him, &. fuch as yow fhall see meet, to afift in that defigne." [*Mafs. Col. Rec.* v : 126.] I find no refponfe to this on the Plymouth Records.

[377] That is, the fame day which Church refers to in his account of fetting his trap for *Tifpaquin.*

[378] Hubbard fays the Plymouth authorities tefted Tifpaquin on his reputation of being impenetrable by bullets, but " he fell down at the firft fhot." [*Narrative*, 107.] The fact probably

was, that the Court, having committed themfelves to the policy of extermination, fo far as the ringleaders of late butcheries were concerned, did not fee fit to gratify Church by making exceptions in thefe eminent cafes. The Home Government at London — if we may judge by the records of the times would have been even more unyielding.

[379] The Court met 1 Nov., 1676.

[380] In the Old Style the o of January, 1676, came after, inftead of before, November and December; the year beginning with 25th March, inftead of 1ft January.

[381] After the *Annawon* expedition, Church's old company feems to have difbanded; and, from the iffue of this new commiffion to him at this time, the force of the old would feem to have expired.

nour *Winſlow*, to Scoure the Woods of ſome of the lurking
Enemy, which they were well informed were there.
Which Commiſſion is as follows: [54]

B*Eing well informed that there are certain parties of our*
Indian Enemies, (remains of the People, or Allies of
Philip, *late Sachem of* Mount-hope, *our Mortal Enemy)*
that are ſtill lurking in the Woods near ſome of our Planta-
tions, that go on to diſturb the Peace of His Majeſty's Subjeɛts
in this & the Neighbouring Colonies, by their frequent Rob-
beries, and other Inſolences. Capt. Benjamin Church *is*
therefore hereby Nominated, Ordered, Commiſſioned, and
Impowred to raiſe a Company of Volunteers, conſiſting of
Engliſh *and* Indians; *ſo many as he ſhall judge neceſſary to*
improve in the preſent Expedition, and can obtain ; And of
them to take the Command, and Conduɛt, and to lead them
forth unto ſuch place or places within this or the Neighbour-
ing Colonies, as he ſhall think fit, and as the Providence of
God, and his Intelligence may lead him ; To Diſcover, Pur-
ſue, Fight, Surprize, Deſtroy, and Subdue our ſaid Indian
Enemy, or any party or parties of them, that by the Provi-
dence of God they may meet with ; Or them, or any of them
to receive to Mercy, if he ſee cauſe (provided they be not Mur-
derous Rogues, or ſuch as have been principal Aɛtors in thoſe
Vilanies.) And for the Proſecution of this deſign, liberty is
hereby granted to the ſaid Capt. Church, *and others, to Arm*
and ſet out ſuch of our friendly Indians, *as he is willing to*
Entertain. And foraſmuch as all theſe our Enemies that
have been taken, or at any time may be taken by our Forces,

have by our Courts and Councils been rendred lawful Captives of War, and condemned to perpetual Servitude; this Council do also determine and hereby declare, That all such Prisoners as by the blessing of God the said Captain and Company, or any of them, shall take, together with their Arms, and other Plunder, shall be their own, and to be distributed amongst themselves, according to such agreement as they may be at one with another: And it shall be lawful, and is hereby warrantable for him and them to make Sale of such Prisoners as their perpetual Slaves; or otherwise to retain and keep them as they think meet, (they being such as the Law allows to be kept:) Finally, the said Capt. Church *herein improving his best judgment and discretion, and utmost ability, faithfully to Serve the Interest of God, his Majesties Interest, and the Interest of the Colony; and carefully governing his said Company at home and abroad; these shall be unto him full and ample Commission, Warrant and Discharge. Given under the Publick Seal.* January 15th. 1676.

Per Josiah Winslow, GOV.

Accordingly Capt. *Church* accompanied with several Gentlemen and others went out, and took divers parties of *Indians;* and in one of which Parties there was a certain old man whom Capt. *Church* seem'd to take particular notice of, and asking him where he belonged, who told him to *Swanzey;* the Captain ask'd his name, who replyed, his name was *Conscience; Conscience* said the Captain (smiling) then the War is over, for that was what they were fearching for, it being much wanting; and then returned the faid *Confcience* to his Poft again at *Swanzey*, to a certain perfon the faid *Indian* defired to be Sold to [382] and fo return'd home.

[382] 22 July, 1676, it had been ordered by the Plymouth Council of War: "Whereas it is apprehended that the p'mition of Indian men that are captiues to fettle and abide within this collonie may proue prejuditiall to our comon peace and fafety, confidering that there hath neuer bin any lycence for fuch foe to doe, it is ordered by the councell and the authoritie thereof, that noe Indian male captiue fhall refide in this gou'ment that is aboue 14 yeers of age att the begiñing of his or theire captiuity, and if any fuch captiues aboue that age are now in the gou'ment, which are not defpofed of out of this jurifdiction by the 15th of October next, fhall forthwith be defpofed of for the vfe of this gou'rment." [*Plym. Col. Rec.* v: 210.] Whether this had been repealed, or whether this old Confcience was made an exception, on account of his age, or name, I am not able to fay.

CHRONOLOGICAL TABLE OF EVENTS.

Chronological Table of Events.

Day of Week.	Day of Month.	Year.	EVENT.	Page.
T.	22 July	1673	Saconet grantees met at Plymouth, and Benj. Church with them	3
F.	10 Apr.	1674	Grantees met at Duxbury, and drew lots for their shares	-
—	—	,,	Church goes down to view his lots, and concludes to settle on them	3
—	—	,,	Builds on his lot No. 19	5
F.	29 Jan.	167⅘	*Sassamon* found murdered at *Assawompsett* .	12
T.	15 June	1675	*Awashonks* has a dance, to which she invites Church. He starts for Plymouth, calling on *Petananuet* and *Weetamoe*	7–14
W.	16 June	,,	He arrives at Plymouth, and calls on the Governor	14
S.	20 June	,,	*Philip* allowed his Indians to plunder in Swansey	15
M.	21 June	,,	A messenger reaches the Governor at Plymouth, who orders the Captains of the towns to march that day to Taunton · ·	16
T.	22 June	,,	Church leads a party of English and friend Indians, ahead of the main army, to Brown's and Myles's Garrisons ·	17
Th.	24 June	,,	First blood, in Philip's War, shed either at Swansey or Fall River . · · · · ·	18–19
M.	28 June	,,	A skirmish at Miles's Bridge, in which William Hammond was killed · · · · · ·	20

24

185

Day of Week.	Day of Month.	Year.	EVENT.	Pag
T.	29 June	1675	The troops, marched into Mount-Hope Neck to *Keekkamuit*, by a blunder, fired upon each other, wounding Ensign Savage; found eight English heads, and *Philip's* staved drums	22-
—	– July		The English begin to build a fort at *Keek-kamuit*	
W.	7 July		Captain Fuller and Church, with six files, start for Pocasset, and get over Bristol Ferry to Rhode Island	
Th.	8 July	,,	Get over to Pocasset in the night .	
F.	9 July	,,	Pease-field Fight.	28-
—	———	,,	Church goes back to Rhode-Island for provisions	
—	———	..	A fruitless expedition starts in pursuit of *Weetamoe*	40-
—	———	,,	It starts again in a sloop for Fall River, has a skirmish, and gets back	42-
Th.	15 July	,,	Our forces go from Mount Hope Neck Fort to Rehoboth	
F.	16 July	,,	To Gardner's Neck	
S.	17 July	,,	To Taunton	
M.	19 July	,,	They march to Pocasset, and attack *Philip*,	
—	———	,,	*Philip* gets away by rafts across the Taunton river, and flees to the *Nipmuk* Country .	44-
—	———	,,	*Acushnet* (Dartmouth) destroyed by the Indians	
—	———	,,	Another Fort built at Pocasset	
—	———	,,	Remainder of the summer "improved" in nursing these Forts, while the Indians were recruiting in the *Nipmuk* Country and west as far as Albany	
F.	10 Dec.	,,	Church starts from Boston with Governor Winslow on an expedition against the Narragansetts, and gets to Rehoboth [to Myles's Garrison?]	

CHRONOLOGICAL TABLE OF EVENTS.

CHRONOLOGICAL TABLE OF EVENTS.

Day of Week.	Day of Month.	Year.	EVENT.	Page.
T.	29 Feb.	167⅚	Plymouth Council of War met at Marshfield; and Church advised the sending of 300 soldiers, one-third to be friend Indians; but the Council demurred	66–6
—	8–11 Mar.	,,	Church removes his family from Duxbury to Rhode-Island	69–7
S.	12 Mar.	,,	Clark's Garrison, in Plymouth, destroyed .	7
—	26–28 Mar.	1676	Rehoboth burned	6
F.	21 Apr.		Captain Wadsworth and his Company swallowed up at Sudbury	6
F.	12 May	,,	Church's second son, Constant, born . . .	7
F.	19 May	,,	Captain Turner surprises the Indians at the great falls of the Connecticut, but is himself killed	6
T.	6 June	,,	Church arrives at Plymouth, and meets the General Court	7
Th.	8 June?	,,	Goes back, and on his way hails the Saconet Indians	73–7
F.	9 June?	,,	Church goes to Newport to get permission to go and see *Awashonks*	7
S.	10 June?		Goes across with Daniel Wilcocks to Treaty Rock, and meets *Awashonks* and her Indians	78–8
W.	21 June	,,	Plymouth army to be ready to start for Taunton	8
—	11–24 June	,,	Fruitless efforts to get a vessel, and failure of Anthony Low to aid the business . . .	86–8
S.	25 June	,,	*Peter* is started from Rhode-Island for Saconet and Plymouth, to carry *Awashonks's* submission	8
M.	26 June	,,	Army arrives at Pocasset	8
T.	27 June	,,	Church goes over to see Major Bradford and the army	8
W.	28 June	,,	Went back to go to *Awashonks* to inform her of the arrival of the army. Saw her, and told her what to do, and returned to the army. *Peter* and his two Saconet companions appear before the Court at Plymouth . .	

CHRONOLOGICAL TABLE OF EVENTS.

Day of Week.	Day of Month.	Year.	EVENT.	Page.
Th.	29 June	1676	Army march to *Punkateese*. Church goes down to Saconet	89
F.	30 June	,	*Awashonks* with her subjects make submission at *Punkateese* to Major Bradford, and are ordered to report at Sandwich in six days, where Church agrees to meet her within a week	90
S.	1 July		Army goes back to Pocasset and over to Mount Hope, missing the Indians digging clams at *Weypoiset*	91–92
T.	6 July		The army having got comfortably back to Miles's Garrison, Church has leave to keep his promise with the Saconets .	93
F.	7 July?	,	He reaches Plymouth, and the same afternoon starts for Sandwich. Major Bradford's army marches after Philip	93, 105
S.	8 July?	,,	He finds *Awashonks* at *Mattapoisett* (Mass.),	95–100
S.	9 July?	,,	He returns to Plymouth	100
M.	10 July?	,,	The Governor commissions him, and he marches the same night for the woods . .	101–102
T.	11 July?		Captures a lot of Indians in Middleborough. An onset is made upon Taunton by the Indians	102, 105
—	12–23 July	,	Captures the *Monponsets*, &c., &c.	103–104
S.	16 July	,	Anthony Collymer writes to his wife . . .	105
—	17–22 July		Church guards some carts to Taunton, and pursues and captures Indians through *Assawompset* neck, *Acushnet*, *Ponaganset*, *Mattapoisett*, and *Sippican*, to Plymouth	104–121
Th.	24 July	,,	Church's commission is enlarged	104
S.	30 July	,,	A post from Bridgewater announces that an army of Indians is threatening to cross the *Titicut* to their town; Church starts "by the beginning of the afternoon exercise," and goes to *Monponset* (in Halifax) that night	123–125

Day of Week.	Day of Month.	Year.	EVENT.	Page.
M.	31 July	1676	The "brisk Bridgewater lads" attack the Indians; and Church, scouting towards the town, hears the firing, but does not join in the pursuit	124-12
T.	1 Aug.	,,	Church pursues the enemy; sees Philip; crosses on the felled tree, and back at the wading-place; and takes many prisoners .	126-12
W.	2 Aug.		Pursues further to a swamp in Rehoboth . .	129-13
Th.	3 Aug.		Back, with his prisoners, to Bridgewater . .	131-1,
F.	4 Aug.		Back safe to Plymouth, with his captives . .	13
—	7-9 Aug.?	,,	An expedition toward Dartmouth, and the capture of *Sam Barrow*	13
F.	11 Aug.		Starts on another expedition to Pocasset, and goes over the ferry to see his wife at Major Sanford's; hears that Philip is at Mount Hope, and hastens immediately to attack him	140-1.
S.	12 Aug.		Philip is killed	145-1,
S.	13 Aug.		Church back at Rhode-Island	1
T.	15 Aug.		Starts on his return to Plymouth	1
—	1-6 Sept.?		Goes out towards *Agawom* (in Wareham), after *Tispequin*	175-1
F.	8 Sept.		Starts again for Rhode-Island after *Annawon*	1
S.	10 Sept.		A post informs him of Indians on *Poppa-squash* neck (in Bristol); he starts and scouts after them	154-1
M.	11 Sept.		Church takes prisoners, follows their guide, reaches *Annawon's* camp in *Squannakonk* swamp (in Rehoboth) about dark, and captures him with all his men, &c., &c. . .	159-1
T.	12 Sept.		Takes his prisoners to Taunton, where they refresh and rest over night	174-1
W.	13 Sept.		Taking *Annawon*, Church goes back to Rhode-Island, sending the rest of his company and prisoners to Plymouth	1
—	15-20 Sep.		Starts for Plymouth, with his wife and children, and *Annawon*	1

CHRONOLOGICAL TABLE OF EVENTS.

Day of Week.	Day of Month.	Year.	EVENT.	Page.
—	— Nov.	1676	Church waits on Governor Leverett in Boston	178
	,,	,,	The General Court of Plymouth Colony tender him a vote of thanks	179
M.	15 Jan.	167⁶⁄₇	Church is again commissioned by Governor Winslow, and goes out, and takes " divers parties of Indians," including old *Conscience* of Swansey ; which ends these Annals of the War	179-182

191

INDEX.

INDEX.

The Arabic figures refer to the page in the body of the work; the Roman numerals to the Introductory portion. Names in *italics* are those of Indians.

INDEX.

Pequot, the word explained, 83.

Perkins, Sir William, his execution, 151.

Petananuet, 11, 77.

Peter Awashonks, xx. 6, 77, 87, 149.

Peter Nunnuit, 11, 77.

Petonowowet, 11.

Pettaquamfcut, 52.

Petuxet River, 47.

PHILIP, xix. xx. xxi. 5, 7, 9, *et paſſim ;* his death, 147; treatment of his dead body, 150; his "royalties," or regalia, furrendered by Annawon to Capt. Church; what became of them? 173, 174.

Pierce, Capt. Michael, 67, 70.

Pinfon, Thomas, 4.

Plymouth, orders of court, xxii. 2; the Court proclaim a faft, 15; Court order refpecting prifoners, 101.

Plummer, Mary, 114.

Pocaffet [Tiverton], xx. xxi. xxii. xxiii. xxiv. xli. 11, 12, 41, 43, 47, 89, 140.

Pokanokett, 15.

Poneganfet, 45, 109.

Pope, Thomas, 4.

Poppafquafh Neck, in Briftol, xxv. xxx. 156, 158.

Pofotoquo, 5.

Potock, 59.

Pouwau, Powow, an Indian conjurer, 177.

Powder-mill, firft in New England, 35.

Pratt, Nathan, 166; Stillman, 125.

Prentice, Capt. Thomas, 18, 20, 49, 52.

Preflong, Nicolas, 4.

Price, John, 4.

Prince, Gov. Thomas, 6; dies, 10.

Prince, Thomas, the annalift, quoted, 30.

Proportion of men and money required from each town in Plymouth Colony, 68.

Proprietors of Saconet, their names, 3; their agreement, 4.

Providence burned, 72.

Prudence Ifland, 155.

Pumham, 50, 61, 117.

Punkateaft, Punkateefet, Punkatees, a neck in Tiverton, alfo called Pocaffet Neck, xviii. xix. xxi. xxiii. xxvii. xxxi. 3, 31, 34, 36, 82.

Punkatees Fight, 33–40.

Q.

Quaboag [Brookfield] deftroyed, 40.

Quannapohut, James, 18.

Quannapohut, Thomas, 18.

Quequechan River, now Fall River, 2, 42.

Quinnapin, Qunnapin, 117, 127, 128.

Quiquequanchett, 12.

R.

Rawfon, Rev. Grindal, 85.

Rattlefnakes, 30.

Reformado, Church was one; meaning of the term, 49.

Revere, Paul, xi. xii.; his portraits of Church, and of Philip, xi.

Reyner, Rev. John, 112.

Reynolds, Mary, xlvi.

Rhode-Ifland, why excluded from the Confederacy, 17.

Richard, Eleazar, 153.

Richards, Alice, 16.

Richmond, Anna, xlvi.; Benjamin, *ibid.;* Charles, *ibid.* ; Elizabeth, *ibid.;* Hannah, *ibid.;* John, xxiii. 4, 77; Mary, xlvi. *bis.;* Perez, *ibid.;* Ruth, *ibid.;* Sarah, *ibid.;* Sylvefter, *ibid.;* Thomas, *ibid.;* William, *ibid.,* *bis.*

W.

Made in United States
North Haven, CT
29 May 2023

37130169R00148